52
Weeks
of Easy
Knits

52 Weeks of Easy Knits

Hardie Grant

BOOKS

Contents

01–13

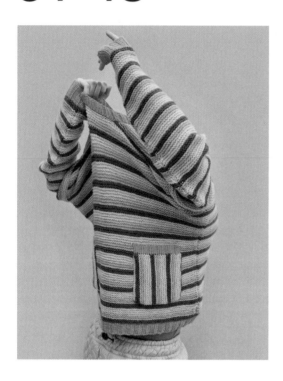

14–26

● SUPER EASY

40–52

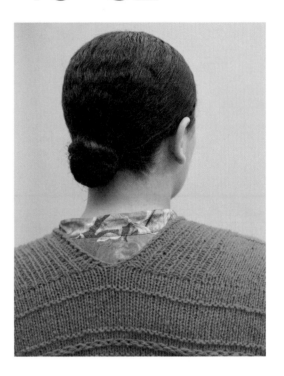

27–39

Preface

Welcome to the world of easy knits!

In recent years, more and more people have discovered the joys of knitting. They have learned how comforting it is to make tactile objects with your hands, and how exhilarating it can be to slip your feet into self-made socks or pull on a beanie fresh off the needles. That is why we wanted to create a book that also reaches out to those who are at the beginning of their knitting journey. Thus, *52 Weeks of Easy Knits* was born.

If you have read our previous *52 Weeks* books, you will find many familiar things, but also something new. Just like before, there is an abundance of knitwear and makers: the book's 52 patterns come from 40 talented designers from all over the world. The beautiful visuals and clear instructions are also something we are known and loved for. What is new, compared with our sock and scarf books, is the variety of subjects. In this book, you will find patterns for many types of knitwear: from sweaters to socks, beanies to mittens and scarves to cardigans. They are fun, modern and wearable, but above all, they are enjoyable to knit.

When we first started planning a book about easy knits, we had to think about what we meant by the word "easy". It can mean quite different things, depending on whether a person has been knitting for thirty years or three months. We wanted to consider both groups: the beginners and the more experienced knitters in search of an effortless comfort knit. That's why there are patterns in this book that meet the needs of both. To make the choices easier, we have used a "Super Easy" label to mark the patterns that are perfect for your very first knitting project. And when your skills grow, you can move on to the more challenging ones.

The patterns in this book use basic techniques or give alternatives for more challenging ones, and there are only a few charts to follow. There may be something in the pattern that requires concentration – for example, a more complex stitch pattern – but to balance that out, the structure of the garment will be straightforward. Or the other way around: the focus of the garment might be on the structure, but otherwise it is knitted in simple garter stitch.

Easiness has also been considered in the pattern writing, and many things have been described more thoroughly than in standard knitting patterns. Abbreviations are used less than usual, and they are all explained in detail at the beginning of the book. You will get the hang of the abbreviations quickly, and after that, they make reading the patterns a lot smoother. Note that even if a pattern is long, this doesn't necessarily mean it is difficult. It just means that each stage of the process has been set out extra-carefully! Often, at first glance some parts of the pattern might seem hard, but once you get to that point in your knitting, they will start to make sense.

At the beginning of the book, we have also gathered information about the techniques used, starting with casting on stitches. And remember that the internet is a treasure trove for knitters. By searching, you will find a vast number of illustrated instructions and videos that help you master the techniques. We have also compiled tutorials on our website, and we aim to make them even more comprehensive in the future.

We wish you happy knitting – rewarding insights and new things to discover, but also those meditative moments when the stitches seem to just fly off the needles!

Laine team

P.S. Want to see more photos of your favourite design? Just go to our website (*lainepublishing.com*).

A Knitter's Basic Tools

What is fingering-weight yarn, and why might circular needles be your go-tos? In this chapter, we talk about different yarns and their characteristics as well as needles and notions.

YARN

WOOL AND ITS COMPANIONS

Yarn can be made of various fibres: wool, linen, cotton, silk, alpaca... and from their blends! So-called natural fibres include animal fibres (such as wool, cashmere and silk) and plant-based fibres (such as cotton and linen). In addition, there are regenerated cellulose fibres, such as viscose and lyocell, and synthetic fibres, such as polyester, nylon and acrylic. The patterns in this book use mostly animal fibres, as they are almost unbeatable when it comes to wearability and are pleasant to knit with, being soft and relatively stretchy.

The feel, durability and look of a yarn depend greatly on the fibre it is made from. For example, a sweater made in linen will have a different drape than one made in rustic wool. Durability is especially important for socks, which need to be hard-wearing. Therefore, sock yarns often include a bit of nylon to make them more durable. Lately, more and more natural, plastic-free sock yarns have also become available.

When choosing yarn for your project, you can of course use the yarn the pattern calls for and just decide on the colour yourself. However, you can also substitute yarns. When doing so, we recommend you choose a yarn with similar fibre content and look (more on this on p. 10). Later, when you get more familiar with different fibres and their characteristics, you can start to play with

other yarn types and modify the look of your knit. If you are unsure about substituting, a local yarn shop or a wise knitting friend can help.

When picking yarn from a shop shelf or pressing the "buy" button, it's good to check the origins of the fibre and evaluate the yarn-making process. If possible, choose yarn from brands whose work and processes are sustainable, transparent, responsible and ecological. And don't forget your local sheep farmers – many of them produce their own yarns!

ABOUT YARN WEIGHTS

Yarns are divided into different groups, depending on their thickness. The term "yarn weight" refers to how thick the thread is. In a knitted fabric, the thicker the yarn, the bigger the individual stitches. Knowing the yarn weight helps, for example, when substituting yarn for patterns (more on this on p. 10). Yarn weights, from thinnest to thickest are: lace, light fingering, fingering (also known as 4ply and sock), sport, DK, worsted, aran, bulky and super bulky (also known as chunky and super chunky).

FROM SKEIN TO BALL

Yarn is most typically sold in balls and skeins. Sometimes you might stumble upon cakes, plates and cones as well. Yarn from balls, cakes, plates and cones is ready to use. Skeins, however, need to be wound before you can cast on. A yarn ball winder is a great investment if you knit a lot. You can also wind yarn by hand. There are multiple methods of doing this: you can ask a friend to hold the opened skein (loop) between outstretched arms or place the loop over the back of a chair. You can also hold the loop yourself, being extra careful not to get tangled. Be sure not to wind the yarn too tightly.

Yarn labels contain important information: what fibres the yarn is made from, yardage, recommended gauge and needle size, care instructions... In addition to the colourway, you will also find a number that stands for the dye lot. Always make sure that the yarns for your project are from the same dye lot, as otherwise, small colour differences may appear. This is especially important for hand-dyed yarns.

NEEDLES

VERSATILE CIRCULARS

When you walk into a yarn shop, you can find several needle types: circular needles (the ones with a cable running between the needles), shorter double-pointed needles (also called DPNs, typically used for socks and other small-circumference knitting) and long straight needles (often known as single-pointed needles). Usually, patterns are written for a specific needle type. You can find this information in the pattern's materials section.

In this book, we mostly use circular needles. They are super versatile, as you can knit both in the round and flat. In addition, circular needles allow you to knit in a more ergonomic position, as your shoulders and arms can relax more easily. Good circular needles have a flexible cable and a smooth transition from cable to the needle, which allows the stitches to glide easily on the needles.

WOOD OR METAL?

Needles are made from different materials, such as wood, bamboo, metal and carbon fibre. Which needle is best depends on your individual tension and yarn. For some yarns, metal needles may feel too slippery while others may catch on wooden ones. Knitters often have their go-tos – ours are Chiaogoo's Red Lace circulars. Test and find your favourites.

IN MANY SIZES

Needle sizes – meaning their thickness – are given in numbers. These vary depending on the country and region. In this book, we give all needles in both US sizes and millimetres, for example US 6 / 4 mm. Patterns state the recommended needle size, but always choose a needle size with which you get the required gauge (more about gauge on p. 12).

When the pattern calls for circular needles, a recommended cable length is also given, for example 16" / 40 mm. The most versatile cable length is 32" / 80 cm. It allows you to knit both larger projects, such as sweaters, as well as smaller circumferences, such as sleeves and socks if using the Magic Loop Method (see p. 21).

NOTIONS

In addition to yarn and needles, and a tapestry needle (for weaving in ends), scissors and a measuring tape, patterns often call for other tools. Maybe the most-used notions are stitch markers and stitch holders.

Stitch markers are useful tools that help you identify important parts of the work. They can, for example, mark where the round begins or show where increases and decreases should be made. Stitch markers are never knitted but simply slipped from the left-hand needle to the right-hand needle. Sometimes locking stitch markers are used. They are attached to the knitted fabric and left in place. Locking stitch markers can be helpful when counting rows, for example. Yarn and craft shops sell stitch markers (from really simple to super fancy) but homemade ones work equally well: simply take a piece of (colourful) yarn and tie a small loop. Just make sure that the stitch marker is easy to notice and slides effortlessly on the needles.

Sometimes a pattern calls for stitch holders. A stitch holder is a tool onto which you can place live stitches while you continue to work other parts of the knit. For example, stitch holders are typically used when knitting a sweater from the top down in one piece: the sleeves are left waiting while you finish the body. Alternatively, you can use scrap yarn, which works equally well.

How to Read Patterns

Knitting patterns can seem rather daunting until you get familiar with their structure and the terms used. If you aren't used to reading patterns, take a look at our notes before casting on.

FINDING THE RIGHT SIZE

The sizing in this book doesn't follow standard clothes sizing. We use numbers to indicate different sizes from small to large, beginning with the number 1. Brackets are used to group sizes and their corresponding numbers and are helpful when you are following a pattern. For example, if you knit a size 4, always follow the fourth number in the pattern.

Choose the size based on actual body measurements. Patterns often give a recommended ease, which describes how the finished piece will fit your body. Positive ease means that the finished garment will be bigger than your actual body measurements, resulting in a relaxed, sometimes oversized look. If a knit has negative ease, it will be smaller than your actual measurements, resulting in a close-fitting knit. Remember that the ease given in any pattern is always just a recommendation: you can choose a size with more or less ease, depending on the fit you are looking for!

For example, when knitting a sweater, start by measuring your chest circumference, as the chest is usually the widest part of the garment. Have a look at the recommended ease or go with your desired fit. Add the ease to your actual chest circumference and choose the size that best corresponds to that. Let's take an example: a sweater comes in sizes 1 (2, 3, 4, 5) (6, 7, 8) and has a recommended ease of 8–9" / 20–25 cm. In the pattern, the final measurements for chest circumference are 41.5 (45.5,

49, 53.5, 60) (64, 67.5, 71.5)" / 106 (115, 125, 136, 153) (162, 172, 181) cm. If your chest circumference is 41" / 105 cm, choose size 3, which gives you approximately 8" / 20 cm of positive ease. When working from the pattern, follow the third number (the second in brackets).

CHOOSING A DIFFERENT YARN

Every pattern mentions which yarn the knit was designed for and photographed in. However, you can always choose a different yarn if you feel like it! The patterns provide information on how much yarn you will need and of which yarn weight. The pattern's yardage information will tell you how many yards or metres you will need of a given yarn weight. When substituting, always use yardage as a guide when estimating how many skeins you need.

When substituting yarn, it's good to have a look at the fibre content of the original yarn. Choose a yarn that has a similar fibre content if you want to knit a piece that looks like the one in the photos. For example, in comparison with a sweater made in 100% alpaca, a sweater using 100% wool yarn will have a completely different fit and drape, even if the yarns are of the same thickness.

If you feel unsure about substituting yarns, always remember that your LYS (local yarn shop) can most probably help!

NEEDLES AND OTHER TOOLS

In the pattern, you can also find information on your most used tools, the needles. The pattern will state a needle size and a cable length if circular needles are used. Remember that the needle sizes are just recommendations: always choose a needle with which you get the required gauge (more on this in Swatch & Get Gauge). The patterns are often written for a specific needle type, for example for circular needles. However, you can of course use DPNs (double-pointed needles) instead of circulars when knitting socks, mittens or sleeves. Just remember that sometimes modifications need to be made when making substitutions.

The pattern also lists any special notions (extra equipment) you will need. You will always need a tapestry needle to weave in the ends, a pair of scissors for cutting the yarn and a measuring tape to check the gauge and dimensions. We talk more about needles and notions on page 9.

SWATCH & GET GAUGE

To ensure that your finished knit will be the right size, always start a new knitting project by making a swatch. A pattern will specify a particular gauge (also known as tension), and the gauge tells you how many stitches and rows you should have in a defined area, usually in a 4 x 4" / 10 x 10 cm square. Every knitter knits with a different tension – some knit super tight, some spot-on, others loose – and that's why swatching is so important. It is also crucial when you are substituting yarns. Some feel that swatching is the most boring part of the process, but see it as an opportunity to get to know the yarn and colourway!

Always knit and finish the swatch the same way as the actual item. If your knit is made in the round, also swatch in the round. When you have knitted your swatch, block it (you can find instructions for blocking on p. 13). Make sure your swatch is large enough.

Swatch as follows: 1) Knit a swatch at least 6 x 6" / 15 x 15 cm in the required stitch pattern. 2) Block the swatch. 3) Take a measuring tape and count how many stitches and rows you have over the required area.

If the numbers are the same as given in the pattern, you can cast on right away! If your gauge differs, you need to adjust the needle size and make a new swatch.

If you have a smaller gauge, meaning you have more stitches/rows than required, change to larger needles. If you have a bigger gauge, meaning you have fewer stitches/rows than required, change to smaller needles. Usually, stitch gauge is more important than row gauge. So make especially sure that your stitch gauge is correct!

USEFUL ABBREVIATIONS

Abbreviations are used in patterns to make them easier to read and follow as well as to keep them short. You can find all abbreviations and their explanations at the beginning of the book (pp. 20–23). Abbreviations can seem like another language but you will learn them quickly, pinky promise!

UNDERSTANDING THE CHARTS

Some patterns include charts. They are often used in colourwork patterns, for example. Every square stands for one stitch. The numbers at the edges of the charts help you keep track of stitches as well as rows and rounds.

Charts are read from bottom to top. When knitting flat, charts are read from right to left on right-side rows and from left to right on wrong-side rows. When knitting in the round, charts are always read from right to left.

Next to the chart, you will find a chart key. The chart key tells you what each chart symbol stands for. "No stitch" means that there is no stitch worked at that point – simply move to the next square!

In some charts, thicker lines are used to mark a specific section of the chart. These lines can mark, for example, a particular size (e.g., the chart for size 2 starts from here) or a stitch pattern sequence that will be repeated during the row or round.

If both written and charted instructions are given, follow whichever you find easier to work from.

Take Time to Finish

You've bound off that last stitch? Great! However, make sure to finish the knit with as much care as you made it – that way, your new wardrobe addition will reach its full potential.

WEAVING IN ENDS

When you bind off your knit and cut the yarn, make sure to leave a tail approximately 4–6" / 10–15 cm long for finishing. Using a blunt-tipped tapestry needle, weave in all the ends on the wrong side of the work, or the side that isn't visible when the item is being worn. For example, for hats with a folded brim, the end at the edge should be woven in on the right side of the brim.

Weave the yarn following the path of the stitches. If the knit features several colours, always weave into same-coloured sections. Different elements, such as an i-cord edge, are great to hide ends in. Be careful not to weave too tightly, so the fabric can relax and doesn't pucker.

BLOCKING

Nearly all knits benefit from blocking. Blocking evens out the fabric, makes the yarn bloom and opens up stitch patterns beautifully, especially lace. When knitting with more rustic wools, blocking also makes the item more comfortable to wear, as it softens the fibres. Blocking is usually the last step when finishing your knit. However, a pattern may recommend blocking individual pieces before joining (for example, when knits are made in pieces rather than seamlessly in a single piece).

Special blocking tools, such as pins, blocking wires, t-pins and blocking combs, are helpful but usually optional. They are, however, important when blocking lace. You can also find special blockers for socks and mittens, which might come in handy. And the next time you knit a hat, try blocking it over a balloon!

Wet-blocking is a common blocking method that works for most knits. Wet-blocking is done as follows:

1) Soak the knit in lukewarm water for about 20 minutes. Make sure the knit is completely submerged. You can add a few drops of wool wash, dish soap or even hair conditioner to the water. If you are using other than rinseless soap, rinse the knit gently.

2) Carefully remove the knit from the water and squeeze excess water out. Take care not to stretch or twist the knit. Lay the piece flat on a clean towel, roll it up and squeeze even more water out.

3) Place your knit on an even, clean surface: a (dry) towel works well (if you aren't using any pins or blocking tools), but you can also use special blocking boards or a firm mattress. Shape the knit to the required measurements: use a tape measure to check that the piece matches the dimensions given in the pattern. If needed, attach the knit to the surface using pins, blocking wires, t-pins or blocking combs. Leave it to dry completely.

If you're in a hurry, you can also steam-block your knit. Steam-blocking is a great option if you have knitted colourwork and are unsure of the colourfastness of one or more of your yarns (whether the colour will run when wet). It's also a good method when you have a fluffy, 3-dimensional knit, such as brioche, that you don't want to squash. Steam-block with a steamer or by placing a damp cloth over your knit and very gently pressing with a warm iron.

STORING AND CLEANING

Always store your knits folded, as placing them on hangers can easily stretch them. Protect your knits from moths and other pests that can harm fibre. You can place blocks of aromatic cedar in your closet or use lavender sachets to keep the little monsters away. If you plan to store your knits for a long time, keep them in storage bags or boxes.

You don't need to clean your wool knits often, as wool is known to have antibacterial and antimicrobial properties. Usually, it's enough to air or steam a knit to freshen it up. You can also take advantage of the cold – air your knit outside on a cold winter day and it will smell fresh again!

Care instructions can be found on yarn labels. Usually, hand-washing is recommended. Remember to use lukewarm water, handle your knit gently and dry it flat. For hand-washing, have a look at the wet-blocking instructions we shared earlier in this chapter. If your laundry machine has a special wool setting, we recommend using this for washing your knits, as it's often the best and most gentle option.

DE-PILLING AND MENDING

Over time, your knit may pill (produce little bobbles). This isn't a sign of low-quality yarn but is often a normal characteristic of natural fibres, especially finer ones, such as cashmere. Brush your knit every now and then (especially great for mohair pieces) or remove pills with a sweater brush, sweater stone or a fabric shaver.

There may come the day when there's a hole in your favourite socks. Panic? No need! Take out your tapestry needle and embrace the craft of mending. Aim for an invisible mend or play with different colours and stitches to make a fashion statement. You can find lots of mending inspiration and tutorials online and in books.

Learning the Techniques

Knitting is all about techniques. Here, we have gathered instructions for the basic techniques used throughout the book. Remember that the internet is also full of helpful tutorials and videos!

GENERAL GUIDELINES

There are hundreds of different techniques used in knitting patterns, whether it's for casting on, binding off, or everything in between. Choosing the best technique has to do with both the characteristics of the garment and the knitter's preferences. If the pattern states a specific technique, it is best to use that one. If a technique isn't specified, you can choose your favourite method or the one that seems the easiest.

CASTING ON STITCHES

LONG-TAIL CAST-ON

This is probably the most widely used cast-on method. When you cast on, make sure that you don't cast on too tightly. To ensure a loose cast-on, some people like to cast on using two needles held together.
Place a slipknot, or a yarn loop, on the tip of your right-hand needle, leaving a long tail (at least three times the length of the total stitches you'll cast on). Place your left thumb and index finger between the two strands, so that the tail is around your thumb and the working end is around your index finger. Hold the yarn ends tightly between the other fingers of your hand. *Insert the right-hand needle into the thumb loop from below. With the needle coming from the right, grab the thread on the index finger and pull it through the thumb loop. Take your thumb out of the loop and tighten the stitch.* Repeat *–* until the required number of stitches has been cast on.

STRETCHY CAST-ON

There are several cast-on methods that ensure a stretchy cast-on edge. These methods are especially suitable for designs with ribbed edges, such as hats and sock cuffs. One of our favourite stretchy cast-ons is the German Twisted Cast-On Method. It is easiest to learn this from a video tutorial and, luckily, there are many available – just search for "German Twisted Cast-On".

BACKWARDS LOOP CAST-ON

With this method, you can add new stitches to an existing row or round. Use it to create new stitches for the underarm when knitting a top-down sweater, for example.
Place the working thread clockwise around your left thumb, insert the right-hand needle into the loop around your thumb from below, remove your thumb from the loop and tighten the loop on the needle. Repeat *–* until the required number of stitches has been cast on.

KNITTED CAST-ON

Just like the Backwards Loop Cast-On, this method allows you to add new stitches to an existing row or round, so it's great for underarm cast-ons and more.
Turn the work. *Insert your right-hand needle into the first stitch on the left-hand needle as if to knit and knit it but do not drop off the stitch you knitted into from the left-hand needle. Slip the new stitch from the right-hand needle onto the left-hand needle.* Repeat *–* until the required number of stitches has been cast on.

CABLE CAST-ON

This method is a variation of the Knitted Cast-On.
Turn the work. *Insert your right-hand needle between the first and second stitch on the left-hand needle. Knit a stitch onto the right-hand needle. Do not drop off a stitch from the left-hand needle. Slip the new stitch from the right-hand needle onto the left-hand needle.* Repeat *–* until the required number of stitches has been cast on.

BINDING OFF STITCHES

REGULAR BIND-OFF

This is the most widely used bind-off method. Most of the time you bind off "in pattern": this means that, for instance, when binding off in ribbing, you knit and purl as established. Be careful to not bind off too tightly: you want to keep the bind-off edge stretchy. To ensure a loose bind-off, you can use a needle a size up.
Knit the first two stitches. You now have two stitches on the right-hand needle. Next, insert the left-hand needle into the first stitch you just knitted (= the right stitch). Pull the right stitch over the left stitch and drop it off the needle. *Knit the next stitch and, again, pull the right stitch over the left stitch and drop it off the needle.* Repeat *–* until one stitch remains on the right-hand needle. Cut the yarn and pull it through the last stitch.
Note! If you bind off stitches in the middle of a row or round (at the underarm, for example) you will be left with a stitch on your right-hand needle.

STRETCHY BIND-OFF

This is an easy method for binding off stitches loosely. A stretchy bind-off is especially suitable for sleeve and sock cuffs.
Knit two stitches. Slip the stitches back to the left-hand needle and knit them together through the back loops. *Knit one stitch. Slip the two stitches on the right-hand needle back to the left-hand needle and knit them together through the back loops.* Repeat *–* until one stitch remains on the right-hand needle. Cut the yarn and pull it through the last stitch.

3-NEEDLE BIND-OFF

This method uses 3 needles for seaming live stitches, for example at the shoulders of a sweater. It can either be done with the wrong side facing outward (the seam will be unnoticeable) or the right side facing outward (the seam will be a visible element in the finished garment).
Hold the two pieces together, with the correct sides facing each other. Hold the two needles parallel. Insert a third needle into the first stitch on each of the two needles. Knit these stitches together. *Knit the next pair of stitches together in the same manner. You now have two stitches on the right-hand needle. Using one of the two parallel needles, pass the first stitch you knitted (= the right stitch) over the left stitch and drop it off the needle.* Repeat *–*.
When you've worked all the stitches on the left-hand needle and one stitch remains on the right-hand needle, cut the yarn and pull it through the last stitch.

GRAFTING

With this method, you can sew together two pieces that are not bound off yet (still on the needles or on waste yarn or stitch holders). Grafting is often used, for example, to finish the toes of socks, as the seam is invisible. This bind-off is worked with a tapestry needle. The standard version, given here, produces knit stitches.
Hold the needles with the stitches so the needle tips point to the right. Thread the tapestry needle (with the tail or a new length of yarn). Put the needle through the first stitch on the front needle as if to purl; leave the stitch on the needle. Next, put the needle through the first stitch on the back needle as if to knit; leave the stitch on the needle. *Put the needle through the first stitch on the front needle knitwise; slip the stitch off the needle. Put the needle through the next stitch on the front needle purlwise; leave the stitch on the needle. Put the needle through the first stitch on the back needle purlwise; slip the stitch off the needle. Put the needle through the next stitch on the back needle knitwise; leave the stitch on the needle.* Repeat *–* until one stitch remains on each needle. Put the needle through the last stitch on the front needle knitwise; slip the stitch off the needle. Put the needle through the last stitch on the back needle purlwise; slip the stitch off the needle. Weave in the yarn end.

PICKING UP STITCHES

Edge stitches are often picked up to work new sections: neckline ribbing, for example. Here, you will find two different ways to pick up stitches.

PICK UP AND KNIT

This is probably the most used and best way to pick up stitches. It's especially good when picking up stitches from neckline curves, for example, as it ensures a neat and sturdy pick-up edge.

Insert the needle from front to back through a stitch along the edge of the fabric. Wrap the working yarn around the needle and pull the loop of yarn through, as if to work a normal knit stitch. Repeat *–* until you have picked up the required amount of stitches.

PICK UP

Sometimes stitches are also picked up without knitting them. It might be used in cases where picking up and knitting would affect the look of the pick-up edge.

Pick up a stitch or yarn loop from the edge onto the needle, making sure it is mounted like a normal knit stitch, without knitting it. Repeat *–* until you have picked up the required amount of stitches.

SEAMING

If a garment, such as a sweater, is knitted in pieces, the pieces have to be seamed together. Usually, this is done by sewing with a tapestry needle, using the main colour or the colour that is dominant on the seam. If the garment is knitted with very thick yarn, you can use a lighter-weight yarn in the same colour for sewing or undo a strand from the original yarn.

Do not make a knot at the beginning of the yarn: instead, leave a short tail. You can also use the tails from the cast-on or bind-off rounds/rows for sewing up – you can leave them longer on purpose. If the yarn runs out while you are sewing, weave in the end and continue with a new strand of yarn. Lastly, tighten the ends without pulling too much and weave the ends into the seams.

There are different ways of seaming. Here, we will give instructions for two of them: Mattress Stitch and Backstitch.

MATTRESS STITCH

Mattress Stitch creates a neat, unnoticeable seam. The pieces are sewn together from the right side of the fabric by grabbing a strand of yarn from each edge. Mattress Stitch works especially well when sewing together straight, vertical edges. Pull the yarn so that the stitch is snug but not too tight: you want to keep the seam flexible.

Whatever kind of fabric you are seaming, start as follows: Thread the length of yarn into a tapestry needle (the yarn should be about twice as long as the length to be seamed). Line up the pieces to be seamed, with the right sides facing up and the edges next to each other. For longer pieces (such as the back and front or sleeves), it is helpful to pin the pieces together at intervals to avoid them from slipping out of line. Start from the beginning of the seam.

For Stockinette Stitch (and ribbing with knit-stitch edges)

Push the needle under the horizontal bar between the first two knit stitches nearest the edge on the right-hand piece and pull yarn through. Push the needle under the corresponding bar on the left-hand piece and pull yarn through. Push the needle under the bar above the previous on the right-hand piece and pull yarn through. Push the needle under the corresponding bar on the left-hand piece and pull yarn through. Continue in this manner, alternating sides as you go. Occasionally stop and tighten the yarn, pulling the two pieces neatly together.

For Garter Stitch

Push the needle under the lower purl bar between the last two stitches on the right-hand piece and pull yarn through. Push the needle under the upper purl bar from the stitch next to the edge stitch on the corresponding row on the left-hand piece and pull yarn through. Continue in this manner, alternating sides as you go. Occasionally stop and tighten the yarn, pulling the two pieces neatly together.

BACKSTITCH

Backstitches are sewn from the wrong side of the fabric, about one row or stitch from the edge (or a bit further away, if the edges of the fabric aren't neat/even). The stitches should be relatively short, around 0.2" / 0.5 cm each, so that the seam will hold well. On a very thick fabric, the stitches can be longer, and on a thin fabric, they can be shorter. Pull the yarn so that the stitch is snug but not too tight: you want to keep the seam flexible.

Place the pieces to be sewn on top of each other, with the right sides facing each other. Pin together the edge that will be seamed. Push the needle from the back to the front about one stitch length away from the beginning of the seam. Now push the needle from front to back at the beginning of the seam. You have one stitch in the

front. Now push the needle from back to front about one stitch length away from the beginning of the last stitch. Now push the needle from front to back at the beginning of the last stitch. You have two stitches in the front. Continue in this manner.

SHORT ROWS

Short rows are rows or rounds that are worked only partly. They allow you to, for example, add extra depth to a certain area of a piece, such as the back neck, and improve fit. There are several ways to work short rows. The most used ones are German Short Rows and the Wrap & Turn Method.

GERMAN SHORT ROWS
Work the number of stitches as stated in the pattern, then turn your work. Slip the first stitch as if to purl with yarn in front, then bring the yarn over the needle to the back of your work. Pull the working yarn tight, so that both legs of the stitch lift onto the needle and create a "double stitch". Work as stated, keeping the yarn pulled tight on the double stitch.
How to resolve double stitches: When working double stitches, treat them as a single stitch by knitting or purling through both legs of the double stitch.

WRAP & TURN
Work the number of stitches as stated in the pattern. Wrap the next stitch by slipping it as if to purl, bring the yarn to the front of your work then slip the stitch back to your left-hand needle. Turn work.
How to resolve Wrap & Turn stitches: When working wrapped stitches, treat them as a single stitch by knitting or purling the stitch and its wrap together.

POMPOMS AND FRINGES

Sometimes knitted garments – especially hats and scarves – are finished with pompoms or fringes. They are fun and easy to make.

MAKING A POMPOM
There are many ways to make a pompom. You can use a pompom-maker, a self-made cardboard template, or simply use your fingers. Here, we will give instructions on how to make a pompom with a cardboard template.

1) **Cut two round cardboard pieces.** The outer diameter should be the same as the pompom you are making. Cut an approximately 1" / 2.5 cm hole in the middle of the cardboard circles so that the templates are doughnut-shaped.

2) **Cut a length of yarn (at least a couple of yds / m).** Using a tapestry needle and holding the cardboard pieces together, start wrapping the yarn snuggly around the rim. If you run out of yarn, just weave the end under the wrapped yarns, cut another length and resume wrapping.

3) **Continue until the cardboard is covered and the hole in the middle is filled with yarn.** Insert a scissor blade in between the two cardboard pieces and cut along the outer rim of the yarn disc. Cut a new 10" / 25 cm length of yarn. Wrap and tie this yarn tightly around the middle of the pompom between the two cardboard pieces. Remove the cardboard pieces.

4) **Trim the pompom with scissors if desired,** but do not cut the ends of the yarn you used to secure the pompom. You will use it to attach the pompom to the garment.

MAKING A FRINGE
You will need a crochet hook for making a fringe. Patterns will specify the length and number of strands you need to cut for a single fringe.
Cut the yarn as instructed in the pattern. Hold the strands of yarn together and fold the bundle in half, forming a loop. Push the crochet hook from front to back through the fabric and pick up the strands from the folded loop. Pull the loop a little way through the stitch, then pull the ends of the strands through the loop and tighten. Trim the fringe with scissors if needed.

FIXING MISTAKES

Sometimes you make mistakes when knitting, but remember that often they can be fixed pretty easily. If you, for example, have one stitch too many or too few, just decrease or increase as you go. It rarely shows in the finished garment! If you drop a stitch, picking it up with a crochet hook is often the easiest way to fix it.

Remember that you can always ask for help from a local yarn shop or a wise knitting friend. Don't be discouraged! Each mistake is a chance to learn.

Terms & Abbreviations

BASIC TERMS & ABBREVIATIONS

approx.
Approximately

BO
Bind off

BOR
Beginning of the round

C
Colour (for example, C1 = colour 1)

CC
Contrast(ing) colour

CN
Cable needle

CO
Cast on

Colourwork
Colourwork knitting means knitting with two or more colours in one row or round to create a pattern. In stranded colourwork knitting, you carry the yarns across the back of the work, which creates horizontal strands (also called floats) on the wrong side of the fabric.

dec('d)
Decrease(d)/decreasing

DPN(s)
Double-pointed needle(s)

Garter Stitch
The most basic stitch pattern is created by knitting every stitch of every row (when knitting flat) or alternating between knit and purl rounds (when knitting in the round). It produces a fully reversible fabric with horizontal ridges.

inc('d)
Increase(d)/increasing

Intarsia
Intarsia is a colourwork technique where the yarns are not carried across the back of the work. Each colour block is its own unit, and when a colour changes, the yarns are twisted together to attach the blocks to each other.

k
Knit

k1tbl / ktbl
Knit through back loop of the stitch (twisted stitch)

k2tog
Knit 2 stitches together (1 stitch decreased)

k2tog tbl
Knit 2 stitches together through back loops (1 stitch decreased)

k3tog
Knit 3 stitches together (2 stitches decreased)

Knitting flat
Knitting flat means knitting back and forth, from alternating sides of the fabric. First, you have stitches on your left-hand needle, then you knit them to your right-hand needle and turn the work around. Knitting is worked in rows and it produces a flat piece of fabric.

Knitting in the round
Knitting in the round (also known as circular knitting) means that the stitches that have been cast on are joined at the ends to form a circle. Knitting is worked in rounds and always from the same side, resulting in a seamless tube. It can be done with either cable needles or double-pointed needles, depending on circumference and knitting technique.

m
Stitch marker

m1l
Make 1 left: With your left-hand needle, pick up the bar between the last stitch you worked and the next stitch on the left-hand needle, bringing the needle from the front to the back, knit into the back of the stitch you just picked up (1 stitch increased)

m1lp
Make 1 left: With your left-hand needle, pick up the bar between the last stitch you worked and the next stitch on the left-hand needle, bringing the needle from the front to the back, purl into the back of the stitch you just picked up (1 stitch increased)

m1r
Make 1 right: With your left-hand needle, pick up the bar between the last stitch you worked and the next stitch on the left-hand needle, bringing the needle from the back to the front, knit into the front of the stitch you just picked up (1 stitch increased)

m1rp
Make 1 right: With your left-hand needle pick up the bar between the last stitch you worked and the next stitch on the left-hand needle, bringing the needle from the back to the front, purl into the front of the stitch you just picked up (1 stitch increased)

Magic Loop
This technique is used to knit small circumferences in the round with a long circular needle. It works well for socks, hats, mittens and sweater sleeves, for example. Magic Loop is an alternative to double-pointed needles (DPNs). You can find tutorials online.

MC
Main colour

p
Purl

p1tbl / ptbl
Purl through back loop (twisted stitch)

p2tog
Purl 2 stitches together (1 stitch decreased)

p2tog tbl
Purl 2 stitches together through back loops (1 stitch decreased)

p3tog
Purl 3 stitches together (2 stitches decreased)

PM
Place marker

pwise
Purlwise

Raglan
Raglan is a sleeve type where the sleeve begins at the neck of the garment and extends diagonally to the underarm. There is no shoulder seam in raglan-shaped sweaters.

Ribbing
Ribbing (or rib stitch) is a common stitch pattern where vertical columns of knit and purl stitches alternate. The width of the columns can vary: in 1 x 1 ribbing, for example,

one knit stitch is followed by one purl stitch (and so on), and in 2 x 2 ribbing, two knit stitches are followed by two purl stitches. Ribbing is often used for cuffs, hems or brims.

RM
Remove marker

rnd(s)
Round(s)

RS
Right side of fabric

sl1
Slip 1 stitch (purlwise with yarn in back on right side and with yarn in front on wrong side, unless otherwise stated)

Slip
Move a stitch from the left-hand needle to the right-hand needle without working it (purlwise with yarn in back on right side and with yarn in front on wrong side, unless otherwise stated)

Slipped stitch
A stitch that is moved from one needle to the other without working it

SM
Slip the stitch marker from the left-hand needle to the right-hand needle

ssk
Slip, slip, knit: Slip 2 stitches one at a time as if to knit, knit them together through back loops (1 stitch decreased)

ssp
Slip, slip, purl: Slip 2 stitches one at a time as if to knit, purl them together through back loops (1 stitch decreased)

Stockinette Stitch
Stockinette stitch is the second most basic stitch pattern. It is created by knitting all stitches (when knitting in the round) or alternating knit and purl rows (when knitting flat). On the right side of the fabric, the stitches are shaped like Vs, and on the wrong side, they form horizontal ridges.

st(s)
Stitch(es)

tbl
Through the back loop

WS
Wrong side of fabric

wyib
With yarn held in back of the work

wyif
With yarn held in front of the work

yds
Yards

yo
Yarn over: Bring yarn between needles to the front, then over right-hand needle ready to knit the next stitch (1 stitch increased)

Yoke
The top part of the garment that fits over the shoulders.

– / ( ) / []
Repeat from * to * / (to) / [to]

SPECIAL ABBREVIATIONS

BORm
Beginning of the round marker

CDD
Central double decrease: Slip 2 stitches together as if to knit to your right-hand needle. Knit the next stitch. Pass the slipped stitches over the knitted stitch. (2 stitches decreased)

DS
Double stitch

Inc 3-into-1
Work *p1, k1, p1* into the same stitch (if the stitch is a purl stitch), or *k1, p1, k1* into the same stitch (if the stitch is a knit stitch) (2 stitches increased)

kDS
Knit double stitch: Knit both legs of a double stitch together

kfb
Knit into the front of the stitch without dropping it from the needle, then knit into the back of the same stitch, then drop it from the needle (1 stitch increased)

kfbf
Knit into the front of the stitch without dropping it from the needle, then knit into the back of the same stitch, then knit into the front of the same stitch again, then drop it from the needle (2 stitches increased)

LLI
Left lifted increase: Lift the left leg of the stitch 2 rows below the stitch on the right-hand needle onto the left-hand needle and knit it through the back loop (1 stitch increased)

mDS
Make double stitch: Slip the next stitch with yarn in front. Bring the yarn over the right-hand needle to the back of your work. Pull the working yarn tight, so that both legs of the slipped stitch lift onto the needle and create a "double stitch" (a stitch with two legs).

pDS
Purl double stitch: Purl both legs of a double stitch together

pfb
Purl into the front and back of the same stitch (1 stitch increased)

psso
Pass slipped stitch over

RLI
Right lifted increase: Insert the right-hand needle from back to front into the right leg of the stitch below the next stitch on the left-hand needle. Lift it and place it on the left-hand needle without twisting it and knit it. (1 stitch increased)

S2KP
Insert right-hand needle into 2 stitches together knitwise and slip onto right-hand needle, k1, pass the 2 slipped stitches over the knit stitch as if to bind off (2 stitches decreased)

skpo
Slip 1 stitch purlwise with yarn in back, knit 1 stitch, pass slipped stitch over the knit stitch (1 stitch decreased)

sssk
Slip, slip, slip, knit: Slip 3 stitches one at a time as if to knit, knit them together through back loops (2 stitches decreased)

w&t
Wrap & turn: Slip the next stitch as if to purl, bring the yarn to the front of your work then slip the stitch back to your left-hand needle. Turn work.
When working wrapped stitches, treat them as a single stitch by knitting or purling the stitch and its wrap together.

13

Jenny Ansah — Ida Wirak Trettevik — Jonna Hietala — Julia Wilkens — Veera Välimäki

Isabell Kraemer — Tiina Arponen — Maddy Moe — Nina Pommerenke — Sasha Hyre

Pauliina Kuunsola — Sylvia Watts-Cherry

Jenny Ansah

01 Give Me the Tee

This cropped, boxy T-shirt is knitted in simple Stockinette Stitch. The pattern is perfect for learning basic sweater-knitting elements such as short rows, increasing and picking up stitches.

SIZES

1 (2, 3, 4, 5) (6, 7, 8)

Recommended ease: 4–6" / 10–15 cm of positive ease.

FINISHED MEASUREMENTS

Bust Circumference: 37.75 (40, 44.25, 48.75, 52.25) (56, 59.75, 64)" / 94.5 (100, 111, 122, 131) (140, 149, 160) cm.
Length from Underarm to Hem (cropped): 6" / 15 cm.
Sleeve Length from Cuff to Underarm: 2" / 5 cm.
Upper Arm Circumference: 15 (16, 17.5, 19, 20.75) (21.5, 23.25, 24.25)" / 37.5 (40, 43.5, 47.5, 52) (53.5, 58, 61) cm.

MATERIALS

Yarn: 3 (3, 4, 4, 4) (5, 5, 5) skeins of Bomulin by Isager (65% cotton, 35% linen, 230 yds / 210 m – 50 g), colourway 58.
3 (3, 4, 4, 4) (5, 5, 6) skeins of Silk Mohair by Isager (75% kid mohair, 25% silk, 232 yds / 212 m – 25 g), colourway 58.

The yarns are held together throughout the pattern.

If you decide to use another yarn, you will need approx. 565 (630, 700, 775, 850) (935, 1030, 1135) yds / 520 (580, 645, 710, 780) (855, 945, 1040) m of light-fingering-weight yarn and approx. 590 (655, 730, 810, 890) (980, 1075, 1185) yds / 540 (600, 670, 745, 815) (900, 985, 1085) m of lace-weight yarn.

Needles: US 2.5 / 3 mm 16" / 40 cm circular needles (for neckband and sleeves), US 2.5 / 3 mm 48" / 120 cm circular needles (for yoke and body).

Notions: Stitch markers, stitch holders or waste yarn.

GAUGE

22 sts and 26 rows to 4" / 10 cm on US 2.5 / 3 mm in Stockinette Stitch knitted in the round holding both yarns together, after blocking.

MODIFICATIONS

You can also knit the sweater with only one strand of yarn. For the one-stranded version, you will need approx. 565 (630, 700, 775, 850) (935, 1030, 1135) yds / 520 (580, 645, 710, 780) (855, 945, 1040) m of sport-weight yarn.

NOTES

You can find the abbreviations and detailed instructions for techniques used in this pattern in the Abbreviations (pp. 20–23) and Techniques (pp. 15–19) sections.

Slip stitch markers as you come across them.

CONSTRUCTION

This sweater is worked top down in the round. The tee has a boxy fit and raglan sleeves. All the edges on the neckline, sleeves and hem are double-folded and hand-sewn in the end.

DIRECTIONS

NECKLINE

With US 2.5 / 3 mm 16" / 40 cm circular needles, cast on 80 (80, 96, 112, 112) (124, 124, 136) sts using the Long-Tail Cast-On Method (or method of choice) holding both yarns together. Join to work in the round and place a stitch marker to mark the beginning of the round (BOR). Be careful not to twist sts when joining in the rnd.

Rnds 1–5: K to end.
Rnd 6: P to end.
Rnds 7–11: K to end.

Option: If you want to join the cast-on edge and the working sts together before continuing to raglan yoke, proceed as follows: Fold the work in double with WS's facing each other. *Insert the right-hand needle through the first st on the left-hand needle and then from the cast-on edge, knit it together.* Repeat *–* with the rest of the sts until the end of the rnd.

YOKE

This is the part where you will divide the front, back and sleeves. To help figure out when to increase, you will add stitch markers. The increases will happen before and after the stitch marker. The BOR will be on the back of the right sleeve.

Set-up rnd: K2, PM, k9 (9, 11, 13, 13) (13, 13, 13), PM, k2, PM, k27 (27, 33, 39, 39) (45, 45, 51), PM, k2, PM, k9 (9, 11, 13, 13) (13, 13, 13), PM, k2, PM, k27 (27, 33, 39, 39) (45, 45, 51).

Back Neck Short Rows
Rnd 1 (RS): K2, SM, k to m, SM, k2, SM, k to m, SM, k2, SM, k to m, SM, k2, SM, k18 (18, 20, 26, 26) (28, 30, 34). Turn work.
Row 2 (WS): MDS, p7 (7, 7, 11, 11) (11, 13, 15). Turn work.

Row 3 (RS): MDS, k to DS, kDS, k2. Turn work.
Row 4 (WS): MDS, p to DS, pDS, p2. Turn work.
Repeat rows 3–4, 4 time in total. After the last repeat, MDS, turn work and k to BOR.

Raglan Increases
Rnd 1 (increase): *SM, k2, SM, m1l, k to next marker, m1r*, repeat *–* a total of 4 times. (8 sts inc'd)
Rnd 2: *SM, k2, SM, k to m*, repeat *–* a total of 4 times.
Repeat rnds 1–2, 26 (26, 28, 28, 28) (30, 30, 30) times in total. You have 61 (61, 67, 69, 69) (73, 73, 73) sts for both sleeves, 79 (79, 89, 95, 95) (105, 105, 111) sts for front and back and 2 sts for each raglan seam.

Next row: *SM, k2, SM, m1l, k next marker, m1r*, repeat *–* a total of 4 times in total. (8 sts inc'd)
Repeat this row 6 (8, 8, 10, 14) (14, 18, 20) times in total. You have 73 (77, 83, 89, 97) (101, 109, 113) sts for both sleeves, 91 (95, 105, 115, 123) (133, 141, 151) sts for front and back, and 2 sts in each raglan seam.

BODY

Separation of Sleeves and Body
Next, you will separate the sleeves and body into individual sections. Each section will be worked in the rnd.

Next rnd: RM, k2, RM, place the right sleeves sts on waste yarn or a stitch holder, RM, using the Backwards Loop Cast-On Method, cast on 4 (5, 6, 7, 8) (8, 9, 10) sts, PM, cast on 5 (6, 7, 8, 9) (9, 10, 11) sts, k2, RM, k to marker, RM, k2, RM, place the left sleeves sts on waste yarn or a stitch holder, RM, cast on 9 (11, 13, 15, 17) (17, 19, 21) sts, k2, RM, k to marker. This is the new BOR.
You have 208 (220, 244, 268, 288) (308, 328, 352) body sts on your needles.

Continue to work in Stockinette Stitch (k all sts) until your work measures 6" / 15 cm from underarm, or desired length.

HEM EDGE

Rnd 1: P to end.
Rnds 2–7: K to end.
Rnd 8: Bind off all sts knitwise.

SLEEVES

Note! You can pick up two extra sts between sleeve sts and cast-on in underarm than recommended in the pattern. It will help to prevent unwelcomed holes from appearing on underarm.

Place the 73 (77, 83, 89, 97) (101, 109, 113) sleeve sts from the scrap yarn or a stitch holder to 2.5 US / 3 mm 16" / 40 cm circular needles. Starting from the centre of the sts cast on for the underarm, pick up and k 4 (5, 6, 7, 8) (8, 9, 10) sts. K 73 (77, 83, 89, 97) (101, 109, 113) sts and pick up and k 5 (6, 7, 8, 9) (9, 10, 11) sts. Place a stitch marker for the BOR. You have 82 (88, 96, 104, 114) (118, 128, 134) sleeve sts.

Work in Stockinette Stitch (k all sts) until sleeve measures 2" / 5 cm or desired length.

Cuff Edge
Rnd 1: P to end.
Rnds 2–7: K to end.
Rnd 8: Bind off all sts knitwise.

FINISHING

Sewing the Sleeve and Hem Edges

Note! When hand-sewing the bind-off edge to the WS bars, do not pull the yarn too tight, as it will wrinkle the garment.

From the fingering (or sport if you knit a one stranded version) yarn ball wrap yarn around the edges two and a half times to measure the amount needed for hand-sewing. Cut the yarn and attach the other end to the yarn hanging from the edge

with a double knot. Pull the other end through the tapestry needle.

Fold the bind-off edge against the WS of the work with WS's facing each other. *Insert the tapestry needle through the first st from the bind-off edge together with the bar above it on the WS of the work. Pull the tapestry needle through them.* Repeat *–* with the rest of the sts until the end of the rnd.

Tie a knot and weave the remaining threads inside the double-folded edge. Remember to fold and sew the neckline similarly, if you haven't done so already.

Blocking

Wet block the sweater to measurements.

Ida Wirak Trettevik

02 Witre

Witre is a warm, oversized vest with high splits at the sides. It is knitted with large needles and three strands of yarn. A quick and rewarding project!

SIZES

1 (2, 3, 4, 5) (6, 7, 8)

Recommended ease: 4–6" / 10–15 cm of positive ease.

FINAL MEASUREMENTS

Chest Circumference: 41 (44.5, 48, 51.5, 55) (58.75, 62.25, 65.75)" / 102 (111, 120, 129, 138) (146.5, 155.5, 164.5) cm.
Length from Shoulder to Hem (front): 26.75 (27.25, 27.75, 28.25, 28.25) (28.75, 29.25, 29.25)" / 68 (69.5, 70.5, 72, 72) (73, 74.5, 74.5) cm.
Armhole Depth: 9 (9.5, 10, 10.5, 10.5) (11, 11.5, 11.5)" / 23 (24.5, 25.5, 27, 27) (28, 29.5, 29.5) cm.
Split Length: 11" / 28 cm (front), 16" / 40.5 cm (back).

MATERIALS

Yarn: 14 (14, 14, 15, 15) (16, 16, 16) balls of Hip Wool (100% Peruvian Highland Wool, 87 yds / 80 m – 50 g), colourway Gingerbread Brown.
3 (3, 3, 4, 4) (4, 4, 4) balls of Hip Mohair (80% mohair, 20% polyamide, 230 yds / 210 m – 25 g), colourway Chestnut Brown.

The vest is worked with both yarns held together throughout the pattern: two threads of Hip Wool and one thread of Hip mohair = three threads held together.

If you decide to use another yarn, you will need approx. 1135 (1175, 1218, 1265, 1305) (1335, 1365, 1392) yds / 1038 (1074, 1120, 1157, 1200) (1221, 1248, 1280) m of aran or bulky-weight yarn and approx. 540 (620, 690, 735, 780) (825, 870, 920) yds / 494 (567, 630, 672, 713) (754, 796, 841) m of lace-weight yarn.

Needles: US 13 / 9 mm 16" / 40 cm (for ribbing) and US 15 / 10 mm 32" / 80 cm (for body and yoke) circular needles.

Notions: Waste yarn or stitch holder, stitch markers.

GAUGE

9 sts x 16 rows to 4" / 10 cm on US 15 / 10 mm needles in Stockinette Stitch, after blocking.
Note! Row gauge is not critical for this project, as the pattern is written based on measurements.

NOTES

You can find the abbreviations and detailed instructions for techniques used in this pattern in the Abbreviations (pp. 20–23) and Techniques (pp. 15–19) sections.

Slip markers as you come across them.

Optional: For a neat edge, stitches at the splits and around the armhole openings are worked as follows: the first stitch is always slipped with yarn in front of the work and the last stitch is always worked as a knit stitch.

CONSTRUCTION

This vest is worked from the bottom up. First, front and back piece are worked flat separately to shape the splits, whereafter both pieces are placed on one needle to be worked in the round. The body is divided into front and back piece again at the armhole openings. They are joined together from the wrong side at the shoulders with a third needle. Finally, stitches are picked up around the neckline for the ribbing which is then folded double. The curled edges around the armhole openings are attached to the WS.

MODIFICATIONS

This vest also works with little ease, thus more fitting. It's all about your personal preferences and how you like to style your garments!

DIRECTIONS

FRONT

With US 13 / 9 mm needles, cast on 48 (52, 56, 60, 64) (68, 72, 76) sts with three threads of yarn held together (two threads of wool yarn and one thread of mohair).

Start to work in ribbing as follows:
Next row (WS): P3, *k2, p2*, repeat *–* to 1 st before end, p1.
Next row (RS): K3, *p2, k2*, repeat *–* to 1 st before end, k1.
Work in established 2 x 2 Ribbing until piece measures 2" / 5 cm. End with a WS row.

Change to a US 15 / 10 mm needles. Work flat in Stockinette Stitch (k all sts on RS rows and p all sts on WS rows), until the slipover measures 11" / 28 cm from cast-on edge. End with a WS row. Place sts on hold on waste yarn or a stitch holder.

BACK

With US 13 / 9 mm needles, cast on 48 (52, 56, 60, 64) (68, 72, 76) sts with three threads of yarn held together (two threads of wool yarn and one thread of mohair).

Start to work in ribbing as follows:
Next row (WS): P3, *k2, p2*, repeat *–* to 1 st before end, p1.
Next row (RS): K3, *p2, k2*, repeat *–* to 1 st before end, k1.
Work in established 2 x 2 Ribbing until piece measures 2" / 5 cm. End with a WS row.

Change to US 15 / 10 mm needles. Work flat in Stockinette Stitch (k all sts on RS rows and p all sts on WS rows), until the slipover measures 16" / 40.5 cm from cast-on edge. End with WS row.
On the following RS row join back and front pieces as follows:

K the back sts until 2 sts left, ssk, PM (this is the BOR m). Take front sts from hold back on needles and k2tog, k to last 2 sts, ssk, PM, k2tog (first two sts of back), k to BOR m.

You should have 92 (100, 108, 116, 124) (132, 140, 148) sts in total: 46 (50, 54, 58, 62) (66, 70, 74) sts for both back and front.

BODY

Continue to work in the rnd in Stockinette Stitch (k all sts) until the front piece measures 18" / 45.5 cm from cast-on edge. Bind off 4 sts on both sides (2 sts before and after each stitch marker). Place a new stitch marker at the centre front. You should have 42 (46, 50, 54, 58) (62, 66, 70) sts for both back and front.

Next, you will continue to work the front piece only, back and forth. Either place the back sts on waste yarn or a stitch holder on hold or keep on your circular needles but don't work them.

Front

Work flat in Stockinette Stitch (k all sts on RS and p all sts on WS) across the front piece until the slipover measures 21 (21, 21.5, 22, 22.5) (23, 23.5, 23.5)" / 53.5 (53.5, 54.5, 56, 57) (58.5, 59.5, 59.5) cm from cast-on edge, ending with WS row. On following RS row bind off the centre 8 (8, 8, 8, 8) (10, 10, 10) sts and k to end of the row [17 (19, 21, 23, 25) (26, 28, 30) sts left for both fronts].

Right Front

The right front is worked flat in Stockinette Stitch (k all sts on RS and p all sts on WS). At the same time, work every RS row as follows: K2, ssk, k to end. Repeat the decrease 4 (5, 5, 5, 5) (5, 6, 6) times in total. You should have 13 (14, 16, 18, 20) (21, 22, 24) sts.

Continue to work flat in Stockinette Stitch (k all sts on RS and p all sts on WS) across remaining sts until the slipover measures 27 (27.5, 28, 28.5, 28.5) (29, 29.5, 29.5)" / 68.5 (70, 71, 72.5, 72.5) (73.5, 75, 75) cm from cast on edge. Place remaining sts on hold on waste yarn or a stitch holder.

Left Front

Start WS row at neckline and work left front piece flat in Stockinette Stitch (k all sts on RS and p all sts on WS). At the same time, work every RS row as follows: K to 4 sts before end, k2tog, k to end. Repeat the decrease 4 (5, 5, 5) (5, 6, 6) times in total. You should have 13 (14, 16, 18, 20) (21, 22, 24) sts.

Continue to work flat in Stockinette Stitch (k all sts on RS and p all sts on WS) across remaining sts, until the slipover measures 27 (27.5, 28, 28.5, 28.5) (29, 29.5, 29.5)" / 68.5 (70, 71, 72.5, 72.5) (73.5, 75, 75) cm from cast-on edge. Place remaining sts on hold on waste yarn or a stitch holder.

Back

Work back piece flat in Stockinette Stitch (k all sts on RS and p all sts on WS), until it measures 32 (32.5, 33, 33.5, 33.5) (34, 34.5, 34.5)" / 81 (82.5, 83.5, 85, 85) (86, 87.5, 87.5) cm from cast-on edge.

On the next WS row, with RS's facing each other, and using the 3-Needle Bind-Off Method, join 13 (14, 16, 18, 20) (21, 22, 24) shoulder sts from both front pieces with the back piece.

Leave 16 (18, 18, 18, 18) (20, 22, 22) neck sts on hold on waste yarn or a stitch holder.

NECKLINE

With US 13 / 9 mm needles, start at the neck's left side and pick up sts as follows: Pick up and k 14 (15, 15, 15, 15) (15, 14, 14) sts evenly along the left side, pick up and k 1 st into each of the 8 (8, 8, 8, 8) (10, 10, 10) front piece sts. Pick up and k the same number of sts evenly along the right side and knit the neck sts onto the needle. You should have 52 (56, 56, 56, 56) (60, 60, 60) sts.

Work in ribbing as follows:
K2, p2, repeat *–* to end.
Continue to work in established 2 x 2 Ribbing until the neckline measures 4.5" / 11.5 cm.

Fold collar double and attach to the WS while at the same time binding off sts. (*Note!* Alternatively, you can bind off all sts and sew the edge to WS.)
Work collar as follows:
Pick up 1 st at the bottom of neckline on WS and knit it together (k2tog) with the 1st st on the left-hand needle. Repeat *–* and bind off sts at the same time (slip the 2nd st from the right-hand needle over the 1st st).

FINISHING

Weave in ends. Wet block the vest to measurements.

The edges around the armhole openings will curl approx. 1" / 2.5 cm. Use a thread of mohair (for a nearly invisible finish), attach the curled edges to the WS by sewing a couple of small sts around the openings.

Jonna Hietala

SUPER EASY!

03 Arthur

Arthur is a quick-to-finish basic hat knitted in thick yarn. This ribbed hat with a folded brim is just as perfect for the streets of New York as for a walk in the forest.

SIZES

1 (2, 3)

To fit a head circumference of approx. 20–21 (21–23, 23–25)" / 51–53 (53–58.5, 58.5–63.5) cm.

FINISHED MEASUREMENTS

Circumference: 12.75 (14, 15.25)" / 32 (35, 38.5) cm.
Height (unfolded): 11.5" / 29 cm.
Note! Because the hat is very stretchy, its circumference is significantly smaller than your head's.

MATERIALS

Yarn: 1 skein of Crazy Sexy Wool by Wool and the Gang (100% wool, 87 yds / 80 m – 200 g), colourway Earthy Orange.

If you decide to use another yarn, you will need approx. 67 (74, 80) yds / 62 (68, 74) m of super-bulky-weight yarn.

Needles: US 13 / 9 mm circular needles, preferably 19" / 50 cm long.

Notions: Stitch marker.

GAUGE

12.5 sts x 11 rows to 4" / 10 cm in 1 x 1 Ribbing, after light steam blocking.

NOTES

You can find the abbreviations and detailed instructions for techniques used in this pattern in the Abbreviations (pp. 20–23) and Techniques (pp. 15–19) sections.

Slip marker as you come across it.

CONSTRUCTION

This hat is knitted from the bottom up in 1 x 1 Ribbing. It features a cosy folded brim and easy crown decreases.

DIRECTIONS

Cast on 40 (44, 48) sts loosely using the German Twisted Cast-On Method, Long-Tail Cast-On Method or method of choice. Place a marker for the beginning of the rnd (BOR) being careful not to twist sts and join to work in the rnd.

Start to work in 1 x 1 Ribbing as follows:
Rnd 1: *K1, p1*, repeat *–* to end.
Work in established ribbing until the piece measures 11" / 28 cm from the cast-on edge.

CROWN

Start to work crown decreases as follows:
Decrease rnd: *K2tog*, repeat *–* to the end. You should have 20 (22, 24) sts. Repeat the decrease rnd once more. You should have 10 (11, 12) sts.

Cut yarn and pull it through the remaining sts.

FINISHING

Weave in ends and steam lightly, if needed.

Julia Wilkens

SUPER EASY!

04 Paula

Paula is a long scarf that features a beautiful Moss Stitch pattern and stripes. It is knitted with two strands, one of which is a mohair yarn, adding luxurious fluffiness to this simple accessory.

SIZE

One Size

FINISHED MEASUREMENTS

Length: 69.5" / 174 cm.
Width: 13.25" / 33.5 cm.

MATERIALS

Yarn A (main colour): 2 skeins of Arwetta by Filcolana (80% wool, 20% nylon, 230 yds / 210 m – 50 g), colourway Natural White 101, and 3 skeins of Ombelle by Fonty (75% mohair, 20% wool, 5% polyamide, 159 yds / 145 m – 50 g), colourway Ecru 1051.
In the pattern, Yarn A refers to these two yarns held together.

Yarn B (contrasting colour): 1 skein of Bicycle by West Wool (90% merino, 10% texel, 390 yds / 350 m – 100 g), colourway Beatrix, and 1 skein of Glowhair by West Wool (72% mohair, 28% silk, 437 yds / 400 m – 50 g), colourway Beatrix.
In the pattern, Yarn B refers to these two yarns held together.

If you decide to use another yarn, you will need approx.
For yarn A: 460 yds / 420 m of fingering-weight yarn and 421 yds / 385 m of lace-weight yarn held together.
For yarn B: 274 yds / 250 m of fingering-weight yarn and 210 yds / 192 m of lace-weight yarn held together.

Needles: US 5 / 3.75 mm 32" / 80 cm circular needles.

Notions: 1 removable stitch marker, tapestry needle, crochet hook of ca. US D-3 – G-6 / 3.25–4 mm.

GAUGE

15 sts x 30 rows to 4" / 10 cm on US 5 / 3.75 mm needles in Moss Stitch, after blocking.

STITCH PATTERNS

Moss Stitch
Row 1: *K1, p1*, repeat *–* to end.
Row 2: *P1, k1*, repeat *–* to end.

NOTES

You can find the abbreviations and detailed instructions for techniques used in this pattern in the Abbreviations (pp. 20–23) and Techniques (pp. 15–19) sections.

CONSTRUCTION

This scarf is knitted flat with two strands of yarn held together thoughout the pattern. The scarf gets its fascinating woven structure sections by changing the colour every row. To achieve this, the stitches are slid back at the end of the row and then knitted again in the same direction.

DIRECTIONS

With yarn A and the Long-Tail Cast-On Method or method of choice, cast on 50 sts.

Yarn A Stripe

Begin working in Moss Stitch.
Row 1 (RS): *K1, p1*, repeat *–* to end.
Row 2 (WS): *P1, k1*, repeat *–* to end. Mark RS with a removable stitch marker.
Rows 3–14: Repeat rows 1–2, 6 times more.

Yarn A/B Stripe

Row 15 (RS): With yarn B, *k1, p1*, repeat *–* to end. Don't turn work.
Row 16 (RS): Slide sts back to the other side of the needle, with yarn A, *p1, k1*, repeat *–* to end.

Row 17 (WS): With yarn B, *k1, p1*, repeat *–* to end. Don't turn work.
Row 18 (WS): Slide sts back to the other side of the needle, with yarn A, *p1, k1*, repeat *–* to end.

Row 19 (RS): With yarn B, *k1, p1*, repeat *–* to end.
Row 20 (WS): With yarn B, *p1, k1*, repeat *–* to end.
Row 21 (RS): Twist yarn A around yarn B once. With yarn B, *k1, p1*, repeat *–* to end.
Row 22 (WS): With yarn B, *p1, k1*, repeat *–* to end.

Row 23 (RS): With yarn A, *k1, p1*, repeat *–* to end. Don't turn work.
Row 24 (RS): Slide sts back to the other side of the needle. With yarn B, *p1, k1*, repeat *–* to end.

Row 25 (WS): With yarn A, *k1, p1*, repeat *–* to end. Don't turn work.
Row 26 (WS): Slide sts back to the other side of the needle. With yarn B, *p1, k1*, repeat *–* to end. Cut yarn B.
Work rows 1–26 (Yarn A and A/B Stripe) for 19 times total.

Work rows 1–14 (Yarn A Stripe) once more.

Bind off loosely.

FRINGES

Cut 3 strands of yarn B to a length of 12" / 30 cm. Repeat until you have 50 fringes. Starting on the right corner of the cast-on edge of the scarf, attach 25 fringes to every other loop of the cast-on sts. Work the same way on the other end of the scarf.

FINISHING

Weave in ends. Wet block to measurements.

Veera Välimäki

05 Sypressi

SUPER EASY!

Sypressi is a fun, oversized sweater with joyful stripes. Thanks to its simple, seamless top-down construction, it's also perfect as a first sweater.

SIZES

1 (2, 3, 4, 5) (6, 7, 8)

Recommended ease: 4–6" / 10–15 cm of positive ease.

FINISHED MEASUREMENTS

Chest Circumference: 37.75 (41.25, 45.75, 50.25, 54.75) (59.5, 62.75, 66.25)" / 94.5 (103, 114.5, 125.5, 137) (148.5, 157, 165.5) cm.
Collar Circumference: 20.5 (20.5, 20.5, 20.5, 21.75) (21.75, 21.75, 21.75)" / 51.5 (51.5, 51.5, 51.5, 54.5) (54.5, 54.5, 54.5) cm.
Upper Arm Circumference: 10.75 (12, 13.25, 14.25, 16) (17.75, 18.75, 20)" / 27 (30, 33, 35.5, 40) (44.5, 47, 50) cm.
Yoke Depth: 8.5 (9.75, 11.5, 10.5, 10.75) (11.5, 12.5, 13.5)" / 21.5 (24.5, 28.5, 26, 27) (28.5, 31, 33.5) cm.
Body Length: 12" / 31 cm.

Cuff Circumference: 8 (8.5, 9.25, 10.25, 10.75) (12.5, 13.25, 13.75)" / 20 (21.5, 23, 25.5, 27) (31.5, 33, 34.5) cm.

MATERIALS

Yarn: Cyrano by De Rerum Natura (100% wool, 164 yds / 150 m – 100 g).
MC: 4 (4, 5, 5, 6) (6, 7, 7) skeins of colourway Genêt (yellow sample) or Baleine Bleue (blue sample).
CC: 1 (1, 2, 2, 2) (2, 2, 2) skein(s) of colourway Bois De Rose (yellow sample) or Erable (blue sample).

If you decide to use another yarn, you will need approx. 580 (640, 720, 800, 870) (960, 1050, 1140) yds / 530 (590, 660, 730, 800) (880, 960, 1040) m of aran-weight yarn in MC and approx. 130 (155, 175, 200, 230) (260, 295, 325) yds / 120 (140, 160, 180, 210) (240, 270, 300) m of aran-weight yarn in CC.

Needles: US 6 / 4 mm (for ribbing) and US 8 / 5 mm (for body and sleeves) 32" / 80 cm circular needles. DPNs in the same sizes for small circumference knitting, if not using the Magic Loop Method.

Notions: Stitch markers, stitch holders or waste yarn.

GAUGE

14 sts x 20 rnds to 4" / 10 cm on US 8 / 5 mm needles in Stockinette Stitch, after blocking.

NOTES

You can find the abbreviations and detailed instructions for techniques used in this pattern in the Abbreviations (pp. 20–23) and Techniques (pp. 15–19) sections.
Slip markers as you come across them.

There's no need to cut the working yarn between stripes. To prevent a jog or ladder at the colour change, always twist the yarn at changing point (e.g., bring the new colour always from above the current colour). Keeping the direction of the twist consistent will make the changes look neat.

CONSTRUCTION

This sweater is knitted seamlessly from the top down with raglan seams. The stripes are worked as follows: three rounds of main colour (MC) followed by one round of contrast colour (CC).

DIRECTIONS

COLLAR

Using US 6 / 4 mm needles and MC, cast on 72 (72, 72, 72, 76) (76, 76, 76) sts using the Long-Tail Cast-On Method or method of choise. Carefully join in the rnd without twisting sts and PM for the beginning of rnd (BOR).

Work 8 rnds in 1 x 1 Ribbing as follows: *K1, p1*, repeat *-* to end.

YOKE

Now you will begin to work the yoke. The yoke is shaped with raglan increases which will be worked in two parts.
Change to US 8 / 5 mm needles.

Next rnd (MC, RS): K12 (12, 12, 12, 12) (12, 12, 12), PM, k24 (24, 24, 24, 26) (26, 26, 26), PM, k12 (12, 12, 12, 12) (12, 12, 12), PM, k24 (24, 24, 24, 26) (26, 26, 26) to BOR.

First Part of Raglan Increases
Continue on RS and attach CC.
Rnd 1 (MC): *K1, m1l, k to 1 st before next m, m1r, k1*, repeat *-* 3 more times to BOR.
Rnd 2 (CC): K to end.
Rnd 3 (MC): *K1, m1l, k to 1 st before next m, m1r, k1*, repeat *-* 3 more times to BOR.
Rnd 4 (MC): K to end.
Repeat rnds 1–4, 1 (2, 2, 2, 2) (2, 3, 3) more time(s). Then work rnds 1–2, 1 (0, 0, 0, 1) (1, 0, 1) more time. You should have 112 (120, 120, 120, 132) (132, 140, 148) sts.

Second Part of Raglan Increases
Sizes 1, 2 and 3 only
Note! Keep striping as established continuing with the correct colour (stripe pattern of 3 rnds in MC and 1 rnd in CC).
Rnd 1: *K1, m1l, k to 1 st before next m, m1r, k1*, repeat *-* 3 more times to BOR.
Rnd 2: K to end.

Rnd 3: *K to m, SM, k1, m1l, k to 1 st before next m, m1r, k1*, repeat *-* once more to BOR.
Rnd 4: K to end.
Repeat rnds 1–4, 7 (8, 10, –, –) (–, –, –) more time(s).

Sizes 4, 5, 6, 7 and 8 only
Note! Keep striping as established continuing with the correct colour (stripe pattern of 3 rnds in MC, 1 rnd in CC).
Rnd 1: *K1, m1l, k to 1 st before next m, m1r, k1*, repeat *-* 3 more times to BOR.
Rnd 2: *K to m, SM, k1, m1l, k to 1 st before next m, m1r, k1*, repeat *-* once more to BOR.
Rnd 3: K to end of rnd.
Repeat rnds 1–3, – (–, –, 12, 12) (13, 14, 15) more time(s).

After all raglan increases you should have 208 (228, 252, 276, 288) (300, 320, 340) sts.

On the next rnd, divide for body and sleeves. *Note!* Remember to continue with correct colour to keep the striping continuous.
Next rnd: *Place all sts before next m on holder, RM, cast on 0 (0, 0, 0, 4) (8, 8, 8) st(s) using the Backwards Loop Cast-On Method or method of choice, k to m*, repeat *-* once.

You should have 132 (144, 160, 176, 192) (208, 220, 232) sts on for the body and 38 (42, 46, 50, 52) (54, 58, 62) sts on each holder for the sleeves.

BODY

Continue with the sts on needle and keep the striping continuous. Work in Stockinette Stitch (k all sts) and stripe pattern until the body measures 10" / 25.5 cm from underarm. End with 2 rnds of MC.

Change to US 6 / 4 mm needles.
Next rnd (decrease): *(K1, p1) 5 times, k1, p2tog*, repeat *-* 9 (9, 11, 11, 13) (13, 15, 15) more times, *k1, p1*, repeat *-* to

end. You should have 122 (134, 148, 164, 178) (194, 204, 216) sts.

Finish the hem with 1 x 1 Ribbing:
K1, p1, repeat *–* to end.
Work in established 1 x 1 Ribbing for 2" / 5 cm. Bind off all sts in ribbing.

SLEEVES

Place the held sts on US 8 / 5 mm needles. Begin with the right colour to keep the striping continuous and starting from the centre of underarm pick up and k 0 (0, 0, 0, 2) (4, 4, 4) st(s), k the sts on needle, pick up and k 0 (0, 0, 0, 2) (4, 4, 4) st(s) to centre of underarm. You should have 38 (42, 46, 50, 56) (62, 66, 70) sts.

Work in Stockinette Stitch (k all sts) and stripes until the sleeve measures 2" / 5 cm from underarm.

Decrease rnd: K1, ssk, k to last 3 sts, k2tog, k1. (2 sts dec'd)
Repeat the decrease rnd 3 (4, 5, 5, 6) (6, 7, 7) more times on every 8th (8th, 8th, 6th, 6th) (6th, 4th, 4th) rnd. You should have 30 (32, 34, 38, 42) (48, 50, 54) sts.

Work in Stockinette Stitch (k all sts) and stripes until the sleeve measures 14" / 35.5 cm from underarm. End with one rnd in MC.
Change to US 6 / 4 mm needles.
Next rnd (decrease): *(K1, p1) 3 times, k1, p2tog*, repeat *–* 1 (1, 1, 1, 3) (3, 3, 5) more time(s), *k1, p1* to end if needed in your size. You should have 28 (30, 32, 36, 38) (44, 46, 48) sts.

Work the cuff in 1 x 1 Ribbing:
K1, p1, repeat *–* to end.
Work in established 1 x 1 Ribbing for 5" / 12.5 cm. Bind off all sts in ribbing.

FINISHING

Weave in all ends. Wet block the sweater to measurements.

Jonna Hietala

SUPER EASY!

06 Audrey

At first a few increases, then some straightforward knitting, and finally a bunch of blissful decreases. It is as simple as that to make this headband, which has echoes from the 1950s.

SIZE

One Size

FINISHED MEASUREMENTS

Length: 24" / 61 cm
Width: 3.25" / 8.5 cm.
Both the length and width of the headband are easily adjustable, if needed.

MATERIALS

Yarn: 1 skein of Acadia by The Fibre Co. (60% merino, 20% baby alpaca, 20% silk, 145 yds / 133 m – 50 g), colourway Sand.

1 ball of Sensai by Ito (60% mohair, 40% silk, 262 yds/ 240 m – 20 g), colourway String.

The headband is worked holding both yarns together.

If you decide to use another yarn, you will need approx. 58 yds / 53 m of DK-weight yarn and approx. 66 yds / 60 m of lace-weight yarn.

Needles: US 6 / 4 mm. You can use circular needles, straight needles or two DPNs – pick your favourite!

GAUGE

23 sts x 30 rows to 4" / 10 cm in Garter Stitch, after blocking.

NOTES

You can find the abbreviations and detailed instructions for techniques used in this pattern in the Abbreviations (pp. 20–23) and Techniques (pp. 15–19) sections.

Audrey is a great stashbuster as it only requires a small amount of yarn. Since the size is so easily adjustable by making more or less increases and rows, use whatever yarns you wish.

CONSTRUCTION

This headband is knitted flat in Garter Stitch. The tapered ends are shaped with increases (at the beginning) and decreases (at the end). Wear it by knotting the ends together.

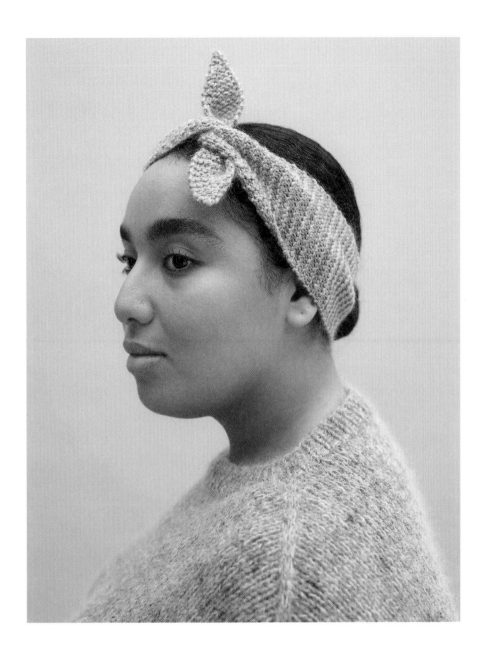

DIRECTIONS

Holding the two yarns together, cast on 2 sts.

Row 1: Sl1 (pwise with yarn in back), k to end.

Row 2: Sl1 (pwise with yarn in back), k to 1 st before the end, yo, k1. (1 st inc'd)

Row 3: K1, k the yo through the backloop (this way, it doesn't create a hole in the fabric), k to end.

Repeat rows 2–3 until you have 20 sts. [The last row is the row 3 (without the increase).]

Continue knitting in Garter Stitch (k all sts) with these sts for 114 more rows. *Note! The length of the headband might seem too short but Garter Stitch stretches quite a bit after blocking. Try the headband on while knitting it and adjust to your liking.*

Finally, it is time to decrease.

Row 4: Sl1 (purlwise with yarn in back), k to 3 sts before the end, k2tog, k1. (1 st dec'd)

Row 5: Sl1 (purlwise with yarn in back), k to end.

Repeat rows 4–5, until you have 2 sts. Bind off.

FINISHING

Weave in the ends and wet block to measurements.

Isabell Kraemer

07 Helmi

Helmi is a basic yoke sweater with a decorative mosaic pattern on the yoke. Mosaic knitting is a fun slipped-stitch colourwork technique in which you work with only one colour at a time.

SIZES

1 (2, 3, 4, 5) (6, 7, 8)

Recommended ease: 2–4" / 5–10 cm of positive ease.

FINISHED MEASUREMENTS

Bust Circumference: 36.25 (40, 44.25, 48, 53) (58, 62, 66)" / 90.5 (100, 110, 120, 132) (145, 155, 165) cm.
Upper Arm Circumference: 12.25 (13, 13.75, 15.25, 17) (19, 20.25, 21.25)" / 30.5 (32.5, 34.5, 38, 43) (47.5, 50.5, 53.5) cm.
Front Neck to Underarm: 7.25 (7.75, 8, 8.75, 9.75) (10, 10, 10.5)" / 18.5 (19.5, 20.5, 22, 25) (25.5, 25.5, 26.5) cm.
Body Length from Underarm (adjustable): 15.25" / 39 cm.
Sleeve Length from Underarm (adjustable): 18" / 46 cm.

MATERIALS

Yarn: Vovó by Retrosaria Rosa Pomar (100% wool, 156 yds / 143 m – 50 g).
MC: 7 (8, 8, 9, 10) (11, 11, 12) skeins of colourway 03.

C1: 1 skein of colourway 20.
C2: 1 skein of colourway 10.

If you decide to use another yarn, you will need approx. 993 (1095, 1179, 1318, 1482) (1593, 1654, 1755) yds / 908 (1001, 1078, 1205, 1355) (1457, 1512, 1605) m of sport-weight yarn in MC, approx. 41 (43, 46, 48, 73) (77, 80, 83) yds / 38 (39, 42, 44, 67) (70, 73, 76) m of sport-weight yarn in C1 and approx. 32 (33, 35, 37, 56) (59, 61, 64) yds / 29 (30, 32, 34, 51) (54, 56, 59) m of sport-weight yarn in C2.

Needles: US 4 / 3.5 mm 16" / 40 cm and 32" / 80 cm circular needles and DPNs (for ribbing), US 5 / 3.75 mm 16" / 40 cm and 32" / 80 cm circular needle and DPNs (for body and sleeves).

Notions: Stitch holders or waste yarn, stitch markers.

GAUGE

21 sts x 33 rows to 4" / 10 cm on US 5 / 3.75 mm needles in Stockinette Stitch, after blocking.

NOTES

You can find the abbreviations and detailed instructions for techniques used in this pattern in the Abbreviations (pp. 20–23) and Techniques (pp. 15–19) sections.

The beginning of the rnd is at the centre back. After dividing the body and sleeves, the beginning of the rnd moves to the right underarm.

Slip stitch markers as you reach them.

After increase or decrease rounds, you will find totals to check your stitch count. When changing colours, cut the unused yarn or carry it up to the next colour change. For the sample yarns have been cut. Sizes 1 to 4 will work 3 sets of stripes, sizes 5 to 8 will work 4 sets of stripes.

CONSTRUCTION

This sweater is worked seamlessly from the top down. Starting with the neck shaping, short rows are worked back and forth to create a higher back neck. The yoke – featuring a simple slipped stitch pattern – is then worked in the round

to sleeve separation. Sleeve stitches are placed on hold to work the body top down to the ribbing first. The sleeves are then worked top down to the cuffs. Optional neck finishing can be worked last.

MODIFICATIONS

Body and sleeves can be lengthened or shortened by working more or less rounds in Stockinette Stitch before starting the ribbing.

The neck can be finished with ribbing. The sample shows the neck unfinished.

DIRECTIONS

YOKE

With MC and shorter US 4 / 3.5 mm circular needles, cast on 100 (104, 104, 108, 108) (112, 112, 112) sts using the Long-Tail Cast-On Method or method of choice. Join to work in the rnd (being careful not to twist sts) and place m for the beginning of rnd (BOR). Rnds begin at the centre of back.

Change to shorter US 5 / 3.75 mm needles.
Rnd 1: K to end.

Size 3 only
Rnd 2 (inc rnd): K10, m1l, *k17, m1l*, repeat *-* to 9 sts before end, k to end. (110 sts)

Size 4 only
Rnd 2 (inc rnd): *K13, m1l, k14, m1l *, repeat *-* to end. (116 sts)

Size 5 only
Rnd 2 (inc rnd): K9, m1l, *k7, m1l*, repeat *-* to 8 sts before end, k to end. (122 sts)

Size 6 only
Rnd 2 (inc rnd): *K7, m1l*, repeat *-* to end. (128 sts)

Size 7 only
Rnd 2 (inc rnd): K4, m1l, *k5, m1l*, repeat *-* to 3 sts before end, k to end. (134 sts)

Size 8 only
Rnd 2 (inc rnd): *K4, m1l*, repeat *-* to end. (140 sts)

Sizes 3, 4, 5, 6, 7 and 8 only
Rnd 3: K to end.

All sizes
You will start to work German Short Rows to make the neck higher.
Short row 1 (RS): K30 (31, 32, 33, 34) (36, 37, 39), turn work.
Short row 2 (WS): Make Double Stitch

(MDS), p to BOR m, SM, p30 (31, 32, 33, 34) (36, 37, 39), turn work.
Short row 3 (RS): MDS, k9 (5, 6, 7, 8) (10, 11, 13), m1l, *k5, m1l*, repeat *-* a total of 3 (4, 4, 4, 4) (4, 4, 4) times, k to BOR m, SM, *k5, m1l*, repeat *-* a total of 4 (5, 5, 5, 5) (5, 5, 5) times, k to DS, knit Double Stitch (kDS), k4, turn work. You should have 108 (114, 120, 126, 132) (138, 144, 150) sts.
Short row 4 (WS): MDS, p to BOR m, SM, p to DS, purl Double Stitch (pDS), p4, turn work.
Short row 5 (RS): MDS, k to BOR m, SM, k to DS, kDS, k4, turn work.
Short row 6 (WS): Repeat short row 4.
Short row 7 (RS): MDS, k to BOR m, SM, k to DS, kDS, k5, turn work.
Short row 8 (WS): MDS, p to BOR m, SM, p to DS, pDS, p5, turn work.
Next row (RS): MDS, k to BOR m.

Next rnd: K to DS, kDS, k to next DS, kDS, k to end.

Work 2 rnds in Stockinette Stitch (k all sts).

Note! Change to longer US 5 / 3.75 mm circular needles when needed to accommodate the increasing number of sts.

Next rnd (inc rnd): *K3, m1l*, repeat *-* to end. You should have 144 (152, 160, 168, 176) (184, 192, 200) sts.

Work 2 rnds in Stockinette Stitch (k all sts).

Slipped Stitch Pattern
With C1,
Rnd 1: K to end.
Rnd 2: P to end.

With C2,
Rnd 3: *K1, sl1 pwise with yarn in back (wyib)*, repeat *-* to end.
Rnd 4: *P1, sl1 pwise wyib*, repeat *-* to end.

With MC,
Rnd 5: K to end.
Rnd 6: K to end.

With C1,
Rnd 7: K to end.
Rnd 8: P to end.

With C2,
Rnd 9: *K1, sl1 pwise wyib*, repeat *–* to end.
Rnd 10: *P1, sl1 pwise wyib*, repeat *–* to end.

With MC,
Work 3 rnds in Stockinette Stitch (k all sts).

Next rnd (inc rnd): K2, m1l, *k4, m1l*, rep *–* to 2 sts before end, k2. You should have 180 (190, 200, 210, 220) (230, 240, 250) sts.

Next rnd: K to end.

Work rnds 1–10 of Slipped Stitch Pattern.

With MC,
Work 3 rnds in Stockinette Stitch (k all sts).

Next rnd (inc rnd): *K5, m1l*, repeat *–* to end. You should have 216 (228, 240, 252, 264) (276, 288, 300) sts.

Next rnd: K to end.

Work rnds 1–10 of Slipped Stitch Pattern.

With MC,
Work 3 rnds in Stockinette Stitch (k all sts).

Next rnd (inc rnd): K3, m1l, *k6, m1l*, repeat *–* to 3 sts before end, k3. You should have 252 (266, 280, 294, 308) (322, 336, 350) sts.

Sizes 1, 2, 3 and 4 only
Work 8 rnds in Stockinette Stitch (k all sts).

Size 1 only
Next rnd (inc rnd): K14, m1l, *k25, m1l*, repeat *–* to 13 sts before end, k13. (262 sts)

Size 2 only
Next rnd (inc rnd): K13, m1l, *k16, m1l*, repeat *–* to 13 sts before end of rnd, k13. (282 sts)

Size 3 only
Next rnd (inc rnd): K14, m1l, *k11, m1l*, repeat *–* to 13 sts before end, k13. (304 sts)

Size 4 only
Next rnd (inc rnd): K18, m1l, *k7, m1l*, repeat *–* to 17 sts before end, k17. (332 sts)

Sizes 5, 6, 7 and 8 only
Next rnd: K to end.
Work rnds 1–10 of Slip Stitch Pattern.
With MC,
Work 3 rnds in Stockinette Stitch (k all sts).
Next rnd (inc rnd): *K7, m1l*, repeat *–* to end. You should have – (–, –, –, 352) (368, 384, 400) sts.
Work 8 rnds in Stockinette Stitch (k all sts).

Size 5 only
Next rnd (inc rnd): K15, m1l, *k19, m1l*, repeat *–* to 14 sts before end, k14. (370 sts)

Size 6 only
Next rnd (inc rnd): *K9, m1l*, repeat *–* to 8 sts before end, k8. (408 sts)

Sizes 7 and 8 only
Next rnd (inc rnd): K4, m1l, *k8, m1l*, repeat *–* to 4 sts before end, k4. You should have – (–, –, –, –) (–, 432, 450) sts.
Work 8 rnds in Stockinette Stitch (k all sts).

Size 7 only
Next rnd (inc rnd): K108, m1l, k216, m1l, k to end. (434 sts)

Size 8 only
Next rnd (inc rnd): K29, m1l, *k56, m1l*, repeat *–* to 29 sts before end, k29. (458 sts)

All sizes
Work in Stockinette Stitch (k all sts) in the rnd until yoke measures 7.25 (7.75, 8, 8.75, 9.75) (10, 10, 10.5)" / 18.5 (19.5, 20.5, 22, 25) (25.5, 25.5, 26.5) cm from cast-on, measured from the centre front down.

DIVIDE FOR BODY AND SLEEVES

Next rnd: K41 (45, 49, 53, 59) (64, 69, 73), place 50 (52, 54, 60, 68) (76, 80, 84) sleeve sts on a holder or waste yarn, using the Backwards Loop Cast-On Method or method of choice, cast on 7 (8, 9, 10, 11) (12, 13, 14) sts, PM (new BOR marker), cast on 7 (8, 9, 10, 11) (12, 13, 14) sts, k81 (89, 98, 106, 117) (128, 137, 145), place 50 (52, 54, 60, 68) (76, 80, 84) sleeve sts on a holder or waste yarn, using the Backwards Loop Cast-On Method, cast on 7 (8, 9, 10, 11) (12, 13, 14) sts, PM (side marker), cast on 7 (8, 9, 10, 11) (12, 13, 14) sts, k40 (44, 49, 53, 58) (64, 68, 72), RM, k to next m (new BOR m). The BOR is now at right underarm. You should have 190 (210, 232, 252, 278) (304, 326, 346) sts for the body: 95 (105, 116, 126, 139) (152, 163, 173) sts for each front and back.

Next rnd: K to end.

BODY

Work in Stockinette Stitch (k all sts), until body measures approx. 5" / 12.5 cm from underarm.

Increase rnd: *K1, m1l, k to 1 st before m, m1r, k1, SM*, repeat *–* to end. You should have 194 (214, 236, 256, 282) (308, 330, 350) sts: 97 (107, 118, 128, 141) (154, 165, 175) sts each for front and back.

Work in Stockinette Stitch (k all sts) until body measures approx. 10.25" / 26 cm from underarm.

Work the increase rnd once more. You should have 198 (218, 240, 260, 286) (312, 334, 354) sts: 99 (109, 120, 130, 143) (156, 167, 177) sts for each front and back.

Work in Stockinette Stitch (k all sts) until body measures approx. 13.75" / 35 cm or 1.5" / 4 cm less than desired length from underarm. Remove the side m on last rnd.

Hem Ribbing
Change to US 4 / 3.5 mm needles.
Next rnd: *K1, p1*, repeat *–* to end. Work in established 1 x 1 Ribbing until body measures approx. 15.25" / 39 cm from underarm. Bind off all sts in pattern using preferred bind-off method.

SLEEVES

Place 50 (52, 54, 60, 68) (76, 80, 84) held sleeve sts on US 5 / 3.75 mm DPNs or 32" / 80 cm circular needles (if using the Magic Loop Method), beginning at the centre of underarm, pick up and k 7 (8, 9, 10, 11) (12, 13, 14) sts from underarm cast-on, k across sleeve sts, pick up and k 7 (8, 9, 10, 11) (12, 13, 14) sts from underarm cast-on, PM for beginning of rnd (BOR).
Note! You may want to pick up one more st at each edge of the underarm cast-on to avoid holes at these points. Decrease these sts on next rnd to achieve the correct

stitch count for your sleeve. You should have 64 (68, 72, 80, 90) (100, 106, 112) sts.

Work in Stockinette Stitch (k all sts) until sleeve measures 2.25" / 5.5 cm from underarm.

Decrease rnd: K1, k2tog, k to last 3 sts, ssk, k1. You should have 62 (66, 70, 78, 88) (98, 104, 110) sts.

Repeat the decrease rnd every 19 (15, 13, 10, 7) (6, 5, 4)th rnd 5 (7, 8, 6, 15) (6, 11, 26) more times, then every – (–, –, 9, –) (5, 4, –)th rnd – (–, –, 5, –) (14, 12, –) more times. You should have 52 (52, 54, 56, 58) (58, 58, 58) sts.

Continue in Stockinette Stitch (k all sts) until sleeve measures approx. 16.5" / 42 cm, or 1.5" / 4 cm less than desired length from underarm.

Ribbing
Change to US 4 / 3.5 mm needles.
Next rnd: *K1, p1*, repeat *–* to end.

Work in established 1 x 1 Ribbing until sleeve measures approx. 18" / 46 cm from underarm. Bind off all sts in pattern.

NECK RIBBING

Note! This step is optional. The sample shows the neck unfinished.

With MC and US 4 / 3.5 mm 16" / 40 cm circular needles, beginning at the centre of back, pick up and k 100 (104, 104, 108, 108) (112, 112, 112) sts around neck, join to work in the rnd and PM for BOR.
Next rnd: *K1, p1*, repeat *–* to end. Work in established 1 x 1 Ribbing until neck ribbing measures approx. 0.75" / 2 cm. Bind off all sts in pattern.

FINISHING

Weave in ends. Wet block to measurements.

Tiina Arponen

08 Iloisa

This long, colourful scarf is knitted in thick, airy wool. As a result, you will get an incredibly warm and cosy piece for your everyday adventures. Great for colourwork novices too!

SIZE

One Size

FINISHED MEASUREMENTS

Width: 12" / 30 cm.
Length: 87" / 220 cm (without pompoms).

MATERIALS

Yarn: 2 skeins of Kos by Sandnes Garn (9% wool, 62 % baby alpaca, 29% polyamide, 164 yds / 150 m – 50 g), colourways blue 6055 (C1), yellow 2023 (C2), powdery pink 3511 (C3), lilac 4631 (C4), orange 2516 (C5) and pink 4614 (C6).

If you decide to use another yarn, you will need approx 1969 yds / 1800 m of bulky-weight yarn, approx. 328 yds / 300 m in each colour.

Needles: US 10 / 6 mm 24" / 60 cm circular needles.

Notions: Stitch marker.

GAUGE

16 sts x 18 rnds to 4" / 10 cm in Stockinette Stitch, after blocking.

NOTES

You can find the abbreviations and detailed instructions for techniques used in this pattern in the Abbreviations (pp. 20–23) and Techniques (pp. 15–19) sections.

Slip stitch marker as you come across it. The charts are read from bottom to top and from right to left.

With this scarf, you can be creative with stitch patterns and colours. In a large scarf, it is not so important that all the patterns are repeated exactly the same way as in the instructions, and small mistakes in colourwork are barely noticeable in the finished piece.

CONSTRUCTION

This long colourwork scarf is knitted from one end to the other in the round, making it extra thick. Pompoms are attached to the ends. First, you will work the triangle beginning by decreasing stitches. After that, you will pick up stitches from the cast-on edge and continue knitting to the other end of the scarf. Finally, you will work another triangle for the end.

DIRECTIONS

The scarf is worked in Stockinette Stitch (k all sts).

With C3 (powdery pink), cast on 100 sts using the Long-Tail Cast-On Method or method of choice. Make sure that you don't cast on too tightly. (If you want, you can also try the Provisional Cast-On Method, which allows you to easily pick up live sts later. Instructions can be found online). Join to work in the rnd and place marker for the beginning of the rnd (BOR).

TRIANGLE BEGINNING

With C3, work 2 rnds in Stockinette Stitch (k all sts).

Work decreases as follows:
Decrease rnd: K2, skpo (= slip 1 st purlwise, k next st, pass the slipped st over the knitted st), k to 4 sts before end, k2tog (= k 2 sts together), k2. (2 sts dec'd) Repeat the decrease rnd, until there are 6 sts left on the needles. Cut yarn, thread it through the remaining sts and pull gently.

MIDDLE SECTION

Vertical Bars
With C1 (blue), pick up and k 100 sts from the cast-on edge. Join to work in the rnd and place marker for the BOR.

Work Chart 1, then continue to work Chart 2. If you want to, you can continue to knit the yellow bars from Chart 1 in Chart 2 until the colour changes to C5 (orange).

Bobbles
With C5 (orange), work 7" / 17 cm in Stockinette Stitch (k all sts). You will later attach bobbles to this section (see Finishing).

Check Pattern
Work Chart 3, 3 times.
Work Chart 4 once.

Horizontal Stripes
Work stripes for 8" / 20 cm, changing colour every third rnd (the stripes will be 2 rnds high). You can knit the stripes randomly with different colours.

Squiggles
Continue to work Chart 5. Work rnds 1–24 twice. Then, work rnds 25–34 once.

Random Lines
With C1, work 8" / 20 cm in Stockinette Stitch. Every now and then, take a 16" / 40-cm-long piece of another colour, attach to the work and hold together with the working yarn. This will create randomly-placed lines.

Diagonal Stripes
Repeat Chart 6, until this section measures approximately 8" / 20 cm.

Sausages
Work 3 rnds in C4 (lilac) in Stockinette Stitch.
Work Chart 7.
Work 2 rnds in C4 (lilac) in Stockinette Stitch.
Work Chart 8.

WEAVING IN ENDS

At this point, weave in ends to the inside of the scarf. Embroider faces to the sausages with blue yarn.

TRIANGLE ENDING

With C1, work end decreases like you did for the beginning triangle.

FINISHING

Bobbles
With C4 (lilac), make bobbles to the orange Bobbles Section, placing them randomly onto the Stockinette Stitch background.

Make bobbles as follows: Pick up a st you want to attach the bobble to. *K into the front loop then into the back loop*, repeat *–* (3 sts increased, 4 sts on your needles). Work 4 rows in Stockinette Stitch (k on RS rows and p on WS rows). Then bind off the sts as follows: k2tog twice, then k2tog once again. Cut yarn, thread it through the remaining st and pull gently. Weave the end to the bottom of the bobble to shape it.

Pompoms
Make two pompoms and attach them to the ends.

Steaming
Steam block to measurements and you're ready to go!

CHART 1

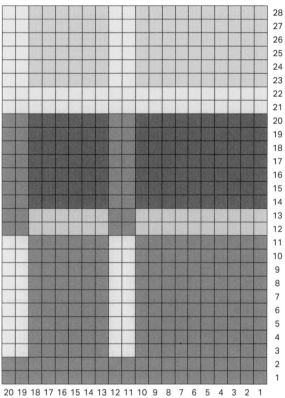

CHART 3

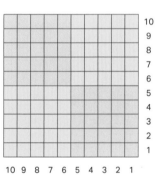

CHART 4

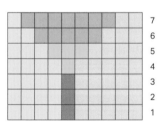

CHART 2

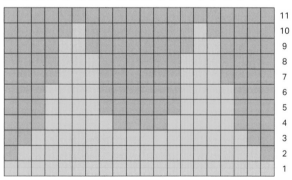

blue = C1

yellow = C2

powdery pink = C3

lilac = C4

orange = C5

pink = C6

CHART 5

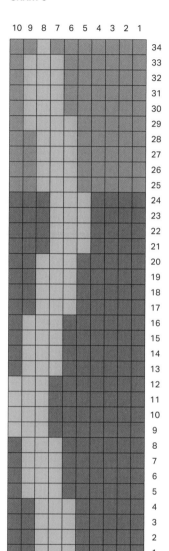

CHART 6

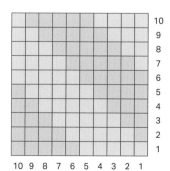

CHART 7

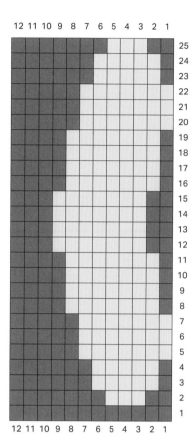

CHART 8

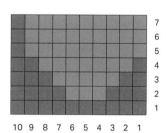

Maddy Moe

09 Grand Staff

Grand Staff are the perfect cosy socks for an evening at home. Throughout the sock, you will only be knitting with one colour on each row – no intricate colourwork involved.

SIZES

1 (2, 3)

Recommended ease: 0–0.5" / 0–1.5 cm of negative ease.

FINISHED MEASUREMENTS

Foot/Leg Circumference: 6.75 (8, 9.25)" / 17 (20, 23) cm.
Foot Length: 9.5" / 24 cm (adjustable).
Leg Length: 6" / 15.25 cm (adjustable).

MATERIALS

Yarn: Socks, Yeah! DK by Coop Knits (75% SW merino, 25% nylon, 122 yds / 112 m – 50 g).
MC: 2 skeins of colourway 205 Dionysus (pink version) or 207 Chiron (rust-coloured version).
CC: 1 skein of colourway 206 Morpheus (pink version) or 205 Dionysus (rust-coloured version).

If you decide to use another yarn, you will need approx. 244 (285, 325) yds / 224 (261, 230) m of DK-weight yarn in MC and approx. 122 (142, 163) yds / 112 (131, 149) m of DK-weight yarn in CC.

Needles: US 2.5 / 3 mm 48" / 120 cm circular needles.

Notions: Stitch markers, tapestry needle.

GAUGE

28 sts x 40 rnds to 4" / 10 cm in Stockinette Stitch, after blocking.

NOTES

You can find the abbreviations and detailed instructions for techniques used in this pattern in the Abbreviations (pp. 20–23) and Techniques (pp. 15–19) sections.

When measuring your foot for sizing, measure around the thickest part of your foot at the base of your ankle. If you are between sizes, it is recommended to size down.

The pattern is written for the Magic Loop Method which is worked with long circular needles. If you want to, you can use DPNs instead. Note, however, that you then need to be able to adjust the instructions accordingly.

Slip markers as you come across them.

As you alternate between stripes, at the beginning of the round, wrap the strand you are about to work from the right side of the strand you just worked. This will help avoid gaps.

As you knit the sock, the slipped stitches on the "front" of the sock will pull the fabric upward, making the front seem shorter. This will even up after blocking your socks, but when you are measuring your sock, measure from the Stockinette section on the "back" side so the sock is not too long.

You may find it helpful to match the stripes as you knit the second sock to ensure that the socks are identical.

It is recommended to use sock blockers to block the socks. This will give the socks a nice shape and clean finish.

CONSTRUCTION

These socks are knitted one at a time, starting at the cuff and ending at the toe. To begin, the cuff and leg are worked in the round. Next, the heel is worked flat using the heel flap method, and finally you will pick up stitches along the heel flap to continue working the foot in the round. After working the foot, you will work decreases to shape the toes, and graft the last few stitches together.

DIRECTIONS

With MC, cast on 48 (56, 64) sts using the Long-Tail Cast-On Method or method of choice. Being careful not to twist sts, begin working in the rnd, placing a m for the beginning of the rnd (BOR).

CUFF AND LEG

Cuff
K2, p2, repeat *–* to end.
Work in the established 2 x 2 Ribbing until your work measures about 1.5" / 4 cm (about 15 rnds total) or preferred cuff length.

We will now rearrange some of the sts so that we can centre the ribbing on the "front" of the sock, which will move the position of the BOR. Read the next rnd carefully.

Set-up rnd: Remove your BOR m, work 1 (3, 1) st(s) in the established ribbing, then PM to mark the new BOR, work around the rest of the sts in the established ribbing and orient them so that you have 24 (28, 32) sts each on the "front" and "back" of the sock.

Join the CC yarn on the next rnd. While working through the leg of the sock there is no need to cut either strand of yarn: you will run them up along the inside of the sock as you add length.

Leg
Rnd 1: With CC, k3 (5, 7), *sl2 pwise wyib, k2*, repeat *–* 5 times, k to BOR.
Rnd 2: With MC, k to end.
Continue working rnds 1–2 until your work measures about 6" / 15 cm from the cast-on edge (22 total repeats worked), or until your preferred length. Note that the heel instructions will add about 2.5" / 6.5 cm to the heel at the back of the work.

After your last repeat, work Leg Rnd 1 once more before beginning the heel.

HEEL

The heel will be worked back and forth across the 24 (28, 32) sts on the back of the sock, using the Heel Flap Method. Work the heel only with MC. Leave the CC yarn attached, as it will be picked up again after working the heel.

Turn your work to begin working the sts you just worked at the end of the rnd.

Using MC, p24 (28, 32) sts. You can leave the remaining 24 (28, 32) sts on the needles, or transfer them to a stitch holder if preferred.

Heel flap
Row 1 (RS): *Sl1 pwise wyib, k1*, repeat *–* to the end.
Row 2 (WS): Sl1 pwise wyif, p to end.
Work rows 1–2 another 11 times. You will have worked 25 rows total for the heel flap. Next, a few rows for the heel turn will be worked. This will turn the heel sts towards the toes.

Heel turn
Row 1 (RS): Sl1 pwise wyib, k12 (14, 16), ssk, k1, turn work.
Row 2 (WS): Sl1 pwise wyif, p3, p2tog, p1, turn work.
Row 3: Sl1 pwise wyib, k to 1 st before gap, ssk, k1, turn work.
Row 4: Sl1 pwise wyif, p to 1 st before gap, p2tog, p1, turn work.
Work rows 3–4 another 3 (4, 5) times, until all sts have been worked, ending after the WS row. You should have 14 (16, 18) sts remaining from the heel flap.

On the next row, sts along the sides of the heel flap will be picked up. You will then continue working in the rnd.

FOOT

Set-up rnd: With MC, sl1 pwise wyib, k across the remaining 13 (15, 17) sts of the heel flap, pick up and k 12 sts along the slipped-st edge of the heel flap, pick up and k 1 additional st at the gap between the heel flap and the sts on hold, SM, k across the sts that were on hold, PM, pick up and k 1 st at the gap between the sts that were on hold and the heel flap, pick up and k an additional 12 sts along the edge of the heel flap. 64 (70, 76) sts on needles.

Foot Shaping

Set-up rnd: K27 (29, 31). You are now at the m at the side of the ankle (where your CC is still attached). You are now at the BOR.

For reference, the 24 (28, 32) sts across the top of the foot with the slipped-st pattern are forming the instep. The remaining 40 (42, 44) sts around the bottom of the heel and side of the foot are forming the gusset. You may find it helpful to rearrange your sts on your needles: the 24 (28, 32) sts across the instep will not change, but we will be working decreases on the gusset.

Rnd 1: With CC, k3 (5, 7), *sl2 pwise wyib, k2*, repeat *–* 5 times, k to m, SM, ssk, k to the last 2 sts, k2tog. (2 sts dec'd)
Rnd 2: With MC, k to end.

Work rnds 1–2 another 7 (6, 5) times. You should have 48 (56, 64) sts. Remove all markers except the BOR m.

Foot

Rnd 1: With CC, k3 (5, 7), *sl2 pwise wyib, k2*, repeat *–* 5 times, k to BOR.
Rnd 2: With MC, k to end.

Work rnds 1–2 until your sock measures about 1.5 (1.5, 1.75)" / 4 (4, 4.5) cm less than the desired length, ending after rnd 2. Cut CC yarn.

TOE

The toe will be worked with MC yarn only.
Set-up rnd: K24 (28, 32), PM, k to end.
Rnd 1: *K1, ssk, k to 3 sts before m, k2tog, k1, SM*, repeat *–* twice. (4 sts dec'd)
Rnd 2: K to end.

Work rnds 1–2 another 5 times. You should have 24 (32, 40) sts.

Work rnd 1 another 2 (3, 4) times. You should have 16 (20, 24) sts.

Graft the remaining sts together, closing the gap at the end of the toes. To set up, cut about 20" / 51 cm of working yarn.

Next, orient your remaining 16 (20, 24) sts across two needles, with 8 (10, 12) sts on each needle. The working yarn will be coming from the back needle. Graft to join the sts. Alternatively, cut yarn and thread the tail through the remaining sts. Pull tight to close the toe.

FINISHING

Weave in ends. Wet block to measurements. Work the second sock.

Nina Pommerenke

10 Diamond Twill

This warm and lightweight vest is knitted in Icelandic unspun Plötulopi yarn. It features a beautiful yet simple-to-knit diamond pattern, which is created with just knit and purl stitches.

SIZES

1 (2, 3, 4, 5) (6, 7, 8)

Recommended ease: 4–7" / 10–18 cm of positive ease.

FINISHED MEASUREMENTS

Bust Circumference: 35 (40, 45, 50, 55) (60, 65, 70)" / 87.5 (100, 112.5, 125, 137.5) (150, 162.5, 175) cm.
Length from Back Hem to Armhole: 9.25 (9.25, 9.25, 10.5, 10.5) (11.25, 11.25, 11.25)" / 23.5 (23.5, 23.5, 26, 26) (28, 28, 28) cm.
Length from Back Hem to Back Neck: 19.25 (19.75, 19.75, 21.5, 21.5) (22.75, 23.25, 23.75)" / 49 (50, 50, 54, 54) (57, 58.5, 60) cm.
Armhole Depth: 10 (10.5, 10.5, 11, 11) (11.5, 12, 12.5)" / 25.5 (26.5, 26.5, 28, 28) (29, 30.5, 32) cm.

MATERIALS

Yarn: 2 cakes of Plötulopi by Ístex (100% unspun Icelandic wool, 328 yds / 300 m – 100 g), colourway Ivory Beige.

Two strands of sport-weight yarn are held together throughout the pattern. Holding two strands of sport-weight yarn together equals one strand of worsted or aran-weight yarn.

If you decide to use another yarn, you will need approx. 330 (380, 435, 490, 545) (545, 600, 655) yds / 300 (350, 400, 450, 500) (500, 550, 600) m of worsted or aran-weight yarn.

Needles: US 6 / 4 mm 24" / 60 cm circular needles for the neck and armhole ribbing. US 7 / 4.5 mm 24" / 60 cm circular needles for the body.

Notions: Stitch markers, waste yarn or stitch holder.

GAUGE

16 sts x 22 rnds to 4" / 10 cm on US 7 / 4.5 mm needles with two strands of yarn held together in Stockinette Stitch, after blocking.

NOTES

You can find the abbreviations and detailed instructions for techniques used in this pattern in the Abbreviations (pp. 20–23) and Techniques (pp. 15–19) sections.

Slip markers as you come across them.

The chart is read from bottom to top and from right to left.

The vest is knitted with two strands of Plötulopi, an unspun Icelandic yarn, held together. You can either take one strand from each plate or only knit from one plate at a time. To do so, take one strand from the middle and the other from the outside of the plate.

Because Plötulopi is an unspun yarn, it can easily break. If it breaks, simply overlap the two ends together and rub them between your palms to combine. If it doesn't combine, add a little bit of water to add moisture and rub again.

CONSTRUCTION

This slipover is knitted from the bottom up. First, the ribbing is knitted flat. After the ribbing, the body is worked in the round and, at the same time, the diamond stitch pattern is worked. After separating for the armholes, the front and back are knitted flat. The shoulders are seamed together. Finally, stitches are picked up for the round neck and armhole ribbings.

MODIFICATIONS

You can also make the vest using only one strand of yarn in which case you should look for aran or worsted-weight yarn. Make sure to swatch to ensure you get gauge.

DIRECTIONS

FRONT HEM RIBBING

With US 7 / 4.5 mm needles and the Long-Tail Cast-On Method or method of choice, cast on 70 (80, 90, 100, 110) (120, 130, 140) sts. You will now start working the hem ribbing flat. Always slip the last st purlwise to achieve a neat edge.

Next row (RS): *K1, p1*, repeat *–* to 2 sts before end, k1, sl1 purlwise with yarn in front.
Next row (WS): *K1, p1*, repeat *–* to 2 sts before end, k1, sl1 purlwise with yarn in front.
Continue in established 1 x 1 Ribbing for 2.5" / 6.5 cm.
Break yarn and put the front hem piece aside, for example on a stitch holder or waste yarn.

BACK HEM RIBBING

Work as Front Hem Ribbing but continue to work in 1 x 1 Ribbing for 3" / 7.5 cm.

BODY

Next, you will join the two pieces to continue working in the rnd. Take the front part and knit across it with the working yarn still attached to the back part. Place a marker to mark the side. Join in the rnd being careful not to twist sts and knit across the back sts.

Place a marker to mark the beginning of the rnd (BOR). Begin to work from the chart. Repeat the chart 7 (8, 9, 10, 11) (12, 13, 14) times per rnd.
Tip! Place a marker after each chart repeat. This will make it easier to keep track of where you are in the pattern.

Sizes 1, 2 and 3 only
Work the chart once. Work rnds 1–17 once again.
Sizes 4 and 5 only
Work the chart twice. Work rnds 1–5 once again.

Sizes 6, 7 and 8 only
Work the chart twice. Work rnds 1–9 once again.

Separate for Armhole Shaping

Put your back sts on separate needles, a stitch holder or a piece of scrap yarn. You will continue to work the front only.

FRONT

Armhole Shaping

Bind off 3 (3, 4, 4, 5) (5, 6, 6) sts in pattern at the beginning of both RS and WS rows. [6 (6, 8, 8, 10) (10, 12, 12) sts dec'd]
Next, bind off 2 sts: 1 (2, 2, 2, 3) (3, 3, 3) time(s), at the beginning of both RS and WS rows.
Next, bind off 1 st: 3 (4, 4, 4, 5) (5, 6, 6) times at the beginning of both RS and WS rows.

Work remaining sts in charted pattern. [16 (22, 24, 24, 32) (32, 36, 36) sts dec'd in total]

You should now have 54 (58, 66, 76, 78) (88, 94, 104) sts.

Continue to work in charted pattern for 6 (6.5, 6.5, 7, 7) (7, 7.5, 7.5)" / 15 (16.5, 16.5, 18, 18) (18, 19, 19) cm, measured from underarm bind-off, ending with a WS row.

FRONT NECK SHAPING

Next row (RS): K21 (23, 26, 30, 31) (35, 38, 43), bind off 12 (12, 14, 16, 16) (18, 18, 18) sts, k to end of row.
Next, you will knit one shoulder at a time.

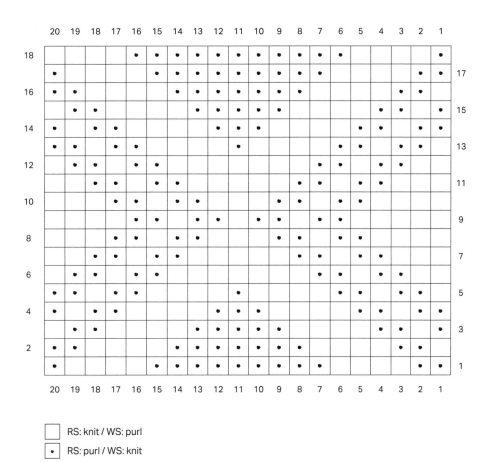

☐ RS: knit / WS: purl

☐ RS: purl / WS: knit

Right Shoulder

Continue to work according to the chart, all WS rows will be worked without decreases. Bind off sts from the RS to form the neck opening as follows:

Bind off 3 sts: 1 (1, 1, 2, 2) (2, 2, 3) time(s).

Next, bind off 2 sts: 3 (3, 4, 4, 4) (6, 7, 7) times.

Next, bind off 1 st: 0 (0, 1, 0, 1) (1, 0, 1) time.

You should now have 12 (14, 14, 16, 16) (16, 18, 19) shoulder sts.

Continue to work in charted pattern until piece measures 10 (10.5, 10.5, 11, 11) (11, 11.5, 11.75)" / 25.5 (26.5, 26.5, 28, 28) (29, 29, 30) cm from underarm bind-off.

Bind off remaining sts. Leave a long tail, so you have enough yarn to later sew together the shoulder seams.

Left Shoulder

The left shoulder is worked as the right shoulder, but this time the decreases to shape the neck opening are made on the WS.

BACK

Work the armhole shaping as for the front piece.

Continue to work in charted pattern until the back measures 8 (8.5, 8.5, 9, 9) (9, 9.5, 9.5)" / 20.5 (21.5, 21.5, 23, 23) (23, 24, 24) cm from underarm bind-off.

Back Neck Shaping

K19 (20, 23, 27, 28) (32, 34, 38), bind off the middle 16 (18, 20, 22, 22) (24, 26, 28) sts, k to end.

Next, you will knit one shoulder at a time.

Left Shoulder

All WS rows will be worked in charted pattern with no decreases.

Bind off all sts from the RS to form the neck opening:

Bind off 3 sts: 1 (1, 1, 2, 2) (3, 3, 4) time(s).

Next, bind off 2 sts: 1 (1, 2, 2, 3) (3, 3, 4) time(s).

Next, bind off 1 st: 2 (1, 2, 1, 0) (1, 1, 0) time(s).

You should now have 12 (14, 14, 16, 16) (16, 18, 18) sts.

Continue to work in charted pattern until the piece measures 10 (10.5, 10.5, 11, 11) (11.5, 12, 12.5)" / 25.5 (26.5, 26.5, 28, 28) (29, 30.5, 32) cm from underarm bind-off.

Bind off remaining sts. Leave a long tail, so you have enough yarn to later sew together the shoulder seams.

Right Shoulder

Start on RS and work one row in charted pattern.

The right shoulder is worked as the left shoulder, but the decreases to shape the neck opening are made on the WS. All RS rows will be worked in charted pattern with no decreases.

After completing the back, sew together the shoulder seams with Mattress Stitch or preferred method.

NECK AND ARMHOLE RIBBING

Neck

With US 6 / 4 mm needles, pick up and knit sts around the neck edge from the RS. Start to pick up sts from the back of the neck. Pick up at a ratio of 1:1 and skip every third or fourth st around the curves. You need to have an even number of sts for the ribbing.

Set-up rnd: *K1, p1*, repeat *–* to end. Work in established 1 x 1 Ribbing for 6 rnds in total.

Bind off all sts.
Note! Do not bind off too loosely, otherwise the neckline may not hold its shape and becomes too loose over time.

Armhole

Work as the neck ribbing. Start picking up the sts at the armpit.

FINISHING

Weave in ends. Wet block to measurements.

Sasha Hyre

11 Marley

Marley is a nod to Sasha Hyre's native country, Jamaica, and her love for Bob Marley's reggae music. As reggae is a fusion of genres, so is this cardigan with different textures and yarns.

SIZES

1 (2, 3, 4, 5) (6, 7, 8)

Recommended ease: 8–10" / 20.5–25.5 cm of positive ease.

FINISHED MEASUREMENTS

Chest Circumference: 41.75 (46.25, 50.25, 53.75, 59.75) (64, 68, 71.75)" / 104.5 (115.5, 125.5, 134.5, 149) (160, 170, 179) cm.
Body Length: 22" / 56 cm.
Yoke Depth: 8.5 (9.5, 10, 10.5, 11.75) (12.5, 13, 13.5)" / 21 (23.5, 25, 26.5, 29.5) (31, 32.5, 33.5) cm.
Upper Arm Circumference: 13.5 (15, 15, 16.25, 17) (18.5, 19.25, 20.25)" / 33.5 (37.5, 37.5, 41, 42.5) (46.5, 48, 51) cm.
Cuff Circumference: 10.25 (10.25, 11, 11, 11.25) (11.25, 11.75, 11.75)" / 25.5 (25.5, 27.5, 27.5, 28) (28, 29, 29) cm.
Sleeve Length: 18" / 45.5 cm.
Back of Neck Width: 8 (8, 8.25, 8.25, 8.75) (8.75, 9, 9)" / 20 (20, 21, 21, 22) (22, 22.5, 22.5) cm.

MATERIALS

Yarn: C1: 2 (2, 3, 3, 3) (4, 4, 4) skeins of Sunday Morning DK by Sonder Yarn Co. (75% BFL, 25% Masham, 268 yds / 245 m – 100 g), colourway Natural.

C2: 2 (2, 2, 3, 3) (4, 4, 4) Bouclé by Julie Asselin (70% alpaca, 30% Highland wool, 240 yds / 220 m – 100 g), colourway Mouton Noir.

C3: 2 (2, 2, 2, 2) (2, 2, 2) skeins of Sunday Morning DK by Sonder Yarn Co. (75% BFL, 25% Masham, 268 yds / 245 m – 100 g), colourway But First Coffee.

If you decide to use another yarn, you will need approx.
C1: 510 (530, 570, 665, 730) (800, 910, 1020) yds / 466 (485, 521, 608, 668) (732, 832, 933) m of DK-weight yarn.
C2: 450 (460, 470, 510, 575) (640, 720, 810) yds / 411 (421, 430, 466, 526) (585, 658, 741) m of worsted-weight bouclé yarn.
C3: 350 (375, 395, 420, 450) (480, 510, 530) yds / 320 (343, 361, 384, 411) (439, 466, 485) m of DK-weight yarn.

Needles: US 7 / 4.5 mm 32" / 80 cm circular needles.

Notions: Stitch markers, waste yarn or stitch holders.

GAUGE

22 sts x 30 rows to 4" / 10 cm on US 7 / 4.5 mm needles with DK-weight yarn in Stockinette Stitch, after blocking.

NOTES

You can find the abbreviations and detailed instructions for techniques used in this pattern in the Abbreviations (pp. 20–23) and Techniques (pp. 15–19) sections.

Slip markers as you come across them.

Intarsia

With intarsia knitting, you have a separate ball of yarn for each area of colour. For the cardigan, you will work with 3 balls of yarn (2 balls of C2 bouclé and 1 ball of C1) for the fronts. Instructions are detailed for the colour change between yarns for the body and sleeve. When working the intarsia sections, twist yarn on the WS whenever changing colours to avoid gaps.

Yarn substitutions

The design uses bouclé which is a textured yarn that knits up into a soft and cosy fabric. A great substitution for bouclé is suri alpaca (held double) or mohair. Ensure to select a fibre that gives a 'fluffy' look and feel. Brands to consider: CaMaRose, Rowan, Drops, Knit Picks, Lana Grossa and many more. The other yarn in the pattern is a rustic yet soft DK-weight wool yarn. When substituting, look for a wool yarn with a similar feel. Anything with silk or cashmere will not have the same appeal and will add more drape than the original design intents.

CONSTRUCTION

This oversized cardigan is knitted in one-piece and worked from the top down seamlessly with a raglan construction. Starting at the neckline, the fronts, shoulders, and back are knitted simultaneously all while creating the V-neck. The sleeves are placed on hold to be completed after the body. You will be working intarsia on the fronts to create an inverted 'V'. Because of the borderless no-rib design, blocking is key to avoid the edges rolling.

DIRECTIONS

With C1, cast on 54 (54, 56, 56, 58) (58, 60, 60) sts.

Next row: P across while placing markers as follows:
P3, PM (left front), p2, PM (left shoulder), p44 (44, 46, 46, 48) (48, 50, 50), PM (right shoulder), p2, PM (right front), p3.
Next row (RS): K1, kfb, m1r, k1, SM, m1l, k to m, m1r, SM, k1, m1l, k to 1 st before m, m1r, k1, SM, m1l, k to m, m1r, SM, k1, kfb, m1l, k1. (10 sts inc'd)
Next row (WS): P to end.

NECKLINE SHAPING

In this section, you will be shaping the neckline all the while making increases on the back, shoulders, and raglans.

1st Increase Section

Row 1 (RS): K to 1 st before m, m1r, k1, SM, m1l, k to m, m1r, SM, k1, m1l, k to 1 st before m, m1r, k1, SM, m1l, k to m, m1r, SM, k1, m1l, k to the end. (8 sts inc'd)
Row 2 (WS): P to end.
Row 3: K2, m1l, k to 1 st before m, m1r, k1, SM, m1l, k to m, m1r, SM, k1, m1l, k to 1 st before m, m1r, k1, SM, m1l, k to m, m1r, SM, k1, m1l, k to the last 2 sts, m1r, k2. (10 sts inc'd)
Row 4: P to end.
Work rows 1–4 a total of 13 (15, 15, 15, 17) (17, 17, 17) times.

You should have a total of 298 (334, 336, 336, 374) (374, 376, 376) sts: 44 (50, 50, 50, 56) (56, 56, 56) sts for each front, 56 (64, 64, 64, 72) (72, 72, 72) sts for each shoulder and 98 (106, 108, 108, 118) (118, 120, 120) sts for the back.

2nd Increase Section

Continue to increase sts on the fronts, shoulders and back.
Work rows 3–4 from 1st Increase Section a total of 4 (3, 1, 3, –) (1, 1, 2) time(s).

You should have a total of 338 (364, 346, 366, 374) (384, 386, 396) sts: 52 (56, 52, 56, 56) (58, 58, 60) sts for each front, 64 (70, 66, 70, 72) (74, 74, 76) sts for each shoulder and 106 (112, 110, 114, 118) (120, 122, 124) sts for the back.

Now, you will continue to increase along the fronts and back only.
Row 5: K2, m1l, k to 1 st before m, m1r, k1, SM, k to m, SM, k1, m1l, k to 1 st before m, m1r, k1, SM, k to m, SM, k1, m1l, k to the last 2 sts, m1r, k2. (6 sts inc'd)
Row 6: P to end.
Work rows 5–6 a total of – (1, 5, 5, 9) (10, 12, 13) time(s).

You should have a total of 338 (370, 376, 396, 428) (444, 458, 474) sts: 52 (58, 62, 66, 74) (78, 82, 86) sts for each front, 64 (70, 66, 70, 72) (74, 74, 76) sts for each shoulder and 106 (114, 120, 124, 136) (140, 146, 150) sts for the back.

SEPARATION OF BODY AND SHOULDER STITCHES

Still working with C1 join the fronts to the back to form the body, place shoulder sts on a holder or waste yarn, and place markers for the intarsia work.

K across left front 52 (58, 62, 66, 74) (78, 82, 86) sts, RM and place left shoulder 64 (70, 66, 70, 72) (74, 74, 76) sts on holder or waste yarn; cast on 10 (12, 16, 20, 22) (28, 32, 36) sts for the left underarm using the Backwards Loop Cast-On method or method of choice; RM, k across back 106 (114, 120, 124, 136) (140, 146, 150) sts, RM and place right shoulder 64 (70, 66, 70, 72) (74, 74, 76) sts on holder or waste yarn; cast on 10 (12, 16, 20, 22) (28, 32, 36) sts for the right underarm using the Backwards Loop Cast-On method or method of choice; RM, k across right front 52 (58, 62, 66, 74) (78, 82, 86) sts.

You should have a total of 230 (254, 276, 296, 328) (352, 374, 394) sts.

Next row (WS): P across and place markers as follows for the intarsia sections: P60 (68, 72, 76, 76) (80, 84, 88), PM (right front), p110 (118, 132, 144, 176) (192, 206, 218), PM (left front), p60 (68, 72, 76, 76) (80, 84, 88).

BODY

Intarsia Set-Up with C2 (bouclé section)

Next row (RS): Join your first ball of C2 (bouclé) and k2, carry C1 yarn and twist it with C2. Continue to k across the body with C1, slip markers as you come across them, until the last 2 sts, join the second ball of C2 (bouclé), twist yarn, k2.
Next row (WS): With C2, p2, carry C1 yarn and twist it and p2 with C2. Continue to p across the body with C1 until the last 4 sts, twist yarn and p4 with C2.

Continue adding 2 sts with C2 on every RS and WS row as established until you have worked all sts until markers. You should have 60 (68, 72, 76, 76) (80, 84, 88) sts.

Note! Remember to twist yarn on the WS whenever changing colours to avoid gaps.

Break C1 and the second ball of C2 yarn. With the first ball of C2, work the body in Stockinette Stitch (k all sts on RS rows and p on WS rows) until the piece measures 10" / 25.5 cm from the underarm or half your desired length.

Intarsia Set-Up with C3

Next row (RS): Join your first ball of C3 and k2, carry C2 yarn and twist it with C3. Continue to k across the body with C2 until the last 2 sts, join the second ball of C3, twist yarn, k2.

Next row (WS): With C3, p2, carry C2 yarn and twist it and p2 with C3. Continue to p across the body with C2 until the last 4 sts, twist yarn and p4 with C3.

Continue adding 2 sts with C3 on every RS and WS row as established until you have worked all sts until markers. You should have 60 (68, 72, 76, 76) (80, 84, 88) sts.

Note! Remember to twist yarn on the WS whenever changing colours to avoid gaps.

Break C2 and the second ball of C3 yarn. With the first ball of C3, work the body in Stockinette Stitch (k all sts on RS rows and p on WS rows) until the piece measures 20" / 51 cm from the underarm cast-on (or desired length).

Border and Bind-Off

Next row (RS): *K1tbl, p1*, repeat *–* to the end.
Next row (WS): Bind off in pattern.

SLEEVES

The sleeves will be worked in the rnd.

Transfer 64 (70, 66, 70, 72) (74, 74, 76) shoulder sts from the holder or waste yarn onto needles.

With C1, starting at the middle of the body underarm sts, pick up and k 5 (6, 8, 10, 11) (14, 16, 18) sts, k across 64 (70, 66, 70, 72) (74, 74, 76) sts from the shoulder, pick up and k 5 (6, 8, 10, 11) (14, 16, 18) sts from the body and place a marker to mark the beginning of the rnd. You should have a total of 74 (82, 82, 90, 94) (102, 106, 112) sts.
K 4 rnds.

Decrease rnd: K1, k2tog, k to 3 sts before m, ssk, k1. (2 sts dec'd)
Work the decrease rnd a total of 9 (13, 11, 15, 16) (20, 21, 24) times every 12 (8, 10, 7, 7) (5, 5, 4)th rnd. You should have a total of 56 (56, 60, 60, 62) (62, 64, 64) sts.

AT THE SAME TIME: Keeping in line with the colourwork of the body, knit the first portion of the sleeve with C1, switch to C2 (bouclé) and finish with C3, while also working the decreases.

With C1, work in Stockinette Stitch (k all sts) for 4.5 (5, 5.25, 5.5, 5.5) (5.75, 6.25, 6.5)" / 11.5 (12.5, 13.5, 14, 14) (14.5, 16, 16.5) cm. Cut C1.

With C2, work in Stockinette Stitch (k all sts) until the sleeve measures 12.5 (13.5, 14, 14.5, 14.5) (15, 15.75, 16.25)" / 32 (34.5, 35.5, 37, 37) (38, 40, 41.5) cm from underarm. Cut C2.

With C3, work the remaining sleeve length in Stockinette Stitch (k all sts) until sleeve measures 18" / 45.5 cm or until desired length.

Border and Bind-Off

Next row: *K1tbl, p1*, repeat *–* to the end.
Next row: Bind off in pattern.

Repeat the instructions for the second sleeve.

FINISHING

Weave in your ends being sure to close all armhole gaps. Wet block to measurements.

Pauliina Kuunsola

12 Duo

These mittens are warm, cosy and simple to knit. You can play with colours and really make them your own. Make a pair for every coat!

SIZES

1 (2, 3)

To fit a hand circumference of approx. 6.5 (8, 10)" / 16.5 (20.5, 25.5) cm.

FINISHED MEASUREMENTS

Circumference: 6.75 (8.5, 10.25)" / 17 (21.5, 25.5) cm.
Height (with folded cuff): Approx. 9.25 (9.75, 10)" / 23.5 (24.5, 25.5) cm.

MATERIALS

Yarn: Manos del Uruguay Cardo (100% Corriedale wool, 109 yds / 100 m – 100 g).
C1: 1 skein, colourway North Sea.
C2: 1 skein, colourway Goldenrod.

If you decide to use another yarn, you will need approx. 60 (75, 91) yds / 55 (69, 83) m of bulky-weight yarn in each colour.

Needles: US 8 / 5 mm DPNs or circular needles suitable for knitting small circumferences in the rnd (16" / 40 cm needles or 32" / 80 cm needles, if using the Magic-Loop Method).

Notions: Stitch holder or scrap yarn, stitch markers.

GAUGE

14 sts x 22 rnds to 4" / 10 cm in Stockinette Stitch, after blocking.

NOTES

You can find the abbreviations and detailed instructions for techniques used in this pattern in the Abbreviations (pp. 20–23) and Techniques (pp. 15–19) sections.

Slip markers as you come across them.

You can alter the length for the cuff by working extra rnds of ribbing. If you need more room for your fingers, add extra rnds of Stockinette Stitch before starting the decreases.

Switch the colours around when knitting the second mitten (working with C2 where it says C1, and C1 where it says C2).

CONSTRUCTION

These mittens are worked from the bottom up in the round. You first work a long rib, which is intended to be worn folded, and then start working the hand in Stockinette Stitch. After separating the thumb stitches, you will change colours and continue in Stockinette Stitch. The decreases for the tip are made on both sides of the mitten.

DIRECTIONS

Cast on 24 (30, 36) sts with C1, using the Long-Tail Cast-On Method or a stretchy cast-on of your choice. PM for the beginning of the rnd (BOR) and join for working in the rnd. Be careful not to twist the sts.

CUFF RIB

Start to work in 1 x 1 Ribbing as follows:
Rib rnd: *K1, p1*, repeat *–* to BOR. Work in established ribbing until it measures 5.5" / 14 cm or desired length.

HAND

Work in Stockinette Stitch (k all sts) for 2.25" / 5.5 cm.

Right mitten only
Thumb rnd: K 3 (4, 4), move the next 4 sts on a stitch holder or scrap yarn for thumb. Cast on 4 sts (either the Backwards Loop or Knitted Cast-On Method is recommended) and continue to work in the rnd, knitting all sts until BOR.

Left mitten only
Thumb rnd: K5 (7, 10), move the next 4 sts on a stitch holder or scrap yarn for thumb. Cast on 4 sts (either the Backwards Loop Method or Knitted Cast-On Method is recommended) and continue to work in the rnd, knitting all sts until BOR.

Both mittens
K 1 more rnd in C1.

Change to C2 and continue to work in Stockinette Stitch (k all sts). *Note!* If you want to hide the jog that appears at the transition point of the two colours, on your second rnd of C2, slip the first st purlwise with yarn in back and then continue knitting in the rnd.

Work in Stockinette Stitch (k all sts) for 2.5" / 6.5 cm from colour change or until 1.75 (2.25, 2.5)" / 4.5 (5.5, 6.5) cm from desired length.

DECREASES

Next, start working the tip decreases.
Set-up rnd: *K1, ssk, k6 (9, 12), k2tog, k1*, PM, repeat *–* to end.
Rnd 1: K to end.
Rnd 2: *K1, ssk, k to 3 sts bef m, k2tog, k1*, SM, repeat *–* to end.
Repeat rnds 1–2, 3 (4, 5) more times. You should now have 8 (10, 12) sts.
Work rnd 1 once more.

Cut yarn and pull through the remaining sts to close the top.

THUMB

Move the 4 sts from holder onto needles and, with C1, pick up and k 8 more sts from around the thumb hole. You should have 12 sts. Place BOR marker and join to work in the rnd.

Work in Stockinette Stitch (k all sts) until thumb is covered.

Dec rnd: *K2tog*, repeat decrease to BOR. (6 sts)

Cut yarn and pull through the remaining stitches to close top.

Knit the other mitten the same (working the correct thumb rnd), but switch the colours around (working with C2 where it says C1, and C1 where it says C2).

FINISHING

Weave in all ends. Wet block to measurements.

Sylvia Watts-Cherry

13 True Stripes

This fun sweater invites you to play with colours, and it features only basic techniques. Don't be afraid of seaming either – it's much easier than you may think.

SIZES

1 (2, 3, 4, 5) (6, 7, 8)

Recommended ease: 5.25–7" / 13.5–18 cm of positive ease.

FINISHED MEASUREMENTS

Chest Circumference: 37.25 (42.75, 46.25, 49.75, 57) (60.5, 64, 67.5)" / 93.5 (106.5, 115.5, 124.5, 142) (151, 160, 169) cm.
Length from Hem to Shoulder: 22 (22.5, 23, 23.5, 24.5) (25, 25.5, 26)" / 56 (57, 58.5, 59.5, 62) (63.5, 65, 66) cm.
Armhole Depth: 7.5 (8, 8.5, 9, 10) (10.5, 11, 11.5)" / 19.5 (20.5, 22, 23, 25.5) (27, 28, 29.5) cm.
Front Neck Drop: 4" / 10 cm.
Back Neck Drop: 1" / 2.5 cm.
Sleeve Length: 19 (18.75, 18.75, 18.75, 18) (18, 17.5, 17.5)" / 48.5 (47.5, 47.5, 47.5, 45.5) (45.5, 44.5, 44.5) cm.
Upper Arm Circumference: 15 (16, 17, 18.25, 20) (21, 22.25, 23)" / 38 (40, 42, 45.5, 50) (52, 55.5, 58.5) cm.
Cuff Circumference: 9 (9.75, 9.75, 9.75, 10.75) (10.75, 11.5, 11.5)" / 22 (24.5, 24.5, 24.5, 26.5) (26.5, 29, 29) cm.

MATERIALS

Yarn: Cascade Yarns 220 Superwash Merino (100% merino, 219 yds / 200 m – 100 g).
MC: 2 (3, 3, 3, 4) (4, 4, 4) skeins of colourway Pastel Turquoise 090.
C1: 1 skein of colourway Camelia 098.
C2: 2 (2, 2, 2, 3) (3, 3, 3) skeins of colourway Dark Teal 034.
C3: 2 (2, 2, 2, 3) (3, 3, 3) skeins of colourway Lime 013.
C4: 1 (1, 1, 2, 2) (2, 2, 2) skein(s) of colourway Artisan Gold 008.

If you decide to use another yarn, you will need approx.
MC: 436 (489, 533, 579, 663) (711, 753, 803) yds / 399 (447, 488, 529, 606) (650, 689, 734) m of DK-weight yarn.
C1: 117 (126, 132, 137, 154) (161, 168, 174) yds / 107 (115, 121, 125, 141) (147, 154, 159) m of DK-weight yarn.
C2: 315 (352, 385, 418, 478) (513, 544, 579) yds / 288 (322, 352, 382, 437) (469, 497, 529) m of DK-weight yarn.
C3: 304 (339, 370, 403, 460) (493, 524, 557) yds / 278 (310, 338, 369, 421) (451, 479, 509) m of DK-weight yarn.
C4: 168 (187, 205, 223, 256) (273, 289, 308) yds / 154 (171, 188, 204, 234) (250, 264, 282) m of DK-weight yarn.

Needles: US 6 / 4 mm (for ribbing) and US 8 / 5 mm 24" / 60 cm circular needles (for the body and sleeves).

Notions: 4 locking stitch markers or waste yarn, stitch holder.

GAUGE

18 sts x 38 rows to 4" / 10 cm on US 8 / 5 mm needles in Garter Stitch, after blocking.

STITCH PATTERNS

Stripe Pattern
Row 1 (RS): Using C2, k to end.
Rows 2–4: K to end.
Row 5 (RS): Change to C3, k to end.
Row 6 (WS): K to end.
Row 7 (RS): Change to C4, k to end.
Row 8 (WS): K to end.
Rows 9–10: Repeat rows 5–6.
Row 11 (RS): Change to MC, k to end.
Rows 12–16: K to end.
These 16 rows form the stitch pattern.

NOTES

You can find the abbreviations and detailed instructions for techniques used in this pattern in the Abbreviations (pp. 20–23) and Techniques (pp. 15–19) sections.

The pieces are worked in a simple 4-colour stripe stitch pattern in Garter Stitch. To avoid too many ends for weaving in at the end, carry the 4 colours up the side of the knitting. A good method for this is to twist the 4 colours at the beginning of the RS row so that the 3 colours you are not using make a wrap around the working yarn. This avoids the long strands that occur when you carry yarn up the side of knitting.

CONSTRUCTION

This striped Garter Stitch sweater is worked in pieces and sewn together in Mattress Stitch. The pieces (back, front and sleeves) are knitted flat from the bottom up. The neckband is worked by picking up stitches along the front and back neck edges after the shoulder seams are sewed together and worked in the round. Two patch pockets are knitted separately and sewn onto the front.

MODIFICATIONS

The sweater length can be altered by altering the length knitted before neck shaping begins.

DIRECTIONS

BACK

Start with the back. With C1 and US 6 / 4 mm needles, cast on 84 (96, 104, 112, 128) (136, 144, 152) sts using the Long-Tail Cast-On Method or preferred method.

Start to work in 2 x 2 Ribbing as follows:
Row 1 (RS): *K2, p2*, repeat *-* to end.
Note! You can place a locking stitch marker to mark the RS.
Row 2 (WS): *K2, p2*, repeat *-* to end.
Continue to work in established 2 x 2 Ribbing until piece measures 1.75" / 4.5 cm. End with a WS row.

Change to US 8 / 5 mm needles.

Establish Pattern
Work Stripe Pattern from written instructions to end. Continue in established 16-row stripe pattern changing yarn as indicated until piece measures 21 (21.5, 22, 22.5, 23.5) (24, 24.5, 25)" / 53.5 (54.5, 56, 57, 59.5) (61, 62, 63.5) cm from the cast-on edge. End with a WS row.

Note! Place locking st marker at each end of work when the piece measures 13.75" / 35 cm from cast-on edge, to mark the beginning of armhole.

SHAPE NECK AND SHOULDERS

Next row (RS): K25 (30, 34, 38, 44) (47, 51, 54) sts, bind off 34 (36, 36, 36, 40) (42, 42, 44) sts, k to end.

Place sts worked before the bind-off sts on holder, and begin working only 25 (30, 34, 38, 44) (47, 51, 54) sts after the bind-off sts for the left side. Continue to work as established in Stripe Pattern.

Left Neck and Shoulder
Work WS row (k all sts).
Next row (RS): K1, k2tog, k to end.
(1 st dec'd)
You should have 24 (29, 33, 37, 43) (46, 50, 53) sts.

You will now bind off the shoulder edge as follows:
Bind off 8 (10, 11, 13, 15) (16, 17, 18) sts at the beginning of the WS row 3 (2, 3, 1, 1) (1, 2, 2) time(s), then bind off – (9, –, 12, 14) (15, 16, 17) stitches on the following WS rows – (1, –, 2, 2) (2, 1, 1) time(s).

Place sts on holder back onto US 8 / 5 mm needles and rejoin yarn to begin the right side beginning with WS row.

Right Neck and Shoulder
Work a WS row (k all sts).
Next row (RS): K to last 3 sts, k2tog, k1.
(1 st dec'd)
You should have 24 (29, 33, 37, 43) (46, 50, 53) sts.

Work a WS row (k all sts).

Bind off 8 (10, 11, 13, 15) (16, 17, 18) sts beginning on next RS row 3 (2, 3, 1, 1) (1, 2, 2) time(s), then bind off – (9, –, 12, 14) (15, 16, 17) sts on the following RS rows – (1, –, 2, 2) (2, 1, 1) time(s).

FRONT

Next, you will work the front piece. Work as for Back until front piece measures 18 (18.5, 19, 19.5, 20.5) (21, 21.5, 22)" / 45.5 (47, 48.5, 49.5, 52) (53.5, 54.5, 56) cm ending with a WS row. You should have 84 (96, 104, 112, 128) (136, 144, 152) sts.

Shape Neck
Next row (RS): K 33 (38, 42, 46, 53) (57, 61, 65) sts, bind off 18 (20, 20, 20, 22) (22, 22, 22) sts, k to the end. 33 (38, 42, 46, 53) (57, 61, 65) sts remain on each side of bind-off sts.

Place sts worked before the bind-off sts on holder and begin working only the sts after the bind-off sts for RS.

Right Neck

Work a WS row (k all sts).
Next row (RS) (decrease): K1, k2tog, k to end. (1 st dec'd)
Next row (WS): K to end.
Repeat the last 2 rows, 8 (8, 8, 8, 9) (10, 10, 11) more times.

Work straight until front armhole matches the back armhole, ending with a RS row.

Shape Shoulder

Bind off 8 (10, 11, 13, 15) (16, 17, 18) sts beginning on next WS row 3 (2, 3, 1, 1) (1, 2, 2) time(s), then bind off – (9, –, 12, 14) (15, 16, 17) sts on the following WS rows – (1, –, 2, 2) (2, 1, 1) time(s).

Left Neck

Place the 33 (38, 42, 46, 53) (57, 61, 65) sts on holder back onto US 8 / 5 mm needles and rejoin yarn to begin the left side beginning with a WS row.

Work a WS row (k all sts).
Next row (RS) (decrease): K to last 3 sts, k2tog, k1. (1 st dec'd)
Next row (WS): K to end.
Repeat the last 2 rows, 8 (8, 8, 8, 9) (10, 10, 11) more times.

Work straight until front armhole matches the back armhole, ending with a WS row.

Shape Shoulder

Bind off 8 (10, 11, 13, 15) (16, 17, 18) sts beginning on next RS row 3 (2, 3, 1, 1) (1, 2, 2) time(s), then bind off – (9, –, 12, 14) (15, 16, 17) sts on the following RS rows – (1, –, 2, 2) (2, 1, 1) time(s).

SLEEVES

With C1 and US 6 / 4 mm needles, cast on 40 (44, 44, 44, 48) (48, 52, 52) sts using the Long-Tail Cast-On Method or preferred method.

Row 1 (RS): *K2, p2*, repeat *–* to end.
Note! You can place a locking stitch marker to mark the RS.
Row 2 (WS): *K2, p2*, repeat *–* to end.
Continue to work in established 2 x 2 Ribbing until piece measures 2" / 5 cm.

Change to US 8 / 5 mm needles.

Establish Pattern

Work Stripe Pattern from written instructions to end.

Continue in established pattern changing yarn as required begin to shape the sleeves as follows:
Work 10 rows in Stripe Pattern.
Next row (RS) (increase): K1, m1r, k to last st, m1l, k1. (2 sts inc'd)
Continue to work in pattern for 9 (9, 7, 5, 5) (3, 3, 3) rows.
Repeat last 10 (10, 8, 6, 6) (4, 4, 4) rows 12 (12, 9, 5, 17) (2, 7, 13) times more. You should have 66 (70, 64, 56, 84) (54, 68, 80) sts.

Work increase row, then work 11 (9, 9, 7, 7) (5, 5, 5) rows. Repeat last – (–, 10, 8, 8) (6, 6, 6) rows – (–, 5, 12, 2) (19, 15, 11) time(s) more. You should have 68 (72, 76, 82, 90) (94, 100, 104) sts.

Without further increases, continue in pattern until sleeve measures 19 (18.75, 18.75, 18.75, 18) (18, 17.5, 17.5)" / 48.5 (47.5, 47.5, 47.5, 45.5) (45.5, 44.5. 44.5) cm from cast-on edge, ending with a WS row. Bind off all sts.

Repeat instructions for second sleeve.

POCKETS

With C2 and US 8 / 5 mm needles, cast on 26 sts using the Long-Tail Cast-On Method or preferred method. Changing yarn as required, work 48 (48, 48, 48, 56) (56, 56, 56) rows in the Stripe Pattern. Bind off all sts.

Turn the pocket to the side, with RS facing, using C1 and US 6 / 4 mm needles, pick up and k 24 (24, 24, 24, 28) (28, 28, 28) sts along the side edge.
Next row (WS): Sll, *p2, k2*, repeat *–* to last 3 sts, p2, k1.
Next row (RS): Sll, *k2, p2*, repeat *–* to last 3 sts, k3.
Repeat last 2 rows twice more.

Bind off all sts.

BLOCKING & SHOULDER SEAMS

Weave all ends, wet block pieces to measurements and allow to dry completely. Using Mattress Stitch, seam together front pieces to back at shoulders.

NECKBAND

With RS facing, using US 6 / 4 mm needles suitable for working small circumferences in the rnd and C1, begin at left shoulder seam, pick up and k 25 (25, 25, 25, 26) (27, 27, 28) sts down left side of front neck, pick up and k 18 (20, 20, 20, 22) (22, 22, 22) sts across front neck, pick up and k 25 (25, 25, 25, 26) (27, 27, 28) sts up right side of front neck, pick up and k 5 sts down right side of back neck, pick up and k 34 (36, 36, 36, 40) (42, 42, 44) sts across back neck, pick up and k 5 sts up left side of back neck. PM to indicate the beginning of the rnd and join to work in the rnd. You should have 112 (116, 116, 116, 124) (128, 128, 132) sts.

Rnd 1: *K2, p2*, repeat *–* to end. Continue to work in established 2 x 2 Ribbing until the neckband measures 1.25" / 3 cm. Bind off all sts.

Sew sleeves to the sweater body ensuring the centre of each sleeve matches the centre of the shoulder seam and the sleeve ends are lined up to the locked stitch marker on the front and back pieces. Sew side and sleeve seams. Sew the pockets to the front of the sweater, position pockets 1" / 2.5 cm above the top of the rib and 1 (1.5, 2, 2.5, 3.5) (4.25, 4.5, 5)" / 2.5 (4, 5, 6.5, 9) (11, 11.5, 12.5) cm from the side seams.

FINISHING

Weave in all remaining ends and block seams and neckband.

14

26

Jonna Hietala — Evgeniya Dupliy — Meiju K-P — Maija Kangasluoma — Sidsel Grau Petersen
Tiina Huhtaniemi — Sini Kramer — Lindsey Fowler — Paula Pereira — Pauliina Kuunsola
Bernice Lim — Elise Damstra

Jonna Hietala

SUPER EASY!

14 Lullaby

Large needles and Garter Stitch – yes, please! This comfy cardigan is knitted top down with shorter sleeves for a lighter look.

SIZES

1 (2, 3, 4, 5) (6, 7, 8)

Recommended ease: 4–8" / 10–20 cm of positive ease.

FINISHED MEASUREMENTS

Chest Circumference: 40.75 (44.25, 47.75, 51.75, 57.5) (62.25, 66.5, 70.5)" / 102 (110.5, 119, 129.5, 143.5) (155.5, 166, 176.5) cm.
Collar Circumference: 21.25 (21.25, 21.25, 22.5, 24) (24, 24, 25.5)" / 53 (53, 53, 56.5, 60) (60, 60, 63.5) cm.
Upper Arm Circumference: 15.25 (15.25, 16.75, 17.5, 18) (19.5, 20.25, 21.5)" / 38 (38, 42, 43.5, 45) (49, 50.5, 54) cm.
Yoke Depth: 7.25 (7.25, 8, 8.5, 8.75) (9.5, 10, 10.75)" / 18 (18, 20, 21, 22) (24, 25, 27) cm.
Body Length: 12" / 30 cm.
Cuff Circumference: 12.5 (12.5, 13.25, 13.25, 14) (14.5, 14.5, 14.5)" / 31 (31, 33, 33, 35) (36.5, 36.5, 36.5) cm.

MATERIALS

Yarn: 5 (5, 6, 6, 7) (7, 8, 9) skeins of Watershed by Hinterland (50% Canadian Rambouillet, 50% home-grown alpaca, 150 yds / 137 m – 112 g), colourway Maple.

If you decide to use another yarn, you will need approx. 663 (704, 785, 857, 949) (1058, 1138, 1245) yds / 606 (643, 717, 783, 867) (966, 1039, 1137) m of bulky-weight yarn.

Needles: US 15 / 10 mm 40" / 100 cm circular needles, US 11 / 8 mm 40" / 100 cm circular needles for ribbing.

Notions: Stitch markers, 6 buttons (approx. 0.75" / 2 cm diameter).

GAUGE

11.5 sts x 20 rnds to 4" / 10 cm on US 15 / 10 mm needles in Garter Stitch, after blocking.

NOTES

You can find the abbreviations and detailed instructions for techniques used in this pattern in the Abbreviations (pp. 20–23) and Techniques (pp. 15–19) sections.

Slip stitch markers as you come across them.

CONSTRUCTION

This cardigan is mostly knitted flat in one piece. The sleeves are worked in the round. Besides the ribbings, sleeves and buttonbands, the piece is worked in knit stitches only.

DIRECTIONS

YOKE

Cast on 37 (37, 37, 41, 45) (45, 45, 49) sts.
Set-up row: K2 (2, 2, 3, 4) (4, 4, 5), PM, k8, PM, k17 (17, 17, 19, 21) (21, 21, 23), PM, k8, PM, k2 (2, 2, 3, 4) (4, 4, 5).
Row 1 (RS): Kfb, k to 1 st before m, m1r, k1, SM, k1, m1l, *k to 1 st before m, m1r, k1, SM, k1, m1l*, repeat *–* once more, k to 1 st before m, m1r, k1, SM, m1l, kfb. (10 sts inc'd)
Row 2 (WS): K to end.
Row 3: Kfb, *k to 1 st before m, m1r, k1, SM, k1, m1l*, repeat *–* 3 more times, k to last st, kfb. (10 sts inc'd)
Row 4: K to end.
Row 5: Kfb, *k to 1 st before m, m1r, k1, SM, k1, m1l*, repeat *–* 3 more times, k to last st, kfb. (10 sts inc'd)
Row 6: K to end.
Row 7: *K to 1 st before m, m1r, k1, SM, k1, m1l*, repeat *–* 3 more times, k to last st, cast on 1 st using the Backwards Loop Cast-On Method. (9 sts inc'd)
Row 8: K to end, cast on 1 st using the Backwards Loop Cast-On Method. (1 st inc'd)
Row 9: *K to 1 st before m, m1r, k1, SM, k1, m1l*, repeat *–* 3 more times, k to end, cast on 3 sts using the Backwards Loop method. (11 sts inc'd)
Row 10: K to end, cast on 3 sts using the Backwards Loop method. (3 sts inc'd)
91 (91, 91, 95, 99) (99, 99, 103) sts [14 (14, 14, 15, 16) (16, 16, 17) sts for both fronts, 18 (18, 18, 18, 18) (18, 18, 18) sts for both sleeves, 27 (27, 27, 29, 31) (31, 31, 33) sts for back].

Row 11: *K to 1 st bef m, m1r, k1, SM, k1, m1l*, repeat *–* 3 more times, k to end. (8 sts inc'd)
Row 12: K to end.
Repeat rows 11–12, 12 (12, 14, 15, 16) (18, 19 21) more times. 195 (195, 211, 223, 235) (251, 259, 279) sts [27 (27, 29, 31, 33) (35, 36, 39) sts for both fronts, 44 (44, 48,

50, 52) (56, 58, 62) sts for both sleeves, 53 (53, 57, 61, 65) (69, 71, 77) sts for back].

DIVIDE FOR BODY AND SLEEVES

K to the first marker and remove it. Place all sts between it and the next marker on a piece of scrap yarn and remove the second marker. Cast on 5 (10, 11, 13, 17) (20, 24, 24) underarm sts using the Backwards Loop Cast-On Method. Knit the back sts to the third marker and remove it. Place all sts between it and the next marker on a piece of scrap yarn and remove the last marker. Cast on 5 (10, 11, 13, 17) (20, 24, 24) underarm sts using the Backwards Loop Cast-On Method and k to end. 117 (127, 137, 149, 165) (179, 191, 203) sts for body.

BODY AND HEM

Continue working in Garter Stitch (every row is a knit row) for approx. 44 rows (they create 22 garter ridges). Note that the cardigan may now seem too short, but the Garter Stitch will stretch quite a bit after blocking. You can, of course, make the cardigan as short or long as you wish.

Ribbing

Change to smaller needles and start ribbing: *P1, k1tbl*, repeat *–* until the last st, p1. Continue ribbing in this way for 9 more rows (or until the rib measures approx. 2.5" / 6 cm). Bind off loosely.

SLEEVES

Place 44 (44, 48, 50, 52) (56, 58, 62) sleeve sts from scrap yarn on bigger circular needles. You can also use DPNs. *Note!* Don't pick any sts from the underarm cast-on.

Join for working in the round and place BOR marker.

Note! Now that you are knitting Garter Stitch in the rnd, every other rnd is a k rnd and every other a p rnd.

Rnd 1: K to end.
Rnd 2: P to end.
Repeat rnds 1–2 for 28 rows (= 14 garter ridges). *Note!* The sample cardigan has short sleeves, but as with the body, you can make the sleeves as short or long as you wish.

Next rnd: K.
Next rnd:
Sizes 1 & 2: On this rnd, decrease 8 sts as follows: *p3, p2tog*, , repeat *–* twice, *p4, p2tog* 4 times, *p3, p2tog* 2 times. 36 sts.
Size 3: On this rnd, decrease 10 sts as follows: p2, p2tog, p2, *p2tog, p3*, repeat *–* 7 times, p2tog, p2, p2tog, p1. 38 sts.
Size 4: On this rnd, decrease 12 sts as follows: p2, *p2tog, p2*, repeat *–* 5 times, p2tog, p3, *p2tog, p2* 5 times, p2tog, p1. 38 sts.
Size 5: On this rnd, decrease 12 sts as follows: p2, *p2tog, p2*, repeat *–* 4 times, *p2tog, p3* 3 times, *p2tog, p2* 4 times, p2tog, p1. 40 sts.
Size 6: On this rnd, decrease 14 sts as follows: p1, *p2tog, p2*, repeat *–* 13 times, p2tog, p1. 42 sts.
Size 7: On this rnd, decrease 16 sts as follows: p1, *p2tog, p2*, repeat *–* 5 times, *p2tog, p1*, repeat *–* 5 times, *p2tog, p2*, repeat *–* 5 times, p2tog. 42 sts.
Size 8: On this rnd, decrease 20 sts as follows: p1, p2tog, p2, *p2tog, p1*, repeat *–* 17 times, p2tog, p2, p2tog. 42 sts.

Ribbing

Change to smaller needles and start ribbing: *K1tbl, p1*, repeat *–* to the end. Continue ribbing in this way for 9 more rows (or until the rib measures approx. 2.5" / 6 cm). Bind off loosely.

NECKLINE

Using smaller needles, with the RS facing,
pick up and knit approx. 61 (61, 61, 65, 69)
(69, 69, 73) sts from the neckline (the exact
amount of sts isn't crucial but it needs to
be an odd number).

Start ribbing: *P1, k1tbl*, repeat *–* until
the last st, p1.
Work in established twisted ribbing for 5
more rows. Bind off loosely.

BUTTONBAND

Using smaller needles, with the RS facing
and beginning at the neck edge of the
left front, pick up and knit 63 (63, 67, 67,
69) (71, 73, 73) sts (the exact amount of
sts isn't crucial but it needs to be an odd
number).

Row 1 (WS): P1, *p1tbl, k1*, repeat *–*
until the 2 last sts, p1tbl, p1.
Row 2 (RS): K1, *k1tbl, p1*, repeat *–*
until the 2 last sts, k1tbl, k1.
Work in established twisted ribbing for 3
more rows. Bind off loosely.

BUTTONHOLE BAND

Using smaller needles, with the RS
facing and beginning at the bottom edge
of the right front, pick up and knit the
same amount of sts as you did with the
buttonband.

Row 1 (WS): P1, *p1tbl, k1*, repeat *–*
until the 2 last sts, p1tbl, p1.
Row 2 (RS): K1, *k1tbl, p1*, repeat *–*
until the 2 last sts, k1tbl, k1.
Row 3: On this row, make 6 buttonholes
evenly placed: *work in established ribbing
to the desired buttonhole location, yo,
k2tog*, repeat *–* throughout the row.
Work in established twisted ribbing for 2
more rows. Bind off loosely.

FINISHING

Sew the underarm holes. Weave in the ends
and block to measurements. Sew buttons.

Evgeniya Dupliy

SUPER EASY!

15 Abgerundet

This scarf has a fun, unusual shape. It uses easy Garter Rib in the middle and Garter Stitch at the rounded ends, which allows you to focus on decreasing stitches.

SIZE

One Size

FINISHED MEASUREMENTS

Length: 68.5" / 172.5 cm.
Width: 10.75" / 27 cm.

MATERIALS

Yarn: 4 balls of Puno by Gepard Garn (68% baby alpaca, 10% merino, 22% polyamide, 120 yds / 110 m – 50 g), colourway 145.

If you decide to use another yarn, you will need approx. 456 yds / 420 m of bulky-weight yarn.

Needles: US 10.5 / 6.5 mm 32–40" / 80–100 cm circular needles.

GAUGE

14 sts x 26 rows to 4" / 10 cm in Garter Stitch, after blocking.

NOTES

You can find the abbreviations and detailed instructions for techniques used in this pattern in the Abbreviations (pp. 20–23) and Techniques (pp. 15–19) sections.

CONSTRUCTION

This scarf is worked flat, beginning with a simple Long-Tail Cast-On and working 2 x 2 Garter Ribbing to create the centre part. The rounded end is shaped with decreases. After that, stitches are picked up at the cast-on edge and the other end is shaped. Both rounded ends are worked in garter stitch to simplify the knitting process and to allow a beginner to focus on decreases.

DIRECTIONS

Cast on 38 sts using the Long-Tail Cast-On Method or method of choice.

Section 1: Central Part in 2 x 2 Garter Ribbing

Work 6 rows in Garter Stitch (k all sts). You will have 3 garter ridges.

Row 7 (WS): K4, *p2, k2*, repeat *–* to last 2 sts, k2.
Row 8 (RS): K to end.
Repeat rows 7–8 until the scarf measures approx. 35.5" / 90 cm. At this point, you have used about two skeins or approx. 240 yds / 220 m of yarn.

Section 2: 1st Rounded End in Garter Stitch

Work 84 rows in Garter Stitch (k all sts). You will have 42 garter ridges.

Next, work decreases to shape the rounded end as follows:
Row 1 (RS): K1, ssk, k to 3 last sts, k2tog, k1. (2 sts dec'd)
Row 2 (WS): K to end.
Row 3: K to end.
Row 4: K to end.
Repeat rows 1–4 once more. You should have 34 sts.
Repeat rows 1–2, 5 times. You should have 24 sts.
Work row 1, 7 times after that. You should have 10 sts.

Next WS row: Bind off all sts. You don't need to bind off loosely, as the width of the edge is shorter than the width of the scarf. For this scarf, it's better to have a firm edge.

Section 3: 2nd Rounded End in Garter Stitch

With RS facing, pick up 38 sts from the cast-on edge. Continue then working with a WS row as follows:

Work 78 rows in Garter Stitch (k all sts) additional to 6 rows from section 1 here. You will have 42 garter ridges.

Work the decreases to shape the rounded end and bind off as in Section 2.

FINISHING

Weave in ends. Wet block the scarf to measurements. It is important to block the scarf well to achieve a nice rounded shape for the ends.

Meiju K-P

16 Enkel

Enkel is a textural striped sweater with half-length puffy sleeves and a cropped hem. It's easy-going and perfect for layering. This lightweight sweater is a relaxing and quick knit.

SIZES

1 (2, 3, 4, 5) (6, 7, 8)

Recommended ease: 2–4" / 5–10 cm of positive ease.

FINISHED MEASUREMENTS

Chest Circumference: 36 (37.75, 41.75, 46.25, 53.75) (55.5, 57.25, 64)" / 90 (94.5, 104.5, 115.5, 134.5) (138.5, 143, 160) cm.
Upper Arm Circumference: 14.75 (15.5, 17.25, 18.75, 22.25) (22.75, 23.5, 24)" / 37 (38.5, 43, 47, 55.5) (57, 58.5, 60) cm.
Front Yoke Depth without the Neck Ribbing: 8.75 (8.75, 9, 10, 12) (12.5, 13.5, 13.5)" / 22 (22, 23, 25.5, 30.5) (32, 34.5, 34.5) cm or desired length.
Body Length from Underarm: 10" / 25.5 cm or desired length.
Sleeve Length: 10" / 25.5 cm or desired length.
Neck Circumference (based on gauge, this measurement will stretch out): Approx. 16 (17.25, 17.75, 19.5, 20.5) (21.25, 22.25, 24)" / 40 (43, 44.5, 48.5, 51.5) (53, 55.5, 60) cm.

MATERIALS

Yarn: 5 (5, 6, 6, 8) (9, 9, 10) skeins of Eco Soft by Isager (56% alpaca, 44% organic cotton, 137 yds / 125 m – 50 g), colourway E4S.

If you decide to use another yarn, you will need approx. 647 (676, 754, 813, 1081) (1143, 1207, 1323) yds / 592 (618, 689, 743, 988) (1045, 1104, 1210) m of similar DK-weight yarn that gives you gauge. *Note!* The yarn used for the photographed sample is a lightweight blow yarn that gives you a lovely fluff. If you want a similar look and feel as the sample, look for a similar kind of DK-weight yarn.

Needles: US 9 / 5.5 mm 24" / 60 cm and 32" / 80 cm circular needles (for Stockinette Stitch on the body and sleeves), US 7 / 4.5 mm 24" / 60 cm and 32" / 80 cm circular needles (for neck and hem ribbing) and US 6 / 4 mm 24" / 60 cm and 32" / 80 cm circular needles (for cuff ribbing). Sleeves can be worked with circular needles or with DPNs.

Notions: Stitch markers (locking/removable markers), scrap yarn/stitch holders.

GAUGE

14 sts x 20 rnds to 4" / 10 cm with US 9 / 5.5 mm needles in Stockinette Stitch, after blocking.

NOTES

You can find the abbreviations and detailed instructions for techniques used in this pattern in the Abbreviations (pp. 20–23) and Techniques (pp. 15–19) sections.

Slip markers as you come across them.

CONSTRUCTION

This oversized yoke sweater is worked seamlessly from the top down. Purl stripes are worked to give texture to the pullover on every 11th rnd. First you will cast on stitches for the neck ribbing. After the ribbing is done, the yoke is shaped with increases. Optional short rows are worked to make the back neck higher than the front. After the yoke is worked to its length, the body and sleeves are separated and the hem is completed. Lastly, the sleeves are worked in the round.

DIRECTIONS

YOKE

With US 7 / 4.5 mm needles, cast on 56 (60, 62, 68, 72) (74, 78, 84) sts using your method of choice. (For example the a bit more advanced Tubular Cast-On Method which creates a very neat edge. Tutorials can be found online.) Join to work in the rnd, PM for the beginning of rnd (BOR). Your BOR marker is on your right back shoulder.

Neck Ribbing
Rnd 1 (RS): *K1, p1*, repeat *–* to end. Continue in established 1 x 1 Ribbing until neck measures approx. 1.5" / 4 cm.

Shape Yoke
Change to US 9 / 5.5 mm needles.

Sizes 1, 3, 4 and 6 only
Set-up rnd: M1l, k to end. (1 st inc'd)

Sizes 2, 5, 7 and 8 only
Set-up rnd: K to end.

You should have 57 (60, 63, 69, 72) (75, 78, 84) sts.

Increase rnd 1: *K3, LLI*, repeat *–* to end. [19 (20, 21, 23, 24) (25, 26, 28) sts inc'd]
You should have 76 (80, 84, 92, 96) (100, 104, 112) sts.

K 1 rnd.

Increase rnd 2: *K4, LLI*, repeat *–* to end. [19 (20, 21, 23, 24) (25, 26, 28) sts inc'd]
You should have 95 (100, 105, 115, 120) (125, 130, 140) sts.

K 1 rnd.

Increase rnd 3: *K5, LLI*, repeat *–* to end. [19 (20, 21, 23, 24) (25, 26, 28) sts inc'd]

You should have 114 (120, 126, 138, 144) (150, 156, 168) sts.

Optional Short Row Section
In this section, use markers in different colours to separate them from each other. The markers are named A, B and C. Short rows are worked to lift the back neck higher than the front for a better fit. In this pattern, instructions for optional German Short Rows are given (if you use another method, adjust pattern if needed). You can skip this section if you do not want to work short rows.

On the next rnd, place markers for short row shaping:
Set-up rnd: K30 (30, 30, 36, 36) (36, 36, 42), PM A, k30 (30, 36, 36, 36) (42, 42, 42), PM B, k30 (30, 30, 36, 36) (36, 36, 42), PM C, k24 (30, 30, 30, 36) (36, 42, 42) to BOR m, SM.

The st count stays the same throughout the whole section, as no increases are worked. Short rows are worked flat, back and forth.
Short row 1 (RS): K to m A, SM, k2, turn work.
Short row 2 (WS): Make double stitch (MDS), p to m A, SM, p to BOR m, SM, p to m C, SM, p to m B, SM, p2, turn work.
Short row 3 (RS): MDS, k to m B, SM, k to m C, SM, k to BOR m, SM, k to m A, SM, k to the last DS and k the DS, k1, turn work.
Short row 4 (WS): MDS, p to m A, SM, p to BOR m, SM, p to m C, SM, p to m B, SM, p to the last DS and p the DS, p1, turn work.
Repeat short rows 3–4, 3 more times.

Next row (RS): K to BOR m.
Continue to work in the rnd.
Next rnd (RS): K to end.
Next rnd: P to end.
Next rnd: K to end.
The optional short row section ends here. You can remove all markers except the BOR marker.

Continue Increasing

Increase rnd 4: *K6, LLI*, repeat *–*
to end. [19 (20, 21, 23, 24) (25, 26, 28)
sts inc'd]
You should have 133 (140, 147, 161, 168)
(175, 182, 196) sts.

K 6 rnds.

Increase rnd 5: *K7, LLI*, repeat *–*
to end. [19 (20, 21, 23, 24) (25, 26, 28)
sts inc'd]
You should have 152 (160, 168, 184, 192)
(200, 208, 224) sts.

K 1 rnd.
P 1 rnd.
K 4 rnds.

Increase rnd 6: *K8, LLI*, repeat *–*
to end. [19 (20, 21, 23, 24) (25, 26, 28)
sts inc'd]
You should have 171 (180, 189, 207, 216)
(225, 234, 252) sts.

K 5 rnds.
P 1 rnd.
K 2 rnds.

Increase rnd 7: *K9, LLI*, repeat *–*
to end. [19 (20, 21, 23, 24) (25, 26, 28)
sts inc'd]
You should have 190 (200, 210, 230, 240)
(250, 260, 280) sts.

You have established a pattern where
every 11th rnd is a purl rnd. Continue in
this pattern throughout the work.

On the next rnd move your BOR m 5 (1, 5,
8, 4) (4, 0, 5) sts left to centre your short
row neck to the middle front. *Note!* If
you didn't work the short row section,
skip this step.

Work extra rnds, if necessary, until your
(front) yoke measures approx. 8.75 (8.75, 9,
10, 12) (12.5, 13.5, 13.5)" / 22 (22, 23, 25.5,
30.5) (32, 34.5, 34.5) cm measured from
below the neck ribbing, remembering to
work every 11th rnd as a purl rnd. End on

a rnd where you have a knit rnd coming
up next, so you don't have to purl when
separating the body and the sleeves.

Separating Body and Sleeves

Remove BOR m, *place 42 (44, 46, 50,
52) (54, 56, 56) sleeve sts on scrap yarn
or st holder, cast on 10 (10, 14, 16, 26)
(26, 26, 28) sts for underarm using the
Backwards Loop Cast-On Method or
method of choice* and PM (for BOR)
in the middle of those sts, work 53 (56,
59, 65, 68) (71, 74, 84) front sts, repeat
– to create the second sleeve, work as
established to end (BOR m). Your BOR is
now under the right arm.
You have 126 (132, 146, 162, 188) (194, 200,
224) sts for body and 42 (44, 46, 50, 52)
(54, 56, 56) sts on hold for each sleeves.

BODY

Continue in pattern: work every 11th rnd
as a purl rnd and knit other rnds. Work
until body measures approx. 8" / 20.5 cm
(or 2" / 5 cm less than desired length)
from underarm.

Change to US 7 / 4.5 mm needles.

Hem ribbing row 1 (RS): *K1, p1*, repeat
– to end.
Work in established 1x1 Ribbing until
it measures 2" / 5 cm. Bind off loosely
in ribbing.

SLEEVES

Work with US 9 / 5.5 mm needles. Continue
working in the same pattern as for the
body: work every 11th rnd as a purl rnd and
knit other rnds. The sleeves are worked
in the rnd.
Move the 42 (44, 46, 50, 52) (54, 56, 56)
sleeve sts to circular needles or DPNs.

Join yarn in the middle of the armhole
opening, pick up and k 6 (6, 8, 9, 14)
(14, 14, 15) sts, k 42 (44, 46, 50, 52) (54,

56, 56) sleeve sts, pick up and k 6 (6, 8,
9, 14) (14, 14, 15) sts, PM in the middle of
underarm to indicate the beginning of
the rnd (BOR). You should have 54 (56,
62, 68, 80) (82, 84, 86) sts.

Sleeve decrease rnd: K5 (5, 7, 8, 13)
(13, 13, 14), k2tog, k to 7 (7, 9, 10, 15)
(15, 15, 16) sts before end, ssk, k to end.
(2 sts dec'd) [You should have 52 (54, 60,
66, 78) (80, 82, 84) sts]

Work in established pattern (work every
11th rnd as a purl rnd and knit other
rnds) until the sleeve measures approx.
8" / 20.5 cm from underarm (from the
underarm pick-up sts).

Change to US 6 / 4 mm needles and begin
ribbing:
Cuff ribbing rnd 1: *K1, p1*, repeat *–*
to end.
Work in established 1 x 1 Ribbing until
ribbing measures 2" / 5 cm. Bind off in
ribbing. The bind-off can be worked a
bit tighter to give the sleeve more of a
balloon shape.

Repeat instructions for the second sleeve.

FINISHING

Weave in all yarn ends. Wet block to
measurements.

Jonna Hietala

SUPER EASY!

17 Birke

Birke is an uncomplicated, asymmetrical shawl knitted with earthy tones – but why not play with the two contrast colours and make the most of all the silk mohair ends in your stash?

SIZE

One Size

FINISHED MEASUREMENTS

Width: 56.75" / 144 cm.
Depth: 20.5" / 52 cm.

MATERIALS

Yarn: MC: 2 skeins of Shear by Harrisville Designs (100% CVM and Romedale, 320 yds / 293 m – 100 g), colourway Shear.
CC1: 2 balls of Sensai by Ito (60% mohair, 40% silk, 262 yds / 240 m – 20 g), colourway 364 Top Dark Grey.
CC2: 2 balls of Soft Silk Mohair by Knitting for Olive (70% mohair, 30% silk, 246 yds / 225 m – 25 g), colourway Linen.
The shawl is worked holding these three yarns together.
If you decide to use another yarn, you will need approx. 634 yds / 580 m of DK-weight yarn in MC and 470 yds / 430 m of lace-weight yarn in each CC.

Needles: US 10.5 or 11 / 7 mm 32–40" / 80–100 cm circular needles.

GAUGE

14 sts x 24 rows to 4" / 10 cm in Garter Stitch, after blocking.

NOTES

You can find the abbreviations and detailed instructions for techniques used in this pattern in the Abbreviations (pp. 20–23) and Techniques (pp. 15–19) sections.

The size of this shawl is easily adjustable by knitting more or fewer rows, therefore you can actually use whatever yarns you wish – or have in your stash, just note that using different weights will mean the yardage needed and shawl size will also change.

CONSTRUCTION

This asymmetrical triangular shawl begins from the narrow tip and is knitted flat in Garter Stitch. A simple yarn over increase is made at the end of every other row. The shawl is bound off on the opposite edge with the I-Cord Bind-Off Method. Tassels are attached to each tip of the shawl.

DIRECTIONS

Holding three yarns together cast on 3 sts.
Row 1 (WS): Sl1 pwise wyib, k to end.
Row 2 (RS): Sl1 pwise wyib, k to 1 st before the end, yo, k1. (1 st inc'd)
Row 3: K1, k the yo through the back loop (this way it doesn't create a hole in the fabric), k to end.
Repeat rows 2–3 (ending with row 3) until you have 107 sts in total.

I-CORD BIND-OFF

Bind off using the I-Cord Bind-Off Method: Cast on 3 sts to the front of the left-hand needle using the Cable Cast-On Method. *K2, sl1 pwise wyib, k1, pass the slipped st over. Lift the 3 sts back on the left-hand needle*. Repeat *–* to end.

FINISHING

Weave in the ends and wet block to measurements. Make three tassels using your favourite method (or look up one of the many tutorials online) and fasten them tightly to each corner.

Maija Kangasluoma

18 Kupla

This boxy sweater features an all-over bubble pattern created with a simple technique. The stitch pattern may seem daunting but don't worry – it's super easy, almost like knitting stripes!

SIZES

1 (2, 3, 4, 5) (6, 7, 8)

Recommended ease: 8–10" / 20–25 cm of positive ease.

FINISHED MEASUREMENTS

Chest Circumference: 40 (45, 48.5, 52, 56) (60.5, 64, 68)" / 102 (114, 123, 132.5, 142) (154, 163, 172.5) cm.
Length from Shoulder to Hem: 21 (21.5, 22, 22, 23) (24, 24, 25)" / 53.5 (54.5, 55.5, 56.5, 58.5) (60.5, 61.5, 63.5) cm.
Sleeve Length: 16.5 (16.5, 16.5, 16.5, 15.5) (15.5, 15.5, 15.5)" / 41.5 (41.5, 41.5, 41.5, 39.5) (39.5, 39.5, 39,5) cm.
Upper Arm Circumference: 13 (14, 14.5, 15.5, 16.5) (18, 19.5, 20.5)" / 32.5 (35, 37, 39.5, 42) (45.5, 49, 52.5) cm.

MATERIALS

Yarn: VIP by Lana Gatto (80% merino, 20% cashmere, 219 yds / 200 m – 50 g).
MC: 5 (5, 6, 6, 7) (7, 8, 8) balls, colourway Muschio.
CC: 4 (5, 5, 6, 6) (7, 7, 8) balls, colourway Rosa Carne.

If you decide to use another yarn, you will need approx. 924 (1037, 1124, 1222, 1319) (1464, 1575, 1710) yds / 845 (948, 1028, 1117, 1206) (1339, 1440, 1564) m of fingering-weight yarn in MC and 836 (933, 1012, 1100, 1188) (1318, 1296, 1539) yds / 764 (853, 925, 1006, 1086) (1205, 1296, 1407) m of fingering-weight yarn in CC.

Needles: US 2.5 / 3 mm and US 4 / 3.5 mm needles (you can either use long, straight needles or 32" / 80 cm circulars).

Notions: Stitch holders or waste yarn, pins or other blocking tools for blocking.

GAUGE

26 sts x 48 rows to 4" / 10 cm on US 4 / 3.5 mm needles in Bubble Pattern, after blocking.

STITCH PATTERN

Bubble Pattern (knitted flat)
(st count divisible by 4 + 3 sts)
Rows 1–6: Start with a RS row. With CC, work in Stockinette Stitch (k all sts on RS, p on WS). Always slip the first st (knitwise with yarn in back on RS rows and purlwise with yarn in front on WS rows).

Row 7 (RS): With MC, k1 (*Note!* On this row, you don't slip the first st). *With the tip of the right-hand needle knit into the st which is located 4 rows down from the st on the left-hand needle (meaning into a CC-coloured st on the 2nd CC row), drop the 1st st of the left-hand needle off the needle: it will slowly unravel to the st you knitted, k3*, repeat *–* to 2 sts before end. Work a dropped st once more, k1.
Rows 8–12: With MC, work in Stockinette Stitch (k all sts on RS, p on WS). Always slip the first st as established.
Row 13 (RS): With CC, k3 (*Note!* On this row, you don't slip the first st). *With the tip of the right-hand needle knit into the st which is located 4 rows below the st on the left-hand needle (meaning into a MC-coloured st on the 2nd MC row), drop the 1st st of the left-hand needle off the needle: it will slowly unravel to the st you knitted, k3*, repeat *–* to end.
Rows 14–18: With CC, work in Stockinette Stitch (k all sts on RS, p on WS). Always slip the first st as established. Repeat rows 7–18 for pattern.

NOTES

You can find the abbreviations and detailed instructions for techniques used in this pattern in the Abbreviations (pp. 20–23) and Techniques (pp. 15–19) sections.

There's no need to cut the yarns between sections. You can carry them along the side of the work.

CONSTRUCTION

This boxy sweater has a relaxed fit and dropped shoulders. The pieces are knitted flat from the bottom up and later seamed together with simple backstitches. Seaming brings more structure to the sweater. You begin with working the back and front pieces with a 2 x 2 Ribbing as well as the sleeves. Then, the other shoulder is seamed and the neckline is worked in 2 x 2 Ribbing. Once the neckline is completed, the other shoulder is seamed. The sleeves are attached and the sleeve and side seams worked.

MODIFICATIONS

This is a great project to use left-overs! Pick for instance a neutral colour, such as grey or white, as the main colour and combine it with different contrasting-coloured yarns of the same weight.

As front and back pieces are worked without any waist or bust shaping, it's easy to modify the size: you can make the sweater longer or more cropped or add ease to the sleeves.

DIRECTIONS

BACK

With MC and US 2.5 / 3 mm needles, cast on 135 (151, 163, 175, 187) (203, 215, 227) sts with the Long-Tail Cast-On Method or method of choice. Work 2 x 2 Ribbing for the hem as follows:

Row 1 (WS): *K2, p2*, repeat *–* to 3 sts before end, k2, p1.
Row 2 (RS): Work the sts as they appear, meaning k the knit sts and p the purl sts. Repeat row 2 until the hem ribbing measures approx. 1.5" / 3.5 cm. End with a WS row.

Change to US 4 / 3.5 mm needles and begin to work in Bubble Pattern beginning with a RS row. Work in Bubble Pattern until the piece measures approx. 20.5 (21, 21.5, 21.5, 22.5) (23.5, 23.5, 24.5)" / 52 (53, 54, 55, 57) (59, 60, 62) cm. Be sure to end with a row 8 or 14.

Neckline and Shoulders

Continue to work with a RS row. Work 39 (46, 51, 56, 62) (69, 74, 79) sts in Bubble Pattern, transfer the next 57 (59, 61, 63, 63) (65, 67, 69) sts (for the neckline) to a stitch holder or piece of waste yarn, transfer the next 39 (46, 51, 56, 62) (69, 74, 79) sts (for the left shoulder) to another stitch holder or piece of waste yarn.

First, work the right back shoulder. Continue to work in Bubble Pattern with the right shoulder sts and, at the same time, decrease for the neckline by binding off 2 sts at the beginning of the WS row. Repeat on the next WS row once more. 35 (42, 47, 52, 58) (65, 70, 75) sts remain. Continue in Bubble Pattern until the back measures approx. 21.5 (21.5, 22, 22.5, 23) (24, 24.5, 25)" / 54 (55, 56, 57, 59) (61, 62, 64) cm in total. Bind off sts loosely. Continue with the back left shoulder. Start with a RS row (at the neck edge), attach yarn and continue in Bubble Pattern. Start working the neckline decreases at the next

RS row by binding off 2 sts at the beginning of the row. Repeat on the next RS row once more. 35 (42, 47, 52, 58) (65, 70, 75) sts remain. Continue in Bubble Pattern until the left back shoulder matches the right shoulder. Bind off loosely.

FRONT

Work as the back until the piece measures approx. 19.5 (20, 20.5, 21, 21.5) (22.5, 23, 23.5)" / 50 (51, 52, 53, 55) (57, 58, 60) cm. Be sure to end with a row 8 or 14. *Note!* If you would like to add depth to your front neckline, begin to work the decreases earlier.

Neckline and Shoulders

You are continuing with a RS row. Work 46 (53, 58, 63, 69) (76, 81, 86) sts, transfer the next 43 (45, 47, 49, 49) (51, 53, 55) sts (for the neckline) to a stitch holder or piece of waste yarn, transfer the next 46 (53, 58, 63, 69) (76, 81, 86) sts (for the right shoulder) to another stitch holder or piece of waste yarn.

First, work the left front shoulder (this is the part that is on the right side of the front piece). Continue in Bubble Pattern and, at the same time, decrease for the neckline at the beginning of every WS row (at the neck edge) as follows:
Decrease row 1 (WS): Bind off 4 sts.
Decrease rows 2–3 (WS): Bind off 2 sts.
Decrease rows 4–6 (WS): Bind off 1 st.
35 (42, 47, 52, 58) (65, 70, 75) sts remain.

Continue to work in Bubble Pattern until the piece measures approx. 21.5 (21.5, 22.5, 23) (24, 24.5, 25)" / 54 (55, 56, 57, 59) (61, 62, 64) cm, the same as the back. Bind off sts loosely.
Continue with the right front shoulder. Start with a RS row (at the neck edge), attach yarn and continue in Bubble Pattern. On the next RS row, start to work decreases at the beginning of every RS row (at the neck edge) as follows:

Decrease row 1 (RS): Bind off 4 sts.
Decrease rows 2–3 (RS): Bind off 2 sts.
Decrease rows 4–6 (RS): Bind off 1 st.
Note! Cut yarn every time you change colour. 35 (42, 47, 52, 58) (65, 70, 75) sts remain.

Continue in Bubble Pattern until the right front shoulder matches the left shoulder. Bind off loosely.

SLEEVES

With MC and US 2.5 / 3 mm needles, cast on 59 (59, 63, 63, 67) (67, 71, 71) sts with the Long-Tail Cast-On Method or method of choice. Work 2 x 2 Ribbing for the cuff as follows:
Row 1 (WS): *K2, p2*, repeat *–* to 3 sts before end, k2, p1.
Row 2: Work the sts as they appear, meaning k the knit sts and p the purl sts. Repeat row 2 until the cuff ribbing measures approx. 2" / 4.5 cm. End with a WS row.

Change to US 4 / 3.5 mm needles and begin to work in Bubble Pattern beginning with a RS row. When the sleeve measures approx. 3.5 (3.5, 3.5, 3, 3) (3, 2.5, 2.5)" / 9 (9, 9, 8, 8) (7, 6, 6) cm, begin increases on a RS row as follows:
Increase Row (RS): Continue to work in Bubble Pattern but knit into the front and back of the first and last st (2 sts increased).
Repeat the increase row every 10th (9th, 8th, 7th, 7th) (6th, 6th, 5th) row another 12 (15, 16, 19, 20) (25, 27, 32) times. 26 (32, 34, 40, 42) (52, 56, 66) sts increased in total. You should have a total of 85 (91, 97, 103, 109) (119, 127, 137) sts for the sleeve.
Note! As new sts are created to the sides, you need to follow the Bubble Pattern based on the previous rows. At this point you're already familiar with this stitch pattern, so you will know where to work the dropped sts. Start to work the Bubble Pattern with the edge sts as soon as it's possible. Just remember not to work a

dropped st with the first or last st of the row and not with a st that's just increased.

When the piece measures approx. 16.5 (16.5, 16.5, 16.5, 15.5) (15.5, 15.5, 15.5)" / 42 (42, 42, 42, 40) (40, 40, 40) cm, bind off all sts loosely.

Repeat for the second sleeve.

BLOCKING

Weave in all ends. Wet block all pieces to measurements and let dry completely. You will see all measurements in Final Measurements but add approx. 0.2" / 0.5 cm for the seams.

NECKLINE RIBBING

Place the RSs together and join the first shoulder with backstitches about 0.2" / 0.5 cm from the edge.

With MC and RSs facing you, pick up and knit beginning from the right neckline edge. Pick up sts evenly, approx. at a ratio of 1:1 and skip every third or fourth st around the curves. When you reach the sts placed on the waste yarn or stitch holder, transfer them to the needles and knit. Work as established until you have picked up and knitted sts around the whole neckline. You should have around 158 (162, 166, 170, 170) (174, 178, 182) sts (or more if you decided to work a deeper neckline). Do not join to work in the rnd. *Note!* Since the neckline ribbing is worked flat and the other shoulder is seamed after that, the exact number of sts isn't important. If you prefer to join both shoulders first and work the neckline ribbing in the rnd, the st count should be divisible by four.

Work in 2 x 2 Ribbing flat for approx. 1" / 2 cm. On the next RS row, bind off loosely.

SEAMING AND FINISHING

Work the other shoulder with backstitches about 0.2" / 0.5 cm from the edge.

Join the sleeves so that the sleeve's centre top point meets the shoulder seam and the sleeves are placed symmetrically for the front and back pieces.

Sew the side and sleeve seams.

Weave in the remaining ends.

Sidsel Grau Petersen

19 Marta

Marta is a vest in all-over Garter Stitch. This is a quick and easy pattern that has a fun construction: it is knitted sideways. Get creative with the embroidered stripes!

SIZES

1 (2, 3, 4, 5) (6, 7, 8)

Recommended ease: 6–8" / 15–20.5 cm of positive ease.

FINISHED MEASUREMENTS

Chest Circumference: 38.75 (44.5, 49.25, 53.75, 58.25) (62.75, 67.5, 72)" / 97 (111.5, 123, 134.5, 145.5) (157, 168.5, 180) cm.
Full Length from Back Neck to Hem: 23 (24.5, 25.25, 25.25, 26) (26.5, 28, 29.25)" / 57.5 (61.5, 63, 63, 66) (66.5, 70, 73) cm.
Body Length from Armhole to Hem: 10.25 (11, 11.75, 11.25, 11.75) (12, 12.25, 13.75)" / 25 (27.5, 29, 27.5, 29) (30, 30, 33.5) cm.

MATERIALS

Yarn: 8 (8, 10, 11, 12) (13, 15, 17) skeins of Fritidsgarn by Sandnes Garn (100%

wool, 77 yds / 70 m – 50 g), colourway Naturmelert 2641.

For the embroidery: 7 (9, 11, 11, 12) (15, 15, 17) packages of DMC Six Strand Embroidery Floss (100% cotton, 9 yds / 8 m – 2 g). For the sample vest 3 colours were used: Pink (3779), Brown (3031) and twice the amount for the Green (934). If four different colours are wanted, you will need 2 (3, 3, 3, 3) (4, 4, 5) packages of DMC Six Strand Embroidery Floss of each colour.

If you decide to use other yarns, you will need approx. 612 (612, 765, 842, 918) (995, 1148, 1300) yds / 560 (560, 700, 770, 840) (910, 1050, 1189) m of bulky-weight yarn for the vest and approx. 53 (70, 88, 88, 101) (123, 123, 140) yds / 48 (64, 80, 80, 92) (112, 112, 128) m of any thread or yarn for embroidering.

Needles: US 9 / 5.5 mm and US 10 / 6 mm 32" / 80 cm circular needles.

Notions: Stitch marker, tapestry needle for embroidering, crochet needle for seaming.

GAUGE

12 sts x 28 rows to 4" / 10 cm on US 10 / 6 mm needles in Garter Stitch, after blocking.

NOTES

You can find the abbreviations and detailed instructions for techniques used in this pattern in the Abbreviations (pp. 20–23) and Techniques (pp. 15–19) sections.

Slip markers as you come across them.

You can place a removable stitch marker to help you count the rows. Note that each Garter Stitch ridge (or bump if you prefer to count those) counts for two rows.

CONSTRUCTION

This vest is knitted sideways in simple Garter Stitch. It is knitted flat and seamed together at the shoulders and sides. You will begin with working the front, then the back. After seaming, the vest is finished with easy-to-make, embroidered stripes. Lastly, the armholes, neckline and hem are finished with a ribbed edge.

MODIFICATIONS

The vest works great without embroidery too, although you shouldn't be scared of learning this technique! If you, however, wish to make a plain vest, simply skip the embroidery and go straight to the ribbing.

Hand-dyed yarns or other special-effect yarns can also be used for embroidery.

DIRECTIONS

FRONT

You will start with the right shoulder and finish with the left shoulder.

With US 10 / 6 mm needles, cast on 58 (62, 64, 64, 66) (68, 72, 76) sts using the Long-Tail Cast-On Method or method of choice.

Work 9 (9, 11, 13, 15) (17, 19, 21) rows in Garter Stitch (k all rows). The first row will be a WS row. You will end with a WS row.

Next row (inc row) (RS): K to 1 st before the end, m1l, k1. (1 st inc'd)
Continue to work in Garter Stitch (k all rows) and repeat the increase row every 10th (10th, 12th, 14th, 16th) (18th, 20th, 22nd) row a total of 3 (4, 4, 4, 4) (4, 4, 4) times. You should have 61 (66, 68, 68, 70) (72, 76, 80) sts.

K 2 rows.
Next, we will start to decrease sts to create the right side of the v-neckline:
Next row (WS): Bind off 2 sts, k to end of row. (2 sts dec'd)
Next row (RS): K to end.
Repeat the previous two rows 17 more times. You should have 25 (30, 32, 32, 34) (36, 40, 44) sts.

K 2 rows.

Next, we will start to increase sts to create the left side of the v-neckline:
Next row (WS): Cast on 2 sts using the Knitted Cast-On Method or method of choice, k to end of row. (2 sts inc'd)
Next row (RS): K to end.
Repeat the previous two rows 17 times. You should have 61 (66, 68, 68, 70) (72, 76, 80) sts.

K 2 rows.

Next row (dec row) (WS): K1, k2tog, k to end of row. (1 st dec'd)

Continue to work in Garter Stitch (k all rows) and repeat the decrease row every 10th (10th, 12th, 14th, 16th) (18th, 20th, 22nd) row a total of 3 (4, 4, 4, 4) (4, 4, 4) times. You should have 58 (62, 64, 64, 66) (68, 72, 76) sts.

K 9 (9, 11, 13, 15) (17, 19, 21) rows.

Bind off all sts loosely.

BACK

You will start with the right shoulder and finish with the left shoulder.

With US 10 / 6 mm needles, cast on 58 (62, 64, 64, 66) (68, 72, 76) sts using the Long-Tail Cast-On Method or method of choice.

Work 9 (9, 11, 13, 15) (17, 19, 21) rows in Garter Stitch (k all rows). The first row will be a RS row. You will end with a RS row.

Next row (inc row) (WS): K to 1 st before end, m1l, k1. (1 st inc'd)
Continue to work in Garter Stitch (k all rows) and repeat the increase row every 10th (10th, 12th, 14th, 16th) (18th, 20th, 22nd) row a total of 3 (4, 4, 4, 4) (4, 4, 4) times. 3 (4, 4, 4, 4) (4, 4, 4) sts inc'd. You should have 61 (66, 68, 68, 70) (72, 76, 80) sts.

Work 78 rows in Garter Stitch (k all rows).

Next row (dec row) (RS): K2tog, k to end of row.
Continue to work in Garter Stitch (k all rows) and repeat the decrease row every 10th (10th, 12th, 14th, 16th) (18th, 20th, 22nd) row a total of 3 (4, 4, 4, 4) (4, 4, 4) times. 3 (4, 4, 4, 4) (4, 4, 4) sts dec'd. You should have 58 (62, 64, 64, 66) (68, 72, 76) sts.
Work 9 (9, 11, 13, 15) (17, 19, 21) rows in Garter Stitch (k all rows).

Bind off all sts loosely.

FINISHING

Seaming

Note! You may find it easier to seam if you wet block the front and back before seaming.

The front and back are seamed together. First, seam together the shoulders using a crochet hook or darning needle for working the Mattress Stitch. Then, seam together the sides leaving an approx. 10 (10.5, 10.5, 11, 11) (11.5, 12.5, 12.5)" / 25.5 (26.5, 26.5, 28, 28) (29, 32, 32) cm deep armhole.

After the vest is seamed, you will embroider the stripes.

Embroidery

Every stripe consists of four lines – the colour combinations are endless! Every line is a horizontal running stitch that goes under the knit sts and over the purl sts. There are 8 sts between every 4-line stripe.

Begin the embroidery approx. 1.5" / 4 cm from the hem in either of the sides by sewing a few sts on the backside to get started. Pull the knitted fabric a bit after embroidering every few sts, so the thread is not too tight.

Begin the first embroidered line approx. 1.5" / 4 cm from the hemline on either the left or right side. Mount the thread on the WS by sewing 3–4 times into the same place. Start stitching leading the thread over a purl st, and under a knit st. Do it very loosely, if you pull the thread too hard, just stretch/pull the knitted garment a little and the thread will fall back into place.

Whenever the thread is almost used, attach it on the backside by sewing 3–4 times into the same place, and begin with a new thread as before. One stripe on the vest consists of 4 embroidered lines. When the first is finished, begin the next one above it. When the 4 embroidered lines are done, count 8 sts upwards, and begin

a new embroidered line on the 9th stitch. Continue the lines upwards. When you reach the neckline, continue the stripes on either side, count the sts to make sure they are symmetrical.

RIBBING

Change to US 9 / 5.5 mm needles.

Work the ribbing along the armholes as follows:
Pick up and k 48 (54, 58, 60, 64) (66, 70, 72) sts. Place a stitch marker for the beginning of the rnd (BOR).

Next rnd: *K1, p1*, repeat *–* to end of rnd.
Work in established 1 x 1 Ribbing for 6 rnds in total.

Bind off all sts.

Work the ribbing along the front hemline as follows (the hemline has a split):
Pick up and k 70 (76, 84, 92, 100) (106, 114, 126) sts.

Next row (RS): *K1, p1*, repeat *–* to end of rnd.
Work in established 1 x 1 Ribbing for 6 rows in total.

Bind off all sts.

Repeat instructions for the back hemline.

Work the neckline ribbing as follows:
Starting from centre front neck, pick up and k 98 (102, 104, 106, 106) (108, 108, 110) sts. Place a stitch marker to mark the beginning of rnd (BOR).

Rnd 1: P to end.
Rnd 2: K to end.
Rnd 3: P to end.
Rnd 4: *K1, p1*, repeat *–* to end of rnd.
Rnd 5 (dec rnd): K1, p2tog, p1, *k1, p1*, repeat *–* until 2 sts left, p2tog. (2 sts dec'd)

Rnd 6: K1, p2, *k1, p1*, repeat *–* until 1 st left, p1.
Rnd 7 (dec rnd): K1, p2tog, *k1, p1*, repeat *–* until 2 sts left, p2tog. (2 sts dec'd)
Rnd 8: *K1, p1*, repeat *–* to end of rnd.
Repeat rnds 5–8 once more.

Bind off all sts.

FINISHING

Weave in all ends. Wet block to measurements.

Tiina Huhtaniemi

20 Marshmallow

Balaclavas are the ultimate winter accessories – they stay in place and keep your head and neck warm. This pattern is knitted with two strands of yarn held together.

SIZES

1 (2, 3)

To fit a head circumference of 20–21 (21–23, 23–25)" / 51–53 (53–58.5, 58.5–63.5) cm.

Little negative to no ease recommended.

FINISHED MEASUREMENTS

Width (measured with the balaclava lying flat): 7.75 (9, 10)" / 19.5 (22.5, 25) cm.

MATERIALS

Yarn: 1 skein of Tukuwool DK by Tukuwool (100% Finnish wool, 273 yds / 250 m – 100 g), colourway Valo (yellow sample) or Sake (pink sample).

1 skein of Silk Mohair by Isager (75% kid mohair, 25% silk, 232 yds / 212 m – 25 g), colourway 22 Yellow (yellow sample) or 19 Pink (pink sample).

The yarns are held together throughout the pattern.

If you decide to use another yarn, you will need approx. 164 (222, 273) yds / 150 (203, 250) m of DK-weight yarn and 157 (194, 231) yds / 144 (178, 212) m of lace-weight yarn.

Needles: US 7 / 4.5 mm (for ribbing) and US 8 / 5 mm (for Garter Stitch) 16" / 40 cm circular needles. DPNs of the same size for small circumference knitting if not using the Magic Loop Technique.

Notions: Stitch marker.

GAUGE

15 sts x 30 rows to 4" / 10 cm on US 8 / 5 mm needles in Garter Stitch, after blocking.

NOTES

You can find the abbreviations and detailed instructions for techniques used in this pattern in the Abbreviations (pp. 20–23) and Techniques (pp. 15–19) sections.

Slip marker as you come across it.

Short rows are worked to shape the back of the head piece. In this pattern, Wrapless Short Rows are used. However, feel free to use another method if preferred.

CONSTRUCTION

This balaclava is knitted seamlessly from the top down. First, you knit the strip at the top of the head and shape the back with simple short rows. Next, you pick up and knit the stitches on the sides and the back of the strip and knit the body part. After neck ribbing you pick up and knit the ribbing around the front edge.

DIRECTIONS

TOP OF THE HEAD

With US 8 / 5 mm needles and both yarns held together, cast on 22 sts with the Long-Tail Cast-On Method or method of choice. You will continue to knit the piece flat.

Work 5 (6, 6.5)" / 12.5 (15, 16.5) cm in Garter Stitch (k all rows).

Work a small triangle with short rows to shape the turning point. It's easy to work short rows when you knit in Garter Stitch: you just turn the work. The hole between the sts won't be visible.

Row 1 (RS): K14, ssk, k1, turn work. (1 st dec'd)
Row 2 (WS): Sl1 pwise wyif, k7, k2tog, k1, turn work. (1 st dec'd)
Row 3: Sl1 pwise wyib, k to 1 st before the gap on the last row, ssk, k1, turn work. (1 st dec'd)
Row 4: Sl1 pwise wyif, k to 1 st before the gap on the last row, k2tog, k1, turn work. (1 st dec'd)
Repeat rows 3–4 once more.

Row 7: Sl1 pwise wyib, k to 1 st before the gap on the last row, ssk, turn work. (1 st dec'd)
Row 8: Sl1 pwise wyif, k to 1 st before the gap on the last row, k2tog. (1 st dec'd)

You now have a total of 14 sts. Cut yarns. Turn the work and start picking up sts on the RS of the work.

SIDES OF THE HEAD PIECE

Next row (RS): Pick up and k 20 (24, 28) sts from the right edge, k 14 sts, pick up and k 20 (24, 28) sts from the left edge. You should now have a total of 54 (62, 70) sts. Continue to work in Garter Stitch (k all rows) until the piece measures 7 (8, 8.5)" / 18 (20.5, 21.5) cm from pick-up edge, ending with a WS row.

Start working increases at the beginning and end of RS rows as follows:
Row 1 (RS): K1, m1l, k to 1 st before end, m1r, k1. (2 sts inc'd)
Row 2 (WS): K to end.
Repeat rows 1–2, 4 more times.
Work row 1 once more and cast on 2 sts at the end of the row using, for example, the Backwards Loop Cast-On or the Knitted Cast-On Method. You should now have 68 (76, 84) sts.

Change to US 7 / 4.5 mm needles. You will now start knitting in the rnd. Add a marker for the beginning of the rnd (BOR).

NECK RIBBING

Start to work in 2 x 2 Ribbing:
Rnd 1: *K2, p2*, repeat *–* to end. Continue to work in ribbing for 14 rnds in total, or until the ribbing has reached the desired length.

Bind off sts loosely in pattern. Cut the yarn.

FRONT RIBBING

Next, you will work a ribbing around the front edges.

With US 7 / 4.5 mm needles, pick up and k 88 (96, 104) sts evenly from the front opening of the balaclava. Pick up sts from each garter ridge to get the neatest look. Add a marker for the beginning of the rnd (BOR).
Rnd 1: *K2, p2*, repeat *–* to end. Continue to work in 2 x 2 Ribbing for 5 rnds in total.

Bind of sts in pattern. Cut the yarn.

FINISHING

Weave in ends. Wet block to measurements.

Sini Kramer

21 Lemonade

Lemonade is a simple but playful sock pattern. Worked in fingering-weight yarn, they are great to wear with shoes. Once you learn how to knit socks, you won't be able to stop!

SIZES

1 (2, 3)

Recommended ease: 0–0.5" / 0–1.5 cm of negative ease.

FINISHED MEASUREMENTS

Circumference: 7 (8, 9)" / 18 (20, 22) cm.
Length: Adjustable.

MATERIALS

Yarn: Heritage by Cascade Yarns (75% superwash merino, 25% nylon, 437 yds / 400 m – 100 g).
MC: 1 skein in colourway 5737 Orange.
CC: 1 skein in colourway 5646 Pink.

If you decide to use another yarn, you will need approx. 219 (256, 273) yds / 200 (225, 250) m of fingering-weight yarn in MC and approx. 126 (142, 157) yds / 115 (130, 144) m of fingering-weight yarn in CC.

Needles: US 1 / 2.25 mm 32–48" / 80–120 cm circular needles.

Notions: Stitch markers.

GAUGE

36 sts x 46 rnds to 4" / 10 cm in Stockinette Stitch, after blocking.

NOTES

You can find the abbreviations and detailed instructions for techniques used in this pattern in the Abbreviations (pp. 20–23) and Techniques (pp. 15–19) sections.

When measuring your foot for sizing, measure around the thickest part of your foot. If you are between sizes, it is recommended to size down.

The pattern is written for the Magic Loop Technique which is worked with long circular needles. If you want to, you can use DPNs instead. Note, however, that you then need to be able to adjust the instructions accordingly.

Slip markers as you come across them.

Choose one or up to three contrast colours.

CONSTRUCTION

These socks are knitted one at a time from cuff to toe. The cuff and leg are worked in the round. Next, the heel is worked flat using the heel flap method. You will then pick up stitches along the heel flap to continue working the foot in the round. After working the foot, you will work decreases to shape the toes. A contrast colour is used for the cuff, heel flap and toes. The colours are changed using a jogless stripe method.

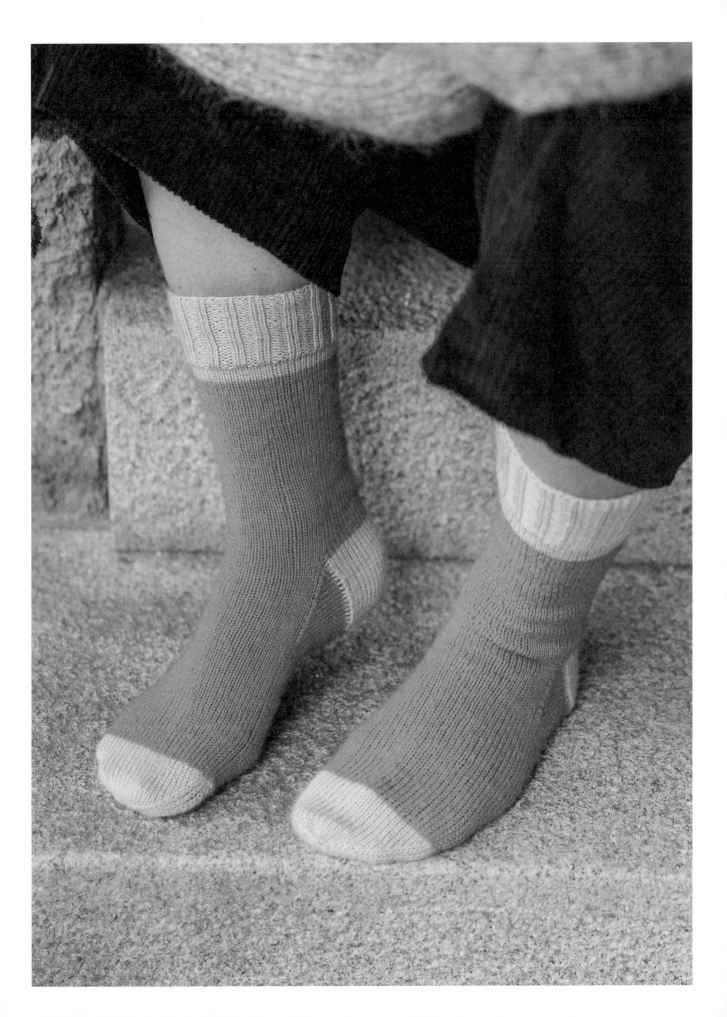

DIRECTIONS

CUFF AND LEG

With CC, cast on 64 (72, 80) sts. If you want to, you can use the German Twisted Cast-On Method which gives a stretchy edge, perfect for socks. You can find tutorials online. Join to knit in the rnd being careful not to twist sts.

Work in 2 x 2 Ribbing (k2, p2) for 26 rnds or for approx. 2.5" / 6 cm.

Then continue for 5 rnds in Stockinette Stitch (k all sts). Cut CC yarn.

Attach MC. K 1 rnd. Twist the yarns (bring the MC yarn over the CC tail back to the right) to prevent a hole. Slip 1 st purlwise with yarn in back. This will create a jogless stripe. Continue in Stockinette Stitch (k all sts) for approx. 5" / 13 cm. At this point, the work measures approx. 7.5" / 19 cm from the cast-on edge. Cut MC.

HEEL

Heel Flap

Attach CC. Turn work and leave the 32 (36, 40) instep sts on hold. You can leave the sts on the needles or transfer them to a stitch holder, if preferred.

Begin to work the heel flap with 32 (36, 40) sts as follows:

Row 1 (WS): Slip 1 st purlwise with yarn in front, p to end.
Row 2 (RS): Slip 1 st purlwise with yarn in back, k to end.
Repeat rows 1–2, 16 (18, 20) times, or until the heel flap measures approx. 3 (3, 3.5)" / 7 (7.5, 8.5) cm, approx. 3/4 of the heel flap width. End with a row 1 which is a WS row.

Heel Turn

Row 1 (RS): Slip 1 st purlwise with yarn in back, k18 (20, 22), ssk, k1, turn work. (1 st dec'd)
Row 2 (WS): Slip 1 st purlwise with yarn in front, p7 (7, 7), p2tog, p1, turn work. (1 st dec'd)
Row 3: Slip 1 st purlwise with yarn in back, k until 1 st before the gap, ssk, k1, turn work. (1 st dec'd)
Row 4: Slip 1 st purlwise with yarn in front, p until 1 st before the gap, p2tog, p1, turn work. (1 st dec'd)
Repeat rows 3–4 until you have worked all sts. The heel turn is now completed.

You should now have 20 (22, 24) sts for the heel. Cut CC yarn.

Gusset
Attach MC.

Next, you will pick up sts along the sides of the heel flap and place a stitch marker for the beginning of the rnd (BOR). You will then continue working in the rnd.

Next row (RS): K 20 (22, 24) heel sts, pick up and k 16 (18, 20) sts along the side of the heel flap, pick up and knit 1 additional st at the gap between the heel flap and the foot sts (to prevent a hole), PM, k the 32 (36, 40) foot sts, PM, pick up and knit 1 additional st at the gap between the heel flap and the foot sts (to prevent a hole), pick up and k 16 (18, 20) sts along the side of the heel flap, k 10 (11, 12) sts. PM for the beginning of the round (BOR).

You should now have a total of 86 (96, 106) sts.

Rnd 1: K to 3 sts before marker, k2tog, k1, SM, k to marker, SM, k1, ssk, k to end. (2 sts dec'd)
Rnd 2: K to end.
Continue to work rnds 1–2, working decreases every 2nd rnd, until 64 (72, 80) sts remain.

Continue in Stockinette Stitch (k all sts) until the pinky toe is covered, or until the foot measures approx. 2 (2.5, 2.5)" / 5 (6, 6.5) cm less than the desired length. On the last rnd, remove the BOR marker. K then to the next marker. This marker is now the new BOR marker (at the beginning of Needle 1, before the instep sts). Cut MC.

TOE

Attach CC. K 1 rnd. Twist the yarns (bring the CC yarn over the MC tail back to the right) to prevent a hole. Slip 1 st purlwise with yarn in back. This will create a jogless stripe. K to end of the rnd.

Next, we will work the toe decreases. The sts are divided evenly on two needles: the first 32 (36, 40) sts are for the instep (on Needle 1), the following 32 (36, 40) sts are for the sole (on Needle 2).

Rnd 1: *Needle 1:* K1, ssk, k to 3 sts before the end of needle, k2tog, k1;
Needle 2: K1, ssk, k to 3 sts before the end of the needle, k2tog, k1. (4 sts dec'd)
Rnd 2: K to end.
Repeat rnds 1–2 a total of 7 (9, 11) times. You now have 18 (18, 18) sts on each needle.

Repeat rnd 1, 5 times more. You now have 8 sts on each needle.

FINISHING

Cut yarn and thread the tail through the remaining sts. If preferred, you can also close the toes by grafting.

Weave in the ends. Block the socks to measurements.

Work the second sock to match.

Lindsey Fowler

22 Fledgling

SUPER EASY!

Fledgling combines wide and narrow stripes and comes in two sizes: a classic scarf and a wider wrap. Optional flannel lining can be added at the end. An easy project to build up your skills.

SIZES

Scarf (Wrap)

FINISHED MEASUREMENTS

Length: 70 (60)" / 180 (151) cm.
Width: 6.5 (17)" / 16 (43) cm.

MATERIALS

Yarn: Corrie Worsted by La Bien Aimée (75% Falkland Corriedale, 25% Gotland, 250 yds / 230 m – 100 g).
C1: 1 (3) skein(s), colourway Winterfell.
C2: 1 (3) skein(s), colourway Coquelicot.

If you decide to use another yarn, you will need approx. 250 (750) yds / 229 (686) m of worsted-weight yarn in C1 and approx. 250 (750) yds / 229 (686) m of worsted-weight yarn in C2.

The wrap-size sample was knitted with Knitting for Olive Heavy Merino (100% non-mulesed merino wool, 137 yds / 125 m – 50 g), colourways Dusty Artichoke (as C1) and Hazel (as C2).

Needles: US 8 / 5 mm straight or 16 (24)" / 40 (60) cm circular needles.

Notions: Stitch markers, crochet hook (to apply fringe), tapestry needle, sewing needle, two fabric strips measuring 7.5 x 36 (19 x 31)" / 19 x 91.5 (48.5 x 78.5) cm (for optional lining), thread to match lining fabric (optional).

GAUGE

18 sts x 25 rows to 4" / 10 cm in Stockinette Stitch, after blocking.

NOTES

You can find the abbreviations and detailed instructions for techniques used in this pattern in the Abbreviations (pp. 20–23) and Techniques (pp. 15–19) sections.

Slip markers as you come across them.

In order to create a clean look and give the piece some extra structure and warmth, adding a lining is an easy way to elevate your accessory. This can also help if you have edges that still curl in after blocking. Instructions on how to add a lining are given at the end of the pattern.

If you do not wish to line your scarf or wrap, it is suggested you substitute a Garter border on both sides of your piece. Rather than k3 and slip 3 sts purlwise with yarn in front on each edge, k3 at the beginning and end of every row on the RS and WS. This will create neat edges. The wrap-size sample is knitted with a Garter border.

Once you have finished your piece, you can add fringes, tassels or pompoms to both ends in C1. Instructions on how to add fringes are given at the end of the pattern.

CONSTRUCTION

This easy knit is made flat in one piece. It features wide and narrow stripes as well as slip stitch columns that runs along the whole length of the work and a simple i-cord edge. An optional lining which helps keep the edges of especially the narrower scarf from rolling is hand-sewn after blocking.

DIRECTIONS

CAST-ON & SET-UP

With C1 and using the Long-Tail Cast-On Method or method of choice, cast on 29 (77) sts.

The following abbreviations are used in this pattern:
sl1 wyib: Slip 1 stitch knitwise with yarn in back.
sl3 wyif: Slip 3 stitches purlwise with yarn in front.

Set-up row (WS): P3, *PM, p5 (11), PM, p1*, repeat *–* a total of 3 (5) times, PM, p5 (11), PM, sl3wyif. The stitch markers are now distributed as follows:
Scarf: 3 / 5 / 1 / 5 / 1 / 5 / 1 / 5 / 3.
Wrap: 3 / 11 / 1 / 11 / 1 / 11 / 1 / 11 / 1 / 11 / 1 / 11 / 3.

WIDE STRIPES

Row 1 (RS): K3, *SM, k5 (11), SM, sl1 wyib*, repeat *–* a total of 3 (5) times, SM, k5 (11), SM, sl3 wyif.
Row 2 (WS): K3, p to last m, SM, sl3 wyif. Repeat rows 1–2 with C1 until stripe measures approx. 7 (6)" / 18 (15) cm from cast-on edge, ending with a row 2. Cut C1. Continue to work in C2 repeating rows 1–2 until the second stripe measures approx. 7 (6)" / 18 (15) cm from colour change.

Continue switching between C1 and C2 until you have five 7 (6)" / 18 (15) cm stripes total (three C1 stripes and two C2 stripes), ending on a row 2 in C1.

The piece should now measure approx. 35 (30)" / 90 (75) cm in total length.

NARROW STRIPES

Begin working with C2.

Continue to repeat rows 1–2, switching the colour on every RS. This means you will work 2 rows per colour. You do not need to cut your yarn when you switch colours in this section. You may carry the colour up on the side, but be mindful not to pull your working yarn too tight when you begin a row where you switch colours.

Repeat until the piece measures 35 (30)" / 89 (76) cm from beginning of the narrow stripes section, ending with C1. The piece should now measure approx. 70 (60)" / 180 (151) cm in total length.

FINISHING

Bind off with C1.
Wash and block to finished dimensions.

Lining
Lining is optional.

Cut two fabric strips measuring 7.5 x 36 (19 x 31)" / 19 x 91.5 (48.5 x 78.5) cm. Using either machine or hand sewing, sew short ends together on one side. Press (use appropriate heat setting for your selected fabric) seam open. Turn in 0.5" / 1.5 cm hem and press on all sides. This lining should fit right inside the i-cord border of the WS of your piece. If it is too narrow, adjust your hems and re-press.

Pin or clip your lining to the WS of your scarf, lining up the middle seam of your lining to the transition from wide stripes to narrow stripes and leaving about 0.5" / 1.5 cm of space at either short edge of the piece for fringe.

Starting in the middle on one side and working your way out, hand sew the lining to your scarf catching the edge of the lining on the fold and fixing it to the inside of your i-cord border so the thread does not show on the front of your piece. Continue working all the way around, removing pins or clips as you come to them. Once you work your way all the way around your piece, secure with a knot buried inside the lining and cut thread.

If needed, steam or gently wet block your scarf again for a crisp finish.

Fringe
Create fringe bundles by cutting 7 (12) strands of C1. Cut 18 (26) bundles of fringe, 9 (13) for each end. Each strand measures 12" / 30.5 cm. Evenly attach bundles on each end.

Paula Pereira

23 Comfy

Comfy is a relaxed pullover worked in Slipped-Stitch Ribbing. The cuff and hem edges in a contrasting colour add that special something. The chart has only slipped stitches, knits and purls.

SIZES

1 (2, 3, 4, 5) (6, 7, 8)

Recommended ease: 3–5.25" / 7.5–13.5 cm of positive ease.

FINISHED MEASUREMENTS

Chest Circumference: 37 (41, 45.25, 49.25, 55.25) (59, 63.25, 67)" / 92.5 (102.5, 113.5, 123.5, 138.5) (147.5, 158.5, 167.5) cm.
Length from Underarm to Hem: 12.25 (12.25, 12.25, 12.25, 13.25) (13.25, 13.25, 13.25)" / 31 (31, 31, 31, 33.5) (33.5, 33.5, 33.5) cm.
Yoke Depth: 7.75 (8.25, 8.75, 9, 9.5) (10, 10.75, 11.25)" / 19.5 (21, 22, 23, 24) (25.5, 27.5, 28.5) cm.
Upper Arm Circumference: 11.25 (12, 13.25, 14.25, 16) (17.25, 19, 21)" / 28.5 (30, 33.5, 36, 40) (43.5, 47.5, 52.5) cm.
Sleeve Length from Underarm: 17.75 (17.75, 18.25, 18.5, 18.25) (18.5, 18.25, 18.75)" / 44 (44.5, 45.5, 46, 45.5) (46, 45.5, 47) cm.
Cuff Circumference: 9 (9.25, 10, 10.75, 11) (12, 12.75, 13)" / 22.5 (23.5, 25, 26.5, 27.5) (30, 31.5, 32.5) cm.

Total Length: 20 (20.5, 21, 21.25, 22.75) (23.25, 24, 24.5)" / 50.5 (52, 53, 54, 57.5) (59, 61, 62) cm.

MATERIALS

Yarn: Worsted by Malabrigo (100% merino, 210 yds / 192 m – 100 g).
MC: 6 (7, 7, 8, 9) (10, 11, 12) skeins of colourway Frank Ochre.
CC: 1 skein of colourway Cactus Flower.

If you decide to use another yarn, you will need approx. 1151 (1294, 1457, 1592, 1868) (2031, 2244, 2463) yds / 1053 (1183, 1332, 1456, 1708) (1857, 2052, 2252) m of worsted-weight yarn in MC and approx. 24 (26, 30, 32, 38) (41, 46, 50) yds / 22 (24, 27, 29, 35) (37, 42, 46) m of worsted-weight yarn in CC.

Needles: US 8 / 5 mm 16" / 40 cm, 24" / 60 cm and 32" / 80 cm circular needles (for body and sleeves), US 6 / 4 mm 16" / 40 cm and 32" / 80 cm circular needles (for ribbing).

Notions: Stitch markers (with one in different colour or shape), stitch holders or waste yarn.

GAUGE

24 sts x 32 rnds to 4" / 10 cm on US 8 / 5 mm needles in Slipped-Stitch Rib, after blocking.
18 sts x 24 rnds to 4" / 10 cm on US 8 / 5 mm needles in Stockinette Stitch, after blocking.

STITCH PATTERNS

Slipped-Stitch Pattern (in the rnd)
Rnd 1: *Sl1 pwise wyib, p1*, repeat *–* to end.
Rnd 2: *K1, p1*, repeat *–* to end.
Repeat rnds 1–2 for pattern.

Slipped-Stitch Pattern (flat)
Row 1 (RS): *Sl1 pwise wyib, p1*, repeat *–* to end.
Row 2 (WS): *K1, p1*, repeat *–* to end.
Repeat rows 1–2 for pattern.

SPECIAL TECHNIQUES

Cable Cast-On on WS

Turn work. At the WS, *insert the right-hand needle from back to front between the first 2 stitches on the left-hand needle. Wrap yarn as if to purl. Draw yarn through to complete the stitch and slip this new stitch to the left-hand needle.* Repeat *–*.

WRITTEN INSTRUCTIONS FOR YOKE CHART

All sts are slipped purlwise with yarn in back.

Increase rnd 1: Sl1, p1, inc 3-into-1, p1, sl1, p1. (2 sts inc'd) (8 sts total)
Rnd 2: *K1, p1*, repeat *–* 4 times.
Rnd 3: *Sl1, p1*, repeat *–* 4 times.
Rnd 4: *K1, p1*, repeat *–* 4 times.
Rnd 5: *Sl1, p1*, repeat *–* 4 times.
Rnd 6: *K1, p1*, repeat *–* 4 times.
Increase rnd 7: *Sl1, p1, sl1, inc 3-into-1, *sl1, p1*, repeat *–* 2 times. (2 sts inc'd) (10 sts total)
Rnd 8: *K1, p1*, repeat *–* 5 times.
Rnd 9: *Sl1, p1, repeat *–* 5 times.
Rnd 10: *K1, p1*, repeat *–* 5 times.
Rnd 11: *Sl1, p1*, repeat *–* 5 times.
Rnd 12: *K1, p1*, repeat *–* 5 times.
Increase rnd 13: *Sl1, p1*, repeat *–* 2 times, inc 3-into-1, *p1, sl1*, repeat *–* 2 times, p1. (2 sts inc'd) (12 sts total)
Rnd 14: *K1, p1*, repeat *–* 6 times.
Rnd 15: *Sl1, p1*, repeat *–* 6 times.
Rnd 16: *K1, p1*, repeat *–* 6 times.
Rnd 17: * Sl1, p1*, repeat *–* 6 times.
Rnd 18: *K1, p1*, repeat *–* 6 times.
Increase rnd 19: *Sl1, p1*, repeat *–* 2 times, sl1, inc 3-into-1, *sl1, p1*, repeat *–* 3 times. (2 sts inc'd) (14 sts total)
Rnd 20: *K1, p1*, repeat *–* 7 times.
Rnd 21: *Sl1, p1*, repeat *–* 7 times.
Rnd 22: *K1, p1*, repeat *–* 7 times.
Rnd 23: *Sl1, p1*, repeat *–* 7 times.
Rnd 24: *K1, p1*, repeat *–* 7 times.
Increase rnd 25: *Sl1, p1*, repeat *–* 3 times, inc 3-into-1, *p1, sl1*, repeat *–* 3 times, p1. (2 sts inc'd) (16 sts total)
Rnd 26: *K1, p1*, repeat *–* 8 times.

Rnd 27: *Sl1, p1*, repeat *–* 8 times.
Rnd 28: *K1, p1*, repeat *–* 8 times.
Rnd 29: *Sl1, p1*, repeat *–* 8 times.
Rnd 30: *K1, p1*, repeat *–* 8 times.
Increase rnd 31: *Sl1, p1, repeat *–* 3 times, sl1, inc 3-into-1, *sl1, p1*, repeat *–* 4 times. (2 sts inc'd) (18 sts total)
Rnd 32: *K1, p1*, repeat *–* 9 times.
Rnd 33: *Sl1, p1*, repeat *–* 9 times.
Rnd 34: *K1, p1*, repeat *–* 9 times.
Rnd 35: *Sl1, p1*, repeat *–* 9 times.
Rnd 36: *K1, p1*, repeat *–* 9 times.
Increase rnd 37: *Sl1, p1*, repeat *–* 4 times, inc 3-into-1, *p1, k1*, repeat *–* 4 times, p1. (2 sts inc'd) (20 sts total)
Rnd 38: *K1, p1*, repeat *–* 10 times.
Rnd 39: *Sl1, p1*, repeat *–* 10 times.
Rnd 40: *K1, p1*, repeat *–* 10 times.
Rnd 41: *Sl1, p1*, repeat *–* 10 times.
Rnd 42: *K1, p1*, repeat *–* 10 times.
Increase rnd 43: *Sl1, p1*, repeat *–* 4 times, sl1, inc 3-into-1, *sl1, p1*, repeat *–* 5 times. (2 sts inc'd) (22 sts total)
Rnd 44: *K1, p1*, repeat *–* 11 times.
Rnd 45: *Sl1, p1*, repeat *–* 11 times.
Rnd 46: *K1, p1*, repeat *–* 11 times.
Rnd 47: *Sl1, p1*, repeat *–* 11 times.
Rnd 48: *K1, p1*, repeat *–* 11 times.
Increase rnd 49: *Sl1, p1*, repeat *–* 5 times, inc 3-into-1, *p1, k1*, rep *–* 5 times, p1. (2 sts inc'd) (24 sts total)
Rnd 50: *K1, p1*, repeat *–* 12 times.
Rnd 51: *Sl1, p1*, repeat *–* 12 times.
Rnd 52: *K1, p1*, repeat *–* 12 times.
Rnd 53: *Sl1, p1*, repeat *–* 12 times.
Rnd 54: *K1, p1*, repeat *–* 12 times.
Increase rnd 55: *Sl1, p1*, repeat *–* 5 times, sl1, inc 3-into-1, *sl1, p1*, repeat *–* 6 times. (2 sts inc'd) (26 sts total)
Rnd 54: *K1, p1*, repeat *–* 13 times.

NOTES

You can find the abbreviations and detailed instructions for techniques used in this pattern in the Abbreviations (pp. 20–23) and Techniques (pp. 15–19) sections.

Slip markers as you come across them.

The chart is read from bottom to top and from right to left.

Change to longer circular needles while working the yoke, when needed.

A marker is positioned at the middle / centre of the back. To keep track, it's helpful to place a stitch marker between each chart repetition too.

The back neck is shaped with short rows for a better fit. The Wrap & Turn Method is suggested. However, you can use your favourite method to work short rows.

To create a rounded effect and prevent underarm holes, the directions indicate to pick up and knit 1 stitch from the round below at the diagonal line between the underarm cast on and the sleeve stitches that were on a holder.

CONSTRUCTION

This sweater is worked seamlessly in the round from the top down. The sleeves are worked in the round from the top down. The collar, back neck shaping, cuff and hem are worked in 1 x 1 Ribbing. The yoke, body and sleeves are worked in 1 x 1 Slipped-Stitch Ribbing. The yoke increases create a motif that looks like brioche increases.

MODIFICATIONS

For a longer sweater, simply work more rounds to the body. Adding more rounds the final yardage will be different and more yarn is needed.

DIRECTIONS

COLLAR

With MC and US 6 / 4 mm needles cast on 114 (114, 120, 126, 132) (138, 138, 138) sts using the Long-Tail Cast-On Method. Place marker for the beginning of the rnd (BOR) and join to knit in the rnd.

Set-up rnd: *K1tbl, sl1 pwise wyif*, repeat *–* to end.
Repeat the rnd once more.

Start to work in 1 x 1 Ribbing as follows:
Rnd 1: *K1, p1*, repeat *–* to end.
Continue in established 1 x 1 Ribbing until the collar measures 2" / 5 cm from the cast-on edge.

Change to US 8 / 5 mm needles.

Back Neck Shaping

Next, you will work short rows for the back neck only to make it higher. This ensures a better fit. The Wrap & Turn Method is recommended but feel free to use another method if preferred. This section is worked back and forth.
Note! When working the back neck short rows, there will be wraps around the st after the number of knit or purl sts indicated. For a neat look, knit these wraps together with their adjacent st as you come across them.

Short row 1 (RS): Work 18 sts in the Slipped-Stitch Pattern, w&t.
Short row 2 (WS): Work in Slipped-Stitch Pattern to m, SM, work 18 sts in Slipped-Stitch Pattern, w&t.
Short row 3: Work in Slipped-Stitch Pattern to marker, SM, work 24 sts in Slipped-Stitch Pattern, w&t.
Short row 4: Work in Slipped-Stitch Pattern to marker, SM, work 24 sts in Slipped-Stitch Pattern, w&t.
Short row 5: Work in Slipped-Stitch Pattern to marker, SM, work 32 sts in Slipped-Stitch Pattern, w&t.

Short row 6: Work in Slipped-Stitch Pattern to marker, SM, work 32 sts in Slipped-Stitch Pattern, w&t.
Short row 7: Work in Slipped-Stitch Pattern to marker, SM, work 42 sts in Slipped-Stitch Pattern, w&t.
Short row 8: Work in Slipped-Stitch Pattern to marker, SM, work 42 sts in Slipped-Stitch Pattern, w&t.
Short row 9: Work in Slipped-Stitch Pattern to marker.
Next rnd: Work to end in Slipped-Stitch Pattern (and pick up and work last wraps together with their adjacent st as you come to them).

For keeping track of the yoke st, it is helpful to place a marker every 6 sts.

YOKE

Continue working the yoke in the rnd. Work rnds 1–32 (32, 38, 38, 44) (44, 50, 56) of the Yoke Chart (or follow the written instructions). You should have 342 (342, 400, 420, 484) (506, 552, 598) sts at the end of the Yoke Chart for chosen size.

Next rnd: *Sl1 pwise wyib, p1*, repeat *–* to end.
Next rnd: *K1, p1*, repeat *–* to end.
Repeat the last two rnds 14 (16, 14, 16, 14) (17, 17, 15) more times. 30 (34, 30, 34, 30) (36, 36, 32) rnds worked in total after Yoke Chart or until the yoke measures 7.75 (8.25, 8.75, 9, 9.5) (10, 10.75, 11.25)" / 19.5 (21, 22, 23, 24) (25.5, 27.5, 28.5) cm.

Next rnd: *Sl1 pwise wyib, p1*, repeat *–* to end.

SEPARATING BODY AND SLEEVES

Next rnd: Work in the second rnd of the Slipped-Stitch Pattern 53 (55, 64, 68, 78) (81, 88, 93) sts (right back sts), transfer 64 (60, 72, 74, 86) (90, 100, 112) sts onto a holder or waste yarn (right sleeve sts), using the Cable Cast-On Method on WS, cast on 4 (12, 8, 12, 10) (14, 14, 14) sts for underarm, work 107 (111, 128, 136, 156) (163, 176, 187) sts (front sts), transfer 64 (60, 72, 74, 86) (90, 100, 112) sts onto a holder or waste yarn (left sleeve sts), using the Cable Cast-On Method on WS, cast on 4 (12, 8, 12, 10) (14, 14, 14) sts for underarm, work 54 (56, 64, 68, 78) (82, 88, 94) sts (left back sts). You should have 222 (246, 272, 296, 332) (354, 380, 402) sts for the body. 64 (60, 72, 74, 86) (90, 100, 112) sts are on hold for each sleeve.

BODY

Continue with the body sts only.
Next rnd: *Sl1 pwise wyib, p1*, repeat *–* to end.
Next rnd: *K1, p1*, repeat *–* to end.
Repeat the previous two rnds, 39 (39, 39, 39, 43) (43, 43, 43) more times or until the body measures approx. 10 (10, 10, 10, 11) (11, 11, 11)" / 25.5 (25.5, 25.5, 25.5, 28) (28, 28, 28) cm from the underarm cast-on. 80 (80, 80, 80, 88) (88, 88, 88) rnds worked in total.

Change to US 6 / 4 mm needles.
Start to work the hem in 1 x 1 Ribbing as follows:
Rnd 1: *K1, p1*, repeat *–* to end.
Repeat rnd 1 until hem ribbing measures 1.75" / 4.5 cm.

Change to CC yarn and work 3 more rounds in 1 x 1 Ribbing for the edge in contrasting colour.

With CC, bind off all sts loosely.

SLEEVES

Return the 64 (60, 72, 74, 86) (90, 100, 112) sleeve sts from hold to US 8 / 5 mm needles.

Sizes 1, 2, 3 and 4 only
With RS facing and beginning at the centre of underarm, pick up and k 1 (5, 3, 5, –) (–, –, –) st(s) along underarm, pick up and k 1 from the rnd below the diagonal line formed between the casted on body sts and the sleeve sts that were on hold, *sll pwise wyib, p1*, repeat *–* over 64 (60, 72, 74, –) (–, –, –) sleeve sts, pick up and k 1 on the rnd below the diagonal line formed between the body casted on sts and the sleeve sts that were on hold, pick up and k 1 (5, 3, 5, 4) (6, 6, 6) st(s). You should have 68 (72, 80, 86, –) (–, –, –) sts.

Place marker for the beginning of the rnd (BOR) and join to work in the rnd.

Next rnd: *K1, p1*, repeat *–* to end.
Next rnd: *Sll pwise wyib, p1*, repeat *–* to end.

Sizes 5, 6, 7 and 8 only
With RS facing and beginning at the centre of underarm, pick up and k – (–, –, –, 4) (6, 6, 6) sts along underarm, pick up and k 1 from the rnd below the diagonal line formed between the casted on body sts and the sleeve sts that were on hold, p1, *sll pwise wyib, p1*, repeat from *–* over over – (–, –, –, 86) (90, 100, 112) sleeve sts, pick up and k 1 on the rnd below the diagonal line formed between the body casted on sts and the sleeve sts that were on hold, pick up and k – (–, –, –, 4) (6, 6, 6) sts. You should have – (–, –, –, 96) (104, 114, 126) sts.

Place marker for the beginning of the rnd (BOR) and join to work in the rnd.

Next rnd: *P1, k1*, repeat *–* to end.
Next rnd: *P1, sll pwise wyib*, repeat *–* to end.

Resume All Sizes
Repeat the previous 2 rnds 1 (1, 3, 3, 3) (0, 6, 5) time(s) more. 4 (4, 8, 8, 8) (2, 14, 12) rnds worked in total.
Decrease rnd: K1, k2tog, work in pattern to 3 sts before m, ssk, k1. (2 sts dec'd)
You should have 66 (70, 78, 84, 94) (102, 112, 124) sts.

Work in pattern for 16 (14, 11, 10, 7) (7, 5, 4) rnds.

Repeat the last 17 (15, 12, 11, 8) (8, 6, 5) rnds (the Decrease Rnd and the rnds following it) 6 (7, 9, 10, 14) (15, 18, 23) more times. You should have 54 (56, 60, 64, 66) (72, 76, 78) sts. Sleeve measures 15.5 (15.5, 16, 16.25, 16) (16.25, 16, 16.5)" / 38.5 (39, 40, 40.5, 40) (40.5, 40, 41.5) cm from underarm.

Cuff

Change to US 6 / 4 mm needles.

Start to work the cuff in 1 x 1 Ribbing as follows:
Sizes 1, 2, 3 and 4 only
Rnd 1: *K1, p1*, repeat *–* to end.
Repeat rnd 1 until the cuff ribbing measures 1.75" / 4.5 cm.
Change to CC yarn and work 3 more rnds in 1 x 1 Ribbing.

With CC, bind off all sts in pattern using preferred method.

Sizes 5, 6, 7 and 8 only
Rnd 1: *P1, k1*, repeat *–* to end.
Repeat rnd 1 until the cuff ribbing measures 1.75" / 4.5 cm.
Change to CC yarn and work 3 more rnds in 1 x 1 Ribbing.

With CC, bind off all sts in pattern using preferred method.

Repeat for the second sleeve.

FINISHING

Weave in ends to the WS. Sew underarm openings if necessary. Wet or steam block to measurements.

YOKE CHART

Legend:

- ☐ Knit
- ∨ Slip 1 st with yarn in back of the work
- • Purl
- ▨ No stitch
- ∨ (p1, k1, p1) into 1 st
- ∨ (k1, p1, k1) into 1 st
- ☐ Repeat

Pauliina Kuunsola

24 Pisama

Pisama is a simple, fun and quick hat design. The contrast-coloured stripes are perfect for using up all those small balls and scraps of yarn you have in your stash.

SIZES

1 (2, 3)

To fit a head circumference of approx. 18.75 (21, 22.75)" / 47 (52.5, 57) cm.

FINISHED MEASUREMENTS

Circumference: 13.75 (16, 17.75)" / 34.5 (40, 44.5) cm.
Height (with folded brim): Approx. 9.25" / 23.5 cm.
(*Note!* Because the hat stretches, its circumference should be significantly smaller than your heads.)

MATERIALS

Yarn: Reborn Wool Recycled by Kremke Soul Wool (65% wool, 25% acryl, 10% nylon, 219 yds / 200 m – 100 g).
MC: 1 skein of colourway Dark Green Melange (12).
CC: Approx. 6.5 (7, 9) yds / 6 (6.5, 8) m of colourway Pastel Pink (03).

If you decide to use another yarn, you will need approx. 219 yds / 200 m of aran-weight yarn in MC and approx. 6.5 (7, 9) yds / 6 (6.5, 8) m of aran-weight yarn in CC (in total in one or more colours).

Needles: US 7 / 4.5 mm 16" / 40 cm circular needles. Or DPNs if preferred for small circumference knitting.

Notions: Stitch marker.

GAUGE

18 sts x 29 rnds to 4" / 10 cm in stitch pattern, after blocking.

NOTES

You can find the abbreviations and detailed instructions for techniques used in this pattern in the Abbreviations (pp. 20–23) and Techniques (pp. 15–19) sections.

Slip markers as you come across them.

Each vertical stripe in contrast colour (CC) is worked from its own length of yarn. Cut your CC yarn into eight approx. 31.5" / 80 cm long pieces.

Do not carry the CC across rounds. For the subsequent rounds, simply pick up the length of CC from a few rounds down, when it is time to knit another CC stitch in that stripe.

The colour you are working a round with is marked in brackets.

CONSTRUCTION

This hat is knitted seamlessly from the brim to crown.

MODIFICATIONS

You can alter the hat height by working more or less repeats.

You can work the vertical stripes using as many colours as you want, making this a perfect project for scrap yarns.

DIRECTIONS

With MC, cast on 62 (72, 80) sts with the Long-Tail Cast-On or a stretchy cast-on of choice. PM for the beginning of rnd (BOR) and join to work in the rnd. Be careful not to twist sts.

Now you will start to work the brim in 1 x 1 Ribbing.

Ribbing rnd: *K1, p1*, repeat *–* to end. Work in established ribbing until the hat measures 5.5" / 14 cm from the cast-on edge.

CONTRAST COLOUR STRIPES

Note! See Notes on how to work with CC.

Sizes 1 and 3 only
Increase 1 st on the first rnd by working the first st as kfb (or use another increase method if preferred). You should have 63 (81) sts.

All sizes
Rnds 1–3 (MC): K to end.
Rnd 4 (MC & CC): K1 with MC, *k1 with CC, k8 with MC*, repeat *–* to 8 sts bef end, k1 with CC, k7 with MC.
Work rnds 1–4, 10 times in total.

Note! You can alter the hat height by working more or less repeats at this point.

CROWN DECREASES

Rnd 1 (MC): K3, *k2tog, k2, k2tog, k3*, repeat *–* to 6 sts before end, k2tog, k2, k2tog. [14 (16, 18) sts dec'd]
You should have 49 (56, 63) sts.

Rnd 2 (MC): K to end.
Rnd 3 (MC & CC): K1 with MC, *k1 with CC, k6 with MC*, repeat *–* to 6 sts before end, k1 with CC, k5 with MC.
From now on, work with MC yarn only.
Rnd 4: K to end.

Rnd 5: K3, *k2tog x 2, k3*, repeat *–* to 4 sts before end, k2tog x 2. [14 (16, 18) sts dec'd]
You should have 35 (40, 45) sts.
Rnds 6–7: K to end.

Size 1 and 3 only
Rnd 8: K1, *k2tog*, repeat *–* to end.
You should have 18 (23) sts.

Size 2 only
Rnd 8: *K2tog*, repeat *–* to end.
You should have 20 sts.

Cut MC leaving a long tail.

FINISHING

Thread the tail to a tapestry needle and pull it through the live sts on the knitting needle. Remove the knitting needle and gently pull to close the hole at the top.

Weave in all ends on the WS. However, if using the brim folded, weave the cast-on end on the RS.

Wet block to measurements.

Bernice Lim

25 Palette

Palette is a playful, short-sleeved V-neck top. The colour-block sweater is worked in pieces with thick yarn and knits up much faster than you would think.

SIZES

1 (2, 3, 4, 5) (6, 7, 8)

Recommended ease: 6–10" / 15–25.5 cm of positive ease.

FINISHED MEASUREMENTS

Bust Circumference: 40 (44, 48, 52, 60) (64, 68, 72)" / 100 (110, 120, 130, 150) (160, 170, 180) cm.
Length from Back Neck to Hem (before working neck and hem ribbing): 15.75 (16, 16.25, 16.5, 17) (17.25, 17.5, 17.75)" / 39.5 (40, 40.5, 41.5, 42.5) (43, 44, 44.5) cm.
Total Length from Back Neck to Hem (including ribbings): 20.75 (21, 21.25, 21.5, 22) (22.25, 22.5, 22.75)" / 52 (52.5, 53, 54, 55) (55.5, 56.5, 57) cm.
Armhole Circumference (before working ribbing): 11.75 (12.25, 12.75, 13.75, 17.5) (19.75, 22, 23.5)" / 29.5 (30.5, 32, 34.5, 44) (49.5, 55, 59) cm.
Depth of Neck Opening (after working neck ribbing): 4.75 (5.25, 5.75, 5.75, 6.75)

(7.25, 7.75, 7.75)" / 12 (13.5, 14.5, 14.5, 17) (18.5, 19.5, 19.5) cm.
Neck Width (after working neck ribbing): 5.75 (6.25, 6.75, 6.75, 8.25) (8.75, 9.75, 9.75)" / 14 (16, 18, 18, 21) (23, 24, 24) cm.

MATERIALS

Yarn: Reborn Wool Recycled by Kremke Soul Wool (65% wool, 25% polyacryl, 10% nylon, 219 yds / 200 m – 100 g).
C1: 1 skein of colourway 11 Emerald.
C2: 1 skein of colourway 03 Pastel Pink.
C3: 1 skein of colourway 19 Turquoise Melange.
C4: 1 skein of colourway 04 Light Orange.
C5: 1 (1, 1, 1, 2) (2, 2, 2) skein(s) of colourway 21 Navy.

The grey sample was knitted in Le Gros Lambswool by Biches & Bûches (100% lambswool, 210 yds / 192 m – 100 g) in the following colourways: Grey Beige (C1), Soft Blue Green (C2), Light Grey (C3), Soft Green Grey (C4) and Off-White (C5).

If you decide to use another yarn, you will need approx. 105 (120, 130, 150, 170) (185, 200, 215) yds / 95 (110, 120, 135, 155) (170, 185, 195) m of aran-weight yarn in C1, C2, C3 and C4 and 170 (185, 195, 215, 245) (270, 285, 295) yds / 155 (170, 180, 195, 225) (245, 260, 270) m in C5.

Needles: US 6 / 4 mm 32" / 80 cm (for body and sleeves) and 24" / 60 cm circular needles (for working neck in the rnd), US 6 / 4 mm circular needles or DPNs (for working small circumference in the rnd).

Notions: Crochet hook in size G-6 / 4 mm, stitch marker, removable stitch marker, stitch holder or waste yarn, tapestry needle.

GAUGE

16 sts x 24 rows to 4" / 10 cm on US 6 / 4 mm needles in Stockinette Stitch, after blocking.

NOTES

You can find the abbreviations and detailed instructions for techniques used in this pattern in the Abbreviations (pp. 20–23) and Techniques (pp. 15–19) sections.

Slip markers as you come across them.

Check your gauge carefully. When knitting a garment sideways, row gauge has an effect on its width while stitch gauge has an effect on its length.

CONSTRUCTION

This v-neck sweater is worked in different-coloured pieces and seamed together. Each colour block is knitted sideways from side to centre. You will start by casting on the side stitches for one of the front colour block pieces. Larger sizes have additional shaping at underarm to maintain a cap-sleeve design that is consistent with smaller sizes.

The shoulders are shaped by increasing stitches at intervals after which the neck is shaped with decreases as you work towards the centre of the tee. A second piece for front is worked, then joined with the first piece using Russian Grafting that creates a decorative seam.

The back pieces are worked by picking up stitches from the side edges of the front, then working towards the centre of the tee before joining using Russian Grafting. Shoulders are joined using Mattress Stitch. Lastly, stitches are picked up and 1 x 1 Ribbing is worked in the round for the hem, armholes and neckline.

DIRECTIONS

FRONT RIGHT

Using C1 and the Long-Tail Cast-On Method or method of choice, cast on 59 (60, 61, 62, 34) (32, 30, 29) sts for the right front.

For sizes 1–4, proceed to All Sizes. For sizes 5–8, begin with underarm shaping as follows:

Sizes 5 (6, 7, 8) only
Row 1 (RS): K to end.
Row 2 (WS): P to end.

Increase row (RS): K to last 2 sts, m1r, k2. (1 st inc'd)
Next row: P to end.
Repeat previous two rows 5 (6, 7, 8) more times. You should have 40 (39, 38, 38) sts. [6 (7, 8, 9) sts inc'd in total]

Next row: K to end, turn work to WS, using the Cable Cast-On Method, cast on 24 (26, 28, 29) sts for armhole. You should have 64 (65, 66, 67) sts.
Next row (WS): P to end.

All sizes
Work 4 (8, 6, 6, 4) (6, 6, 6) rows in Stockinette Stitch (k all sts on RS rows and p all sts on WS rows).
Increase row (RS): K to last 3 sts, m1l, k3. (1 st inc'd)

*Work 7 (7, 9, 11, 9) (9, 9, 11) rows in Stockinette Stitch.
Increase row (RS): K to last 3 sts, m1l, k3. (1 st inc'd)*
Repeat *–* twice more. (4 sts inc'd in total) You should have 63 (64, 65, 66, 68) (69, 70, 71) sts.

Work 3 (3, 3, 3, 3) (3, 5, 3) more rows in Stockinette Stitch. You have worked 32 (36, 40, 46, 54) (58, 62, 68) rows after the

Long-Tail Cast-On row. The piece now measures 5.25 (6, 6.75, 7.75, 9) (9.75, 10.25, 11.25)" / 13.5 (15, 16.5, 19, 22.5) (24, 26, 28.5) cm.

Neck Shaping
Row 1 (RS): K to last 3 sts, k2tog, k1. (1 st dec'd)
Row 2 (WS): P1, p2tog, p to end. (1 st dec'd)
Repeat rows 1–2, 13 (14, 15, 15, 17) (18, 19, 19) more times. You should have 35 (34, 33, 34, 32) (31, 30, 31) sts. [28 (30, 32, 32, 36) (38, 40, 40) sts dec'd in total]

The piece now measures 10 (11, 12, 13, 15) (16, 17, 18)" / 25 (27.5, 30 32.5, 37.5) (40, 42.5, 45) cm after the Long-Tail Cast-On row.

Break yarn. Transfer sts to a stitch holder or waste yarn.

FRONT LEFT

Using C2 and the Long-Tail Cast-On Method or method of choice, cast on 59 (60, 61, 62, 34) (32, 30, 29) sts for the left front.

For sizes 1–4, proceed to All Sizes. For sizes 5–8, begin with underarm shaping as follows:

Sizes 5 (6, 7, 8) only
Row 1 (RS): K to end.
Row 2 (WS): P to end.

Increase Row (RS): K2, m1l, k to end. (1 st inc'd)
Next row: P to end.
Repeat previous two rows 5 (6, 7, 8) more times. You should have 40 (39, 38, 38) sts. [6 (7, 8, 9) sts inc'd in total]

With RS facing and using the Cable Cast-On Method, cast on 24 (26, 28, 29) sts for armhole. You should have 64 (65, 66, 67) sts.

All sizes

Work 4 (8, 6, 6, 4) (6, 6, 6) rows in Stockinette Stitch (k all sts on RS rows and p all sts on WS rows).

Increase row (RS): K3, m1r, k to end. (1 st inc'd)

*Work 7 (7, 9, 11, 9) (9, 9, 11) rows in Stockinette Stitch (k all sts on RS rows and p all sts on WS rows).

Increase row (RS): K3, m1r, k to end. (1 st inc'd)*

Repeat *–* twice more. (4 sts inc'd in total) You should have 63 (64, 65, 66, 68) (69, 70, 71) sts.

Work 3 (3, 3, 3, 3) (3, 5, 3) more rows in Stockinette Stitch (k all sts on RS rows and p all sts on WS rows). You have worked 32 (36, 40, 46, 54) (58, 62, 68) rows after the Long-Tail Cast-On row. The piece now measures 5.25 (6, 6.75, 7.75, 9) (9.75, 10.25, 11.25)" / 13.5 (15, 16.5, 19, 22.5) (24, 26, 28.5) cm.

Neck Shaping

Row 1 (RS): K1, ssk, k to end. (1 st dec'd)
Row 2 (WS): P to last 3 sts, ssp, p1. (1 st dec'd)

Repeat rows 1–2, 13 (14, 15, 15, 17) (18, 19, 19) more times. You should have 35 (34, 33, 34, 32) (31, 30, 31) sts. [28 (30, 32, 32, 36) (38, 40, 40) sts dec'd in total]

The piece measures 10 (11, 12, 13, 15) (16, 17, 18)" / 25 (27.5, 30 32.5, 37.5) (40, 42.5, 45) cm after the Long-Tail Cast-On row.

Break yarn. On your needles, the st on the neck edge is the first st that will be worked in the joining row. Transfer held sts for front right onto the spare needle so that the st on the neck edge is also the first st that will be worked in the joining row below. The joining row is made without using any working yarn. You will need a crochet hook in size G-6 / 4 mm, or a size that matches your knitting needles.

Joining row: Hold WS of both pieces facing each other, then join all live sts from neck edge to hem using Russian Grafting as follows:

Set-up step 1: With WS of pieces facing each other, insert crochet hook through the first st on the back needle as if to knit, slide it off the needle.
Set-up step 2: Insert crochet hook through the first st on the front needle as if to knit, slide it off the needle, then pull it through the st on the hook.
Step 1: Insert crochet hook through the next st on the back needle as if to knit, slide it off the needle, then pull it through the st on the hook.
Step 2: Insert crochet hook through the next st on the front needle as if to knit, slide it off the needle, then pull it through the st on the hook.

Repeat steps 1–2 until all the live sts on both needles have been grafted. Pull the yarn tail near the last live stitch through the last st on the hook to secure the join.

BACK LEFT

With RS of front left facing you and using C3, pick up and k 35 (35, 35, 34, 34) (32, 30, 29) sts from the side edge, beginning from the hem.

Sizes 1 (2, 3, 4) only
Turn work to the WS, using the Cable Cast-On Method, cast on 24 (25, 26, 28) sts for armhole. You should have 59 (60, 61, 62) sts.
Keeping work on the WS, p to end, then proceed to All Sizes.

Sizes 5 (6, 7, 8) only
Next row (WS): P to end.
Increase row (RS): K to last 2 sts, m1r, k2. (1 st inc'd)
Next row: P to end.
Repeat previous two rows 5 (6, 7, 8) more times. You should have 40 (39, 38, 38) sts. [6 (7, 8, 9) sts inc'd in total]

Next row: K to end, turn work to WS, using the Cable Cast-On Method, cast on 24 (26, 28, 29) sts for armhole. You should have 64 (65, 66, 67) sts.
Next row (WS): P to end.

All sizes

Work 2 (6, 4, 4, 2) (4, 4, 4) rows in Stockinette Stitch (k all sts on RS rows and p all sts on WS rows).

Increase row (RS): K to last 3 sts, m1l, k3. (1 st inc'd)

*Work 7 (7, 9, 11, 9) (9, 9, 11) rows in Stockinette Stitch (k all sts on RS rows and p all sts on WS rows).

Increase row (RS): K to last 3 sts, m1l, k3. (1 st inc'd)*
Rep *–* twice more. (4 sts inc'd in total) You should have 63 (64, 65, 66, 68) (69, 70, 71) sts.

Work 31 (33, 35, 35, 39) (41, 45, 43) more rows in Stockinette Stitch (k all sts on RS rows and p all sts on WS rows). The last row worked is a WS row. The piece now measures 10 (11, 12, 13, 15) (16, 17, 18)" / 25 (27.5, 30 32.5, 37.5) (40, 42.5, 45) cm from pick up row.

Break yarn. Transfer sts to a stitch holder or waste yarn.

BACK RIGHT

With RS of front right facing, place a removable stitch marker on the 35th (35th, 35th, 34th, 34th) (32nd, 30th, 29th) st on the side edge, counting from the hem.

Sizes 1 (2, 3, 4) only
Using C4 and the Long-Tail Cast-On Method, cast on 24 (25, 26, 28) sts for the armhole.
Keeping front right on RS and holding needle with casted-on sts on right-hand needle, pick up and k 35 (35, 35, 34) sts from the side edge, beginning with the marked st and working towards the hem.

You should have 59 (60, 61, 62) sts on the needles. RM. On WS, p to end, then proceed to All Sizes.

Sizes 5 (6, 7, 8) only
Keeping Front Right on RS, using C4, pick up and k 34 (32, 30, 29) sts from the side edge, beginning with the marked st and working towards the hem. RM.
Next row (WS): P to end.

Increase row (RS): K2, m1l, knit to end. (1 st inc'd)
Next row: P to end.
Repeat previous two rows 5 (6, 7, 8) more times. You should have 40 (39, 38, 38) sts. [6 (7, 8, 9) sts inc'd in total]

With RS facing and using the Cable Cast-On Method, cast on 24 (26, 28, 29) sts for armhole. You should 64 (65, 66, 67) sts.

All sizes
Work 2 (6, 4, 4, 2) (4, 4, 4) rows in Stockinette Stitch (k all sts on RS rows and p all sts on WS rows).
Increase row (RS): K3, m1r, k to end. (1 st inc'd)

*Work 7 (7, 9, 11, 9) (9, 9, 11) rows in Stockinette Stitch (k all sts on RS rows and p all sts on WS rows).
Increase row (RS): K3, m1r, k to end. (1 st inc'd)*
Repeat *–* twice more. You should have 63 (64, 65, 66, 68) (69, 70, 71) sts. (4 sts inc'd in total)

Work 31 (33, 35, 35, 39) (41, 45, 43) more rows in Stockinette Stitch (k all sts on RS rows and p all sts on WS rows). The last row worked is a WS row. The piece now measures 10 (11, 12, 13, 15) (16, 17, 18)" / 25 (27.5, 30 32.5, 37.5) (40, 42.5, 45) cm from pick up row.

Break yarn. On your needle, the st on the neck edge is the first st that will be worked in the joining row. Transfer held sts for back left onto the spare needle such that the st on the neck edge is also the

first st that will be worked in the joining row below.

Joining row: Hold WS of both pieces facing each other, then, as for front, join all live sts from neck edge to hem using Russian Grafting.

SHOULDER SEAMS

Using Mattress Stitch, seam the right shoulder using C1 or C4 and the left shoulder using C2 or C3 as follows:
Step 1: Thread a tapestry needle with a strand of yarn for seaming the shoulder. You will need approximately twice as much yarn as the length of the seam.

Step 2: Line up the two shoulder seams row by row with the RS facing you.
Step 3: Identify the first column of sts on the right piece and insert the needle under the first bar between the first two knit sts nearest the edge. Pull your yarn through.
Step 4: Identify the first column of sts on the left piece and insert the needle under the first bar between the first two knit sts nearest the edge. Pull your yarn through.
Step 5: Insert the needle under the bar above the previous on the right piece. Pull your yarn through.
Step 6: Insert the needle under the bar above the previous on the left piece. Pull your yarn through.
Repeat steps 5–6 until all rows along the shoulder have been seamed.

HEM

Using C5, you will pick up sts around the hem with RS facing, beginning from either of the side seams. Pick up and k 40 (44, 48, 52, 60) (64, 68, 72) sts from each quarter of the hem (from each colour) at a rate of 2 sts every 3 rows. You should have 160 (176, 192, 208, 240) (256, 272, 288) sts. PM and join to work in the rnd.

Begin to work in 1 x 1 Ribbing as follows:
Rnd 1: *K1, p1*, repeat *–* to end.
Work in established 1 x 1 Ribbing until the hem ribbing measures 3.25" / 8.5 cm. Bind off all sts in pattern using your preferred bind-off method. Break yarn.

ARMHOLE

Change to preferred needle for working small circumference in the rnd. Using C5, you will pick up sts around the armhole with RS facing, beginning from underarm.

Sizes 1 (2, 3, 4) only
Pick up and k 23 (24, 25, 27) sts from each half of the armhole (pick up every st). You should have 46 (48, 50, 54) sts. PM and join to work in the rnd.

Sizes 5 (6, 7, 8) only
Pick up and k 11 (13, 15, 16) sts along the slanting edge of the armhole (at a rate of 5 sts every 6 rows), 23 (25, 27, 28) sts up the vertical edge of the armhole (pick up every st), 23 (25, 27, 28) sts down the other vertical edge of the armhole (pick up every st), and 11 (13, 15, 16) sts along the slanting edge of the armhole towards your starting point (5 sts from every 6 rows). You should have 68 (76, 84, 88) sts. PM and join to work in the rnd.

All sizes
Begin to work in 1 x 1 Ribbing as follows:
Rnd 1: *K1, p1*, repeat *–* to end.
Work in established 1 x 1 Ribbing for 9 more rnds. The cuff ribbing measures approx. 1.75" / 4 cm. Bind off all sts in

pattern using your preferred bind-off method. Break yarn.

Repeat the instructions for the other cuff.

NECK

Change to circular needles for working the neck in the rnd. Using C5, you will be picking up sts around the neck with RS facing, beginning from the left shoulder seam. Pick up and k 28 (30, 32, 32, 36) (38, 40, 40) sts (one st from every row) down the neck, 1 st from the grafted join at the bottom of the v-neck and place a removable stitch marker on this st, 28 (30, 32, 32, 36) (38, 40, 40) sts (one st from every row) up the neck and 37 (41, 43, 43, 49) (51, 53, 53) sts across the back neck (2 sts from every 3 rows). You should have 94 (102, 108, 108, 122) (128, 134, 134) sts. PM and join to work in the rnd.

Rnd 1: *K1, p1*, repeat *–* to marked st, k1 on marked st, p1, *k1, p1*, repeat *–* to end.
Rnd 2: *K1, p1*, repeat *–* to 2 sts before marked st, k1, RM, work Central Double Decrease (CDD), replace marker on the decreased st, *k1, p1, repeat *–* to end. (2 sts dec'd)
Rnd 3: *K1, p1*, repeat from *–* to 1 st before marked st, k1, work k1 on marked st, *k1, p1*, repeat *–* to end.
Rnd 4: *K1, p1*, repeat *–* to 1 st before marked st, RM, work CDD, replace marker on the decreased st, p1, *k1, p1*, repeat *–* to end. (2 sts dec'd)
Repeat rnds 1–4 one more time, then repeat rnds 1–2 one more time, removing markers.

Bind off all sts in pattern using your preferred bind-off method. Break yarn.

FINISHING

Weave in all ends. Wet block to measurements.

Elise Damstra

26 Dip Dye

SUPER EASY!

The Dip Dye scarf may be long but it is worked entirely in Linen Stitch, so once you get the hang of it, just keep going! This repetitive stitch pattern looks more like weaving than knitting.

SIZE

One Size

FINISHED MEASUREMENTS

Length (without fringe): 84" / 213.5 cm.
Length (with fringe): Approx. 90" / 228.5 cm.
Width: 12" / 30 cm.

MATERIALS

Yarn: Børstet Alpakka by Sandnes Garn (96% brushed alpaca, 4% nylon, 120 yds / 110 m – 50 g).
MC: 6 skeins of colourway 2024.
CC: 3 skeins of colourway 3553.
Yarn is held double throughout the pattern.

If you decide to use another yarn, you will need approx. 984 yds / 900 m of bulky-weight yarn.

Needles: US 11 / 8 mm 16–32" / 40–80 cm circular or straight needles.

Notions: Crochet hook.

GAUGE

14 sts x 25 rows to 4" / 10 cm in linen stitch holding two strands of yarn together, after blocking.

NOTES

You can find the abbreviations and detailed instructions for techniques used in this pattern in the Abbreviations (pp. 20–23) and Techniques (pp. 15–19) sections.

The scarf is worked by holding two colours of yarn double throughout the pattern creating a faded look. You start with the CC, then gradually change to the MC, then back to the CC at the end.

The dense structure of the Linen Stitch means that the edges of the scarf do not curl.

CONSTRUCTION

This scarf is worked seamlessly back and forth. You start with a short edge and knit until you achieve the desired length. The scarf is finished with optional fringes.

DIRECTIONS

With two strands of CC held together, cast on 42 sts using the Long-Tail Cast-On Method or method of choice.

Start to work in Linen Stitch as follows:
Row 1 (WS): *P1, slip 1 st purlwise with yarn in the back of the work*, repeat *–* to end.
Row 2 (RS): *K1, slip 1 st purlwise with yarn in front of the work*, repeat *–* to end.
Continue to work rows 1–2 for the Linen Stitch pattern.

When the scarf measures 10" / 25.5 cm from the cast-on edge, cut one strand of CC and replace with one strand of MC. You are now working with one strand of MC and one strand of CC, held together. Continue to work in Linen Stitch for a further 2" / 5 cm, or until the scarf measures 12" / 30.5 cm from the cast-on edge.

Cut the remaining strand of CC and replace with a strand of MC. You are now working with two strands of MC. Continue to work in Linen Stitch for a further 60" / 152.5 cm (or 72" / 183 cm from the cast-on edge).

Cut one strand of MC and replace with a strand of CC. You are now working with one strand of MC and one strand of CC, held together. Work a further 2" / 5 cm.

Cut the remaining strand of MC and replace with a strand of CC. You are now working with two strands of CC. Work a further 10" / 25.5 cm.

Bind off loosely using preferred method.

FINISHING

Weave in ends. Add fringe if desired. Wet block to measurements.

Fringe
Optional fringe can be added to this scarf. A piece of fringe is looped through every second st on both ends of the scarf. This means you will make 21 pieces of fringe for each end.
To make a piece of fringe, cut three 6" / 15 cm lengths of CC.

27

39

Megumi Shinagawa — Anna Heino — Luuanne Chau — Dami Hunter — Tuuli Huhtala

Elena Solier Jansà — Jonna Hietala — Faïza Mebazaa — Natalya Berezynska

Maija Kangasluoma — Maaike van Geijn — Rebekka Mauser

Megumi Shinagawa

27 Koralli

Koralli is a short-sleeved sweater with a relaxed fit. Mosaic knitting creates a colourwork pattern on the neckline and hem – a less challenging option for stranded knitting.

SIZES

1 (2, 3, 4, 5) (6, 7, 8)

Recommended ease: 2.75–8" / 7–20 cm of positive ease.

FINISHED MEASUREMENTS

Chest Circumference: 37 (44, 48, 52, 56) (60, 64, 68)" / 92.5 (110, 120, 130, 140) (150, 160, 170) cm.
Yoke Depth: 8.25 (9, 9.5, 10.5, 11.25) (11.75, 12, 12.5)" / 21 (22.5, 24, 26, 28) (29, 30, 31.5) cm.
Upper Arm Circumference: 12 (14, 16, 17, 19) (20, 21.5, 22.5)" / 30 (35, 40, 42.5, 47.5) (50, 54, 56.5) cm.
Length From Underarm To Hem: 12" / 30 cm.
The total length of the back is approx. 1" / 2.5 cm longer than the front.

MATERIALS

Yarn: Shelter by Brooklyn Tweed (100% Targhee Columbia wool, 140 yds / 128 m – 50 g).

MC: 4 (5, 5, 6, 7) (7, 8, 8) skeins of colourway Almanac.
CC1: 1 skein of colourway Fossil.
CC2: 1 skein of colourway Camper.

If you decide to use another yarn, you will need approx. 543 (645, 700, 780, 868) (922, 1006, 1070) yds / 497 (590, 640, 713, 794) (843, 920, 978) m of worsted-weight yarn in MC, approx. 21 (24, 26, 28, 30) (32, 34, 35) yds / 19 (22, 24, 26, 27) (29, 31, 32) m of worsted-weight yarn in CC1 and approx. 19 (22, 24, 26, 28) (30, 31, 33) yds / 17 (20, 22, 24, 26) (27, 29, 30) m of worsted-weight yarn in CC2.

Needles: US 7 / 4.5 mm 16" / 40 cm (or DPNs) (for sleeves), 24" / 60 cm (for neck) and 32" / 80 cm (for hem) circular needles. US 9 / 5.5 mm 16" / 40 cm (or DPNs) (for sleeves), 24" / 60 cm (for neck and German short rows) and 32" / 80 cm (for body) circular needles.

Notions: 8 stitch markers, stitch holders or waste yarn.

GAUGE

16 sts x 23 rnds to 4" / 10 cm on US 9 / 5.5 mm needles in Stockinette Stitch, after blocking.

16 sts x 12 rnds to 4" / 10 cm x 2" / 5 cm on US 9 / 5.5 mm needles in Slipped-Stitch Pattern, after blocking.

STITCH PATTERNS

Broken Rib
Rnd 1: *K1, p1*, repeat *–* to end.
Rnd 2: K to end.
Repeat rnds 1–2 for pattern.

SPECIAL TECHNIQUES

At Slipped-Stitch Pattern, refer to the following.
When you knit it in the rnd, first, put MC, CC1, and CC2 yarn balls from left to right. Work rnds 1–2. Move MC yarn ball to the right of CC2 yarn ball.
Work rnd 3. Move CC1 to the right of MC.

Work rnds 4–5. Move CC2 to the right of CC1.

Work rnd 6. Move MC to the right of CC2.

Work rnd 7. Move CC1 to the right of MC.

Work rnd 8. Move CC2 to the right of CC1.

Work rnd 9. Move MC to the right of CC2.

Work rnd 10. Cut CC1 yarn, and move CC2 to the right of MC.

Work rnd 11. Cut CC2 yarn.

Work rnd 12.

As a result, you can knit it in the rnd smoothly without getting tangled.

WRITTEN INSTRUCTIONS FOR CHARTS

Slipped-Stitch Pattern

Sts are slipped purlwise with yarn in front.

For Neck

Rnd 1 (CC1): *K1, sl1 wyif*, repeat *–* to end.

Rnd 2 (CC2): K to end.

Rnd 3 (MC): K2, *sl1 wyif, k1*, repeat *–* to end.

Rnd 4 (CC1): *K1, p1*, repeat *–* to end.

For Hem

Rnd 1 (CC1): *K1, sl1 wyif*, repeat *–* to end.

Rnd 2 (CC2): K to end.

Rnd 3 (MC): K2, *sl1 wyif, k1*, repeat *–* to end.

Rnd 4 (CC1): *K1, p1*, repeat *–* to end.

Rnd 5 (CC2): *K1, sl1 wyif*, repeat *–* to end.

Rnd 6 (MC): K to end.

Rnd 7 (CC1): K2, *sl1 wyif, k1*, repeat *–* to end.

Rnd 8 (CC2): *K1, p1* to end.

Rnd 9 (MC): *K1, sl1 wyif*, repeat *–* to end.

Rnd 10 (CC1): K to end.

Rnd 11 (CC2): K2, *sl1 wyif, k1*, repeat *–* to end.

Rnd 12 (MC): *K1, p1*, repeat *–* to end.

NOTES

You can find the abbreviations and detailed instructions for techniques used in this pattern in the Abbreviations (pp. 20–23) and Techniques (pp. 15–19) sections.

Use a marker in a different colour to mark the beginning of the round (BOR).

Be careful not to knit too tight when working the slipped stitches.

The charts are read from bottom to top and from right to left.

You can see in brackets in which colourway the round is to be worked.

After the German Short Rows 2 Section, the back becomes approx. 1" / 2.5 cm longer than the front. This provides a more relaxed fit.

CONSTRUCTION

This sweater is knitted top down with a raglan yoke featuring simple Stockinette Stitch and Broken Rib for neck, hem and sleeves. A mosaic pattern, worked with easy slipped stitches, is worked for the neckline and hem. Short rows are used at the neckline and lower body to add shape and ensure a great fit.

MODIFICATIONS

If you want to make the body shorter or longer, you can knit less or more Stockinette Stitch rounds before the German Short Rows 2 Section.

DIRECTIONS

NECK

With MC and US 7 / 4.5 mm needles, cast on 80 (88, 88, 88, 96) (96, 96, 96) sts using the Long-Tail Cast-On Method or method of choice. Place marker for the beginning of rnd (BOR) and join to knit in the rnd, being careful not to twist sts.

Start to work in Broken Rib as follows:

Rnd 1: *K1, p1*, repeat *–* to end.

Rnd 2: K to end.

Rnd 3: *K1, p1*, repeat *–* to end.

Change to US 9 / 5.5 mm needles.

Rnd 4: K to end.

You will now work the Slipped-Stitch Pattern for Neck, beginning with rnd 5. Join CC1.

Rnds 5–8: Work the Slipped-Stitch Pattern for Neck once. Work from chart or written instructions.

Cut CC1 & CC2 and continue to work in MC.

Rnd 9: K to end.

Sizes 1, 2, 3, 4, 5 and 6 only

Rnd 10 (MC): K to end.

Sizes 7 and 8 only

Rnd 10 (MC): *M1l, k8*, repeat *–* to end. (12 sts inc'd)

You should have 80 (88, 88, 88, 96) (96, 108, 108) sts.

GERMAN SHORT ROWS – FIRST SECTION

Set-up rnd: P1, k2, p1, PM, k6 (6, 6, 4, 6) (4, 6, 4), PM, p1, k2, p1, PM, k26 (30, 30, 32, 34) (36, 40, 42), PM, p1, k2, p1, PM, k6 (6, 6, 4, 6) (4, 6, 4), PM, p1, k2, p1, PM, k to BOR m.

You should have 80 (88, 88, 88, 96) (96, 108, 108) sts: 26 (30, 30, 32, 34) (36, 40, 42) sts for the front, 6 (6, 6, 4, 6) (4, 6, 4) sts for each sleeve, 4 sts for each raglan seam and 26 (30, 30, 32, 34) (36, 40, 42) sts for the back.

Start working short rows to shape the neck and back.

Row 1 (RS): P1, k2, p1, SM, m1l, k to m, m1r, SM, p1, k2, p1, SM, m1l, k to m, m1r, SM, p1, k2, p1, SM, m1l, k to m, m1r, SM, p1, k2, p1, SM, m1l, k2, turn work. (7 sts inc'd)

Row 2 (WS): MDS, p to m, *SM, k1, p2, k1, SM, p to m*, repeat *–* twice more, SM, k1, p2, k1, SM (BOR m), m1rp, p2, turn work. (1 st inc'd)

Row 3 (RS): MDS, k to BOR m, *SM, p1, k2, p1, SM, m1l, k to m, m1r*, repeat *–* twice more, SM, p1, k2, p1, SM, m1l, k to DS, kDS, k2, turn work. (7 sts inc'd)

Row 4 (WS): MDS, p to m, *SM, k1, p2, k1, SM, p to m*, repeat *–* twice more, SM, k1, p2, k1, SM (BOR m), m1rp, p to DS, pDS, p2, turn work. (1 st inc'd)

Row 5 (RS): MDS, k to BOR m, *SM, p1, k2, p1, SM, m1l, k to m, m1r*, repeat *–* twice more, SM, p1, k2, p1, SM, m1l, k to DS, kDS, k3, turn work. (7 sts inc'd)

Row 6 (WS): MDS, p to m, *SM, k1, p2, k1, SM, p to m*, repeat *–* twice more, SM, k1, p2, k1, SM (BOR m), m1rp, p to DS, pDS, p3, turn work. (1 st inc'd)

Row 7 (RS): MDS, k to BOR m, *SM, p1, k2, p1, SM, m1l, k to m, m1r*, repeat *–* twice more, SM, p1, k2, p1, SM, m1l, k to DS, kDS, k4, turn work. (7 sts inc'd)

Row 8 (WS): MDS, p to m, *SM, k1, p2, k1, SM, p to m*, repeat *–* twice more, SM, k1, p2, k1, SM (BOR m), m1rp, p to DS, pDS, p4, turn work. (1 st inc'd)

Row 9 (RS): MDS, k to BOR m.

You should have 112 (120, 120, 120, 128) (128, 140, 140) sts: 34 (38, 38, 40, 42) (44, 48, 50) sts for the front, 14 (14, 14, 12, 14) (12, 14, 12) sts for each sleeve, 4 sts for each raglan seam and 34 (38, 38, 40, 42) (44, 48, 50) sts for the back.

YOKE

Set-up rnd 1: *P1, k2, p1, SM, m1l, k to m, m1r, SM*, repeat *–* twice more, p1, k2, p1, SM, m1l, *k to DS, kDS*, repeat *–* once more, k to BOR m, m1r. (8 sts inc'd)

Set-up rnd 2: *P1, k2, p1, SM, k to m, SM*, repeat *–* twice more, p1, k2, p1, SM, k to BOR m.

Rnd 1: *P1, k2, p1, SM, m1l, k to m, m1r, SM*, repeat *–* twice more, p1, k2, p1, SM, m1l, k to BOR m, m1r. (8 sts inc'd)

Rnd 2: *P1, k2, p1, SM, k to m, SM*, repeat *–* twice more, p1, k2, p1, SM, k to BOR m.

Repeat rnds 1–2, 13 (17, 19, 21, 23) (26, 27, 29) more times. [104 (136, 152, 168, 184) (208, 216, 232) sts inc'd]

Size 1 only

Rnd 29: *P1, k2, p1, SM, m1l, k to m, m1r, SM, p1, k2, p1, SM*, k to m, SM, repeat *–* once more, k to BOR m. (4 sts inc'd)

Rnd 30: *P1, k2, p1, SM, k to m, SM*, repeat *–* twice more, p1, k2, p1, SM, k to BOR m.

You should have 236 (272, 288, 304, 328) (352, 372, 388) sts: 64 (76, 80, 86, 92) (100, 106, 112) sts for the front, 46 (52, 56, 58, 64) (68, 72, 74) sts for each sleeve, 4 sts for each raglan seam and 64 (76, 80, 86, 92) (100, 106, 112) sts for the back.

All sizes resume

Work in Stockinette Stitch (k all sts) for 6 (4, 3, 4, 4) (1, 1, 0) rnd(s), while following the established pattern (p1, k2, p1) for the 4 raglan sts.

SEPARATING BODY & SLEEVES

Set-up rnd 1: *P1, k2, p1, RM, put next 46 (52, 56, 58, 64) (68, 72, 74) sts on st holder or waste yarn, RM, cast on 1 (2, 4, 5, 6) (6, 7, 8) st(s) using the Backward Loop Cast-On Method or method of choice, PM, cast on 1 (2, 4, 5, 6) (6, 7, 8) st(s) using the Backwards Loop Cast-On Method or method of choice, p1, k2, p1, RM, k to m*, RM, repeat *–* once more, RM (BOR m),

k to m (this m is new BOR m).

Rnd 1: K to m, SM, k to BOR m.

You should have 148 (176, 192, 208, 224) (240, 256, 272) sts for the body.

Continue to work in Stockinette Stitch (k all sts) for approx. 7.5" / 19 cm.

GERMAN SHORT ROWS – SECOND SECTION

Start working short rows to shape the back hem and making it a bit longer than the front. You will work the following rows flat.

Row 1 (RS): K to m, SM, k14 (16, 18, 20, 20) (22, 24, 26), turn work.

Row 2 (WS): MDS, *p to m, SM*, repeat *–* once more, p14 (16, 18, 20, 20) (22, 24, 26), turn work.

Row 3 (RS): MDS, *k to m, SM *, repeat *–* once more, k7 (8, 9, 10, 10) (11, 12, 13), turn work.

Row 4 (WS): MDS, *p to m, SM*, repeat *–* once more, p7 (8, 9, 10, 10) (11, 12, 13), turn work.

Row 5 (RS): MDS, *k to m*, SM, repeat *–* once more, turn work.

Row 6 (WS): MDS, p to m, turn work.

Continue to work in the rnd again.

Rnd 1: MDS, *k to DS, kDS*, RM, repeat *–* 4 more times, k to BOR m.

Rnd 2: KDS, k to end.

HEM – STRIPES

Note! Please refer to Special Techniques, Written Instructions for Charts and/or Chart.

Work hem stripes in Slipped-Stitch Pattern for Hem.
Join CC1.

Rnds 1–12: Work the Slipped-Stitch Pattern for Hem once. Work from chart or written instructions.

Rnd 13: K to end.

**SLIPPED-STITCH
PATTERN FOR NECK**

**SLIPPED-STITCH
PATTERN FOR HEM**

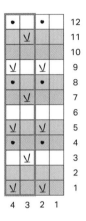

	knit
•	purl
∨	slip 1 st with yarn in front
	repeat
	MC
	CC1
	CC2

HEM – BROKEN RIB

Change to US 7 / 4.5 mm needles. Work in Broken Rib as follows:
Rnd 1: *K1, p1*, repeat *–* to end.
Rnd 2: K to end.
Rnds 3–8: Repeat rnds 1–2, 3 more times.
Rnd 9: *K1, p1*, repeat *–* to end.

Change to US 9 / 5.5 mm needles. Bind off all sts purlwise loosely.

SLEEVES

Place 46 (52, 56, 58, 64) (68, 72, 74) sleeve sts onto US 9 / 5.5 mm needles.
Join MC yarn.

Set-up rnd: Pick up and k 1 (2, 4, 5, 6) (6, 7, 8) st(s) from the centre of cast-on edge, k to CO edge, pick up and k 1 (2, 4, 5, 6) (6, 7, 8) st(s) from cast-on edge, PM. You should have 48 (56, 64, 68, 76) (80, 86, 90) sts for the sleeve.
Rnds 1–5: K to end.

Change to US 7 / 4.5 mm needles. Work in Broken Rib as follows:
Rnd 6: *K1, p1*, repeat *–* to end.
Rnd 7: K to end.
Rnds 8–9: Repeat rnds 6–7 once more.
Rnd 10: *K1, p1*, repeat *–* to end.

Change to US 9 / 5.5 mm needles. Bind off all sts purlwise loosely.

Repeat instructions for the second sleeve.

FINISHING

Weave in all ends. Wet block to measurements.

Anna Heino

28 Hilppa

This long, symmetrical shawl is worked in Garter Stitch and decorated with 'nupps' (bobbles) in different colours. A perfect way to use yarns left over from other projects!

SIZE

One Size

FINISHED MEASUREMENTS

Length: 78.75" / 200 cm.
Width: 12.5" / 32 cm.

MATERIALS

Yarn: Tukuwool Fingering (100% Finnish wool, 219 yds / 200 m – 50 g).
MC: 4 skeins, colourway Runo.
CC1: 1 skein, colourway Repo.
CC2: 1 skein, colourway Rohto.
CC3: 1 skein, colourway Ujo.

If you decide to use another yarn, you will need approx. 875 yds / 800 m of MC and 55 yds / 50 m of each CC in fingering-weight yarn.

You can alter the number of CCs according to your preferences. If making changes, take this into account in the yardages.

Needles: US 6 / 4 mm 40" / 100 cm circular or straight needles.

Notions: Stitch markers.

GAUGE

24 sts x 34 rows to 4" / 10 cm in Garter Stitch, after blocking.

NOTES

You can find the abbreviations and detailed instructions for techniques used in this pattern in the Abbreviations (pp. 20–23) and Techniques (pp. 15–19) sections.

For a neat edge, slip the first stitch of each row purlwise with yarn in back.

Move the stitch markers when you encounter them. Stitch markers are always placed 4 sts before the nupp (bobble). The nupp is easier to work when the stitch markers is not directly next to it.

Begin new skeins at the beginning of the row. This way the tails are easier to weave into the edge.

The CCs are only used in the nupps. Work all other sts with MC.

You can decide which CC to use for each nupp.

CONSTRUCTION

This shawl is worked flat from tip to tip. The long, parallelogram shaped shawl has symmetrical ends.

DIRECTIONS

With MC, cast on 3 sts with the Long-Tail Cast-On Method or method of choice.

Section 1: Increases
Row 1: K3.
Rows 2–3: Sl1, k2.
You have now worked the tip of the shawl. Begin to increase sts at the end of the rows so that the shawl will gradually start to grow.
Row 4 (RS): Sl1, kfb, k1. (1 st inc'd)
Row 5 (WS): Sl1, k to end.
Row 6: Sl1, k to last 2 sts, kfb, k1. (1 st inc'd)
Row 7: Sl1, k to end.
Repeat rows 6–7 a total of 16 times. (20 sts)

Next, begin to work nupps. Work each nupp as follows: work the nupp with one of the CC yarns. Into the same st, k1, yo, k1, yo, k1, turn work, p5, turn work, k5, turn work, p5, turn work, k5tog through back loops. Once the nupp has been worked, move the final st back to the left-hand needle. Cut CC and continue with MC. Leave a tail of about 4" / 10 cm to the beginning and end of the nupp to be woven in later.

Row 8 (place marker): Sl1, k5, PM, k to last 2 sts, kfb, k1. (1 st inc'd)
Row 9: Sl1, k to end.
Row 10 (nupp row): Sl1, k to marker, SM, k4. Work nupp with CC. K to last 2 sts, kfb, k1. (1 st inc'd)
Row 11: Sl1, k to end.
Rows 12–13: Repeat rows 6–7.
Repeat rows 12–13 a total of 9 times. (31 sts)

Row 14 (place marker): Sl1, k to marker, SM, k11, PM, k to last 2 sts, kfb, k1. (1 st inc'd)
Row 15: Sl1, k to end.
Row 16 (nupp row): Sl1, k to marker, SM, k to marker, SM, k4. Work nupp with CC. K to last 2 sts, kfb, k1. (1 st inc'd)
Row 17: Sl1, k to end.

Rows 18–19: Repeat rows 6–7.
Repeat rows 18–19 a total of 9 times. (42 sts)

Row 20 (place marker): Sl1, *k to marker, SM*, repeat *–* once, k11, PM, k to last 2 sts, kfb, k1. (1 st inc'd)
Row 21: Sl1, k to end.
Row 22 (nupp row): Sl1, k to marker, SM, k4. Work nupp with CC. K to marker, SM, k to marker, SM, k4. Work nupp with CC. K to last 2 sts, kfb, k1. (1 st inc'd)
Row 23: Sl1, k to end.
Rows 24–25: Repeat rows 6–7.
Repeat rows 24–25 a total of 9 times. (53 sts)

Row 26 (place marker): Sl1, *k to marker, SM*, repeat *–* a total of 3 times, k11, PM, k to last 2 sts, kfb, k1. (1 st inc'd)
Row 27: Sl1, k to end.
Row 28 (nupp row): Sl1, *k to marker, SM*, repeat *–* once, k4. Work nupp with CC. K to marker, SM, k to marker, SM, k4. Work nupp with CC. K to last 2 sts, kfb, k1. (1 st inc'd)
Row 29: Sl1, k to end.
Row 30–31: Repeat rows 6–7.
Repeat rows 30–31 a total of 9 times. (64 sts)

Row 32 (place marker): Sl1, *k to marker, SM*, repeat *–* a total of 4 times, k11, PM, k to last 2 sts, kfb, k1. (1 st inc'd)
Row 33: Sl1, k to end.
Row 34 (nupp row): Sl1, k to marker, SM, k4. Work nupp with CC. K to marker, SM, k to marker, SM, k4. Work nupp with CC. K to marker, SM, k to marker, SM, k4. Work nupp with CC. K to last 2 sts, kfb, k1. (1 st inc'd)
Row 35: Sl1, k to end.
Rows 36–37: Repeat rows 6–7.
Repeat rows 36–37 a total of 9 times. (75 sts)

Row 38 (place marker): Sl1, *k to marker, SM*, repeat *–* a total of 5 times, k11, PM, k to last 2 sts, kfb, k1. (1 st inc'd)
Row 39: Sl1, k to end.
Row 40 (nupp row): Sl1, *k to marker,

SM*, repeat *–* once, k4. Work nupp with CC. K to marker, SM, k to marker, SM, k4. Work nupp with CC. K to marker, SM, k to marker, SM, k4. Work nupp with CC. K to end. (1 st inc'd)
Row 41: Sl1, k to end.
Repeat row 41, 20 more times.

There are now 76 sts and you are at the beginning of a RS row. Continue knitting a nupp row every 22nd row.

Section 2: Middle
Row 42 (nupp row): Sl1, k to marker, SM, k4. Work nupp with CC. K to marker, SM, k to marker, SM, k4. Work nupp with CC. K to marker, SM, k to marker, SM, k4. Work nupp with CC.
Row 43: Sl1, k to end.
Repeat row 43, 20 more times.

Row 44 (nupp row): Sl1, *k to marker, SM*, repeat *–* once, k4. Work nupp with CC. K to marker, SM, k to marker, SM, k4. Work nupp with CC. K to marker, SM, k to marker, SM, k4. Work nupp with CC. K to end.
Row 45: Sl1, k to end.
Repeat row 45, 20 more times.

Repeat Section 2 a total of 9 times.

Section 3: Decreases
Row 46 (nupp row): Sl1, k to marker, SM, k4. Work nupp with CC. K to marker, SM, k to marker, SM, k4. Work nupp with CC. K to marker, SM, k to marker, SM, k4. Work nupp with CC. K to end.
Row 47: Sl1, k to end.
Repeat row 47, 20 more times.

Row 48 (nupp row): Sl1, *k to marker, SM*, repeat *–* once, k4. Work nupp with CC. K to marker, SM, knit to marker, SM, k4. Work nupp with CC. K to marker, SM, k to marker, PM, k4. Work nupp with CC. K to end.
Row 49: Sl1, k to end.
Row 50: Sl1, k to last 3 sts, ssk, k1. (1 st dec'd)
Row 51: Repeat row 49.

Repeat rows 50–51 a total of 10 times. (66 sts)

Row 52 (nupp row): Sl1, k to marker, SM, k4. Work nupp with CC. K to marker, SM, k to marker, SM, k4. Work nupp with CC. K to marker, SM, k to marker, RM, k4. Work nupp with CC. K to last 3 sts, ssk, k1. (1 st dec'd)
Row 53: Sl1, k to end.
Row 54: Sl1, k to last 3 sts, ssk, k1. (1 st dec'd)
Row 55: Repeat row 53.
Repeat rows 54–55 a total of 10 times. (55 s)

Row 56 (nupp row): Sl1, *k to marker, SM*, repeat *–* once, k4. Work nupp with CC. K to marker, SM, k to marker, RM, k4. Work nupp with CC. K to last 3 sts, ssk, k1. (1 st decreased)
Row 57: Sl1, k to end.
Row 58: Sl1, k to last 3 sts, ssk, k1. (1 st dec'd)
Row 59: Repeat row 57.
Repeat rows 58–59 a total of 10 times. (44 sts)

Row 60 (nupp row): Sl1, k to marker, SM, k4. Work nupp with CC. K to marker, SM, k to marker, RM, k4. Work nupp with CC. K to last 3 sts, ssk, k1. (1 st dec'd)
Row 61: Sl1, k to end.
Row 62: Sl1, k to last 3 sts, ssk, k1. (1 st dec'd)
Row 63: Repeat row 61.
Repeat rows 62–63 a total of 10 times. (33 sts)

Row 64 (nupp rows): Sl1, k to marker, SM, k to marker, RM, k4. Work nupp with CC. K to last 3 sts, ssk, k1. (1 st dec'd)
Row 65: Sl1, k to end.
Row 66: Sl1, k to last 3 sts, ssk, k1. (1 st dec'd)
Row 67: Repeat row 65.
Repeat rows 66–67 a total of 10 times. (22 sts)

Row 68 (nupp row): Sl1, k to marker, RM, k4. Work nupp with CC. K to last 3 sts, ssk, k1. (1 st dec'd)

Row 69: Sl1, k to end.
Row 70: Sl1, k to last 3 sts, ssk, k1. (1 st dec'd)
Row 71: Repeat row 69.
Repeat rows 70–71 until there are 3 sts left on the needles. Cut yarn and pull it through the last sts. Tighten.

FINISHING

Weave in all ends. Wet block to measurements.

Finishing the Nupps
Tighten the yarn ends of the nupp by tying them together with a knot. You can tighten all the nupps once you have finished knitting or after working a few rows after each nupp row as follows: Shape the nupp on the RS and tighten it with the yarn ends on the WS. Then tie the ends together tightly.

If you don't want the ends to show on WS, you can weave in the ends inside the nupp. Make sure not to pull the yarns too tightly while doing this so the nupp doesn't flatten!

Luuanne Chau

29 Rattan

This cropped sweater is knitted in simple Stockinette Stitch that comes alive with a textured bouclé yarn. The V-neck and the hem are worked in a different yarn in a slipped-stitch motif.

SIZES

1 (2, 3, 4, 5) (6, 7, 8)

Recommended ease: 8–10" / 20.5–25.5 cm of positive ease.

FINISHED MEASUREMENTS

Bust Circumference: 42.5 (46.75, 50.5, 54.75, 60) (64.5, 68, 72.5)" / 106 (117, 126, 137, 150) (161, 170, 181) cm.
Sleeve Length from Underarm: 17.5 (17.5, 17.5, 17.5, 17.75) (17.5, 17.75, 17.5)" / 44.5 (44.5, 44.5, 44.5, 45) (44, 45, 44) cm.
Lower Sleeve Circumference: 8 (8.75, 8.75, 9.5, 9.5) (10.5, 10.5, 10.5)" / 20 (22, 22, 24, 24) (26, 26, 26) cm.
V-Neck Depth: 7.5 (8, 8, 8.5, 8.5) (9, 9, 9.5)" / 19 (20, 20, 21.5, 21.5) (22.5, 22.5, 24) cm.
Length from Shoulder to Hem: 18.5 (19, 19.5, 20.5, 21) (22, 22.5, 23)" / 47 (48, 49.5, 52, 53.5) (55.5, 57, 58.5) cm.
Body Length from Underarm to Hem: 11" / 28 cm.

Upper Sleeve Circumference: 15.25 (16, 16.75, 19.25, 20) (21.5, 23.25, 24)" / 38 (40, 42, 48, 50) (54, 58, 60) cm.
Back Neck Length: 8.5 (8.75, 9.25, 8.75, 9.25) (9.5, 10, 10.5)" / 21 (22, 23, 22, 23) (24, 25, 26) cm.

MATERIALS

Yarn: MC: 3 (3, 4, 4, 5) (5, 5, 6) skeins of Flette Bulky by Woolfolk (100% merino, 131 yds / 120 m – 100 g), colourway FB04 (dark red sample) or colourway FB10 (pink sample).
CC: 1 (1, 1, 1, 2) (2, 2, 2) skein(s) of Luft by Woolfolk (55% merino, 45% Pima cotton, 109 yds / 100 m – 50 g), colourway L15 (dark red sample) or colourway L14 (pink sample).

If you decide to use another yarn, you will need approx. 350 (390, 430, 480, 540) (600, 640, 690) yds / 320 (357, 393, 439, 494) (549, 585, 631) m of bulky-weight bouclé yarn in MC (*Note!* 2 strands of DK-weight bouclé yarn held together can be used to substitute) and approx. 90 (95, 100, 105, 110) (115, 120, 125) yds / 82 (87, 91, 96, 101) (105, 110, 114) m of bulky-weight yarn in CC.

Needles: US 10.5 / 6.5 mm 40" / 100 cm circular needles and DPNs, US 9 / 5.5 mm 40" / 100 cm circular needles and DPNs (or preferred needles for small circumference knitting). Spare circular needles for 3-Needle Bind-Off.

Notions: 4 stitch markers, removable/locking stitch markers, stitch holders or waste yarn.

GAUGE

10 sts x 16 rnds to 4" / 10 cm on US 10.5 / 6.5 mm needles in Stockinette Stitch with MC, after blocking.

NOTES

You can find the abbreviations and detailed instructions for techniques used in this pattern in the Abbreviations (pp. 20–23) and Techniques (pp. 15–19) sections.

Placement of stitch markers in pattern is to guide the knitter without having to count stitches or rows. Slip markers (except the locking stitch markers) when you come across them. Use removable/ locking stitch markers to help keep track of rows/rounds in between decreases.

When slipping yarn with yarn in front, always bring yarn back to work another stitch to avoid creating a yarn over.

CONSTRUCTION

Rattan is a relaxed and slightly oversized, drop-shoulder sweater. The sweater is worked seamlessly from the bottom up. The body is worked in the round with increases for an optional waist shaping until reaching the underarms. After this the back and front are worked flat. Shoulders are seamed with the 3-Needle Bind-Off Method. Stitches are picked up around the armholes and the sleeves are worked in the round. Finally, stitches for the neckline are picked up to be worked in the round.

MODIFICATIONS

Waist shaping can be omitted if preferred. The sample is shown with waist shaping.

For the pink sample, the shoulders were seamed from the right side of the fabric creating a visible seam.

DIRECTIONS

With US 9 / 5.5 mm circular needles and CC, cast on 94 (104, 114, 124, 138) (148, 158, 168) sts using the Long-Tail Cast-On Method or method of choice. If omitting waist shaping, cast on 106 (116, 126, 136, 150) (160, 170, 180) sts. Join to knit in the rnd and PM for the beginning of rnd (BOR).

HEM

The hem is worked in a decorative slipped stitch pattern. Begin working the 1 x 1 Ribbing.
Rnd 1: *K1, p1*, repeat *–* to end.
Continue in established 1 x 1 Ribbing for 3 rnds more. 4 rnds worked in total.

Rnd 5: *K1, slip 2 sts pwise wyif*, repeat *–* until 1 (2, 0, 1, 0) (1, 2, 0) st(s) before end, k1 (1, 0, 1, 0) (1, 1, 0), slip 0 (1, 0, 0, 0) (0, 1, 0) pwise wyif.
Rnd 6: Repeat rnd 5.
Rnd 7: *K1, p1*, repeat *–* to end.
Rnd 8: *Slip 1 pwise wyif, k1, slip 1 pwise wyif*, repeat *–* until 1 (2, 0, 1, 0) (1, 2, 0) st(s) before end, slip 1 (1, 0, 1, 0) (1, 1, 0) pwise wyif, k0 (1, 0, 0, 0) (0, 1, 0).
Rnd 9: Repeat rnd 8.
Rnd 10: *K1, p1*, repeat *–* to end.
Rnds 11–12: Repeat rnds 5–6.
Work 3 rnds in 1 x 1 Ribbing.

BODY

Change to US 10.5 / 6.5 mm needles.

Omitting Waist Shaping

Work this section if you do not want to do waist shaping.
Next rnd: Drop CC. With MC, k26 (29, 31, 34, 37) (40, 42, 45), PM1, m1l 0 (1, 0, 1, 0) (1, 0, 1) time(s), k1 (0, 1, 0, 1) (0, 1, 0), PM2, k26 (29, 31, 34, 37) (40, 42, 45), PM3, k to end.
[0 (1, 0, 1, 0) (1, 0, 1) st(s) inc'd]

You should have 106 (117, 126, 137, 150) (161, 170, 181) sts.

Next rnd: K to end.
Continue in Stockinette Stitch (k all sts) until fabric reaches 11" / 28 cm from hem or 7.5 (8, 8.5, 9.5, 10) (11, 11.5, 12)" / 19 (20, 21.5, 24, 25.5) (27.5, 29, 30.5) cm short of desired body length. Proceed to Separate Front and Back.

Including Waist Shaping

Work this section if you want to do waist shaping.
Next rnd: Drop CC. With MC, k23 (26, 28, 31, 34) (37, 39, 42), PM1, m1l 0 (1, 0, 1, 0) (1, 0, 1) time(s), k1 (0, 1, 0, 1) (0, 1, 0), PM2, k23 (26, 28, 31, 34) (37, 39, 42), PM3, k23 (25, 28, 30, 34) (36, 39, 41), PM4, k1 (2, 1, 2, 1) (2, 1, 2), PM5, k to end. [0 (1, 0, 1, 0) (1, 0, 1) st(s) inc'd]
You should have 94 (105, 114, 125, 138) (149, 158, 169) sts.
Work 9 rnds in Stockinette Stitch (k all sts).

Increase rnd: K to M1, m1r, SM1, k to M2, SM2, m1l, k past M3 to M4, m1r, SM4, k to M5, SM5, m1l, k to end. (4 sts inc'd)
You should have 98 (109, 118, 129, 142) (153, 162, 173) sts.

Continue in Stockinette Stitch (k all sts). Repeat increase rnd every 12th rnd twice more. You should have 106 (117, 126, 137, 150) (161, 170, 181) sts.

Continue in Stockinette Stitch (k all sts) until the piece reaches 11" / 28 cm from hem or until it measures 7.5 (8, 8.5, 9.5, 10) (11, 11.5, 12)" / 19 (20, 21.5, 24, 25.5) (27.5, 29, 30.5) cm short of desired body length.

SEPARATE FRONT AND BACK

Next, you will separate the front and back and continue working them back and forth, separately.

Note! Sizes 1 and 2 will follow directions different from that of sizes 3, 4, 5, 6, 7 and 8 until directed otherwise.

Size 1 (2) only
Next rnd: K to 3 sts before m1, k2tog, k1, RM1, place next 27 (30) sts onto a stitch holder or waste yarn, RM3, then slip remaining 53 (58) sts onto another st holder while removing any remaining markers. Turn work. (1 st dec'd)
You should have 25 (28) sts for the front.

Sizes 3 (4, 5, 6, 7, 8) only
Next rnd: K to m3, place remaining 63 (68, 75, 80, 85, 90) sts onto a stitch holder or waste yarn while removing any remaining markers. Turn work. You should have 63 (69, 75, 81, 85, 91) sts for the front.
Row 1 (WS): P to end.
Continue in Stockinette Stitch (k all sts on RS rows, p all sts on WS rows) for 0 (2, 4 6, 8, 8) more row(s) or until the piece measures 0.5 (1, 1.5, 2, 2.5, 2.5)" / 1.5 (2.5, 4, 5, 6.5, 6.5) cm from front/back split. End with WS row.
Next row (RS): K to 3 sts before m1, k2tog, k1, RM1, place remaining 32 (35, 38, 41, 43, 46) sts onto a stitch holder or waste yarn. Turn work. (1 st dec'd)
You should have 30 (33, 36, 39, 41, 44) sts for the front.

All sizes
LEFT FRONT NECK SHAPING

Next row (WS): P to end.
Dec row (RS): K to 3 sts to end, k2tog, k1. (1 st dec'd)
You should have 24 (27, 29, 32, 35) (38, 40, 43) sts.

Continue in Stockinette Stitch (k all sts on RS rows, p all sts on WS rows). Repeat decrease row every RS row 7 (8, 8, 7, 7) (8, 8, 9) more times, then repeat decrease row every other RS row 3 (3, 3, 4, 4) (4, 4, 4) more times. [10 (11, 11, 11, 11) (12, 12, 13) sts dec'd]
You should have 14 (16, 18, 21, 24) (26,

28, 30) sts.

Next row (WS): P to end.
Place left shoulder sts onto a stitch holder or waste yarn and cut yarn, leaving a tail of approx. 6" / 15 cm.

RIGHT FRONT NECK SHAPING

Return right front sts from stitch holder back onto US 10.5 / 6.5 mm needles. You should have 27 (30, 32, 35, 38) (41, 43, 46) sts.
Decrease row (RS): Rejoin MC yarn, bind off 1 st while RM2, ssk, k to end. (2 sts dec'd)
Next row (WS): P to end.
Decrease row (RS): K1, ssk, k to end. (1 sts dec'd)
You should have 24 (27, 29, 32, 35) (38, 40, 43) sts.

Continue in Stockinette Stitch (k all sts on RS rows, p all sts on WS rows). Repeat decrease row every RS row 7 (8, 8, 7, 7) (8, 8, 9) more times, then repeat decrease row every other RS row 3 (3, 3, 4, 4) (4, 4, 4) more times. [10 (11, 11, 11, 11) (12, 12, 13) sts dec'd]
You should have 14 (16, 18, 21, 24) (26, 28, 30) sts.

Next row (WS): P to end.
Place right shoulder sts onto a stitch holder or waste yarn and cut yarn, leaving a tail of approx. 6" / 15 cm.

BACK

Next, you will continue to work the back. Return back sts from stitch holder onto US 10.5 / 6.5 mm needles. You should have 53 (58, 63, 68, 75) (80, 85, 90) sts.
Next row (RS): Rejoin MC yarn and k to end.
Next row (WS): P to end.

Continue in Stockinette Stitch (k all sts on RS rows, p all sts on WS rows) until

the piece measures 6.75 (7.25, 7.75, 8.75, 9.25) (10.25, 10.75, 11.25)" / 17 (18, 19.5, 22, 23.5) (25.5, 27, 28.5) cm from front/back split. End with a WS row.

Next row (RS): K16 (18, 20, 23, 26) (28, 30, 32), bind off 21 (22, 23, 22, 23) (24, 25, 26) sts, k remaining 16 (18, 20, 23, 26) (28, 30, 32) sts.
You should have 16 (18, 20, 23, 26) (28, 30, 32) sts remaining for each shoulder.

LEFT BACK SHOULDER

Next row (WS): P16 (18, 20, 23, 26) (28, 30, 32), turn work.
Next row (RS): K1, sssk, k to end. (2 sts dec'd)
Next row (WS): P14 (16, 18, 21, 24) (26, 28, 30). Place the 14 (16, 18, 21, 24) (26, 28, 30) sts onto a stitch holder or waste yarn. Cut yarn, leaving an approx. 30" / 76 cm tail.

RIGHT BACK SHOULDER

Return to the remaining 16 (18, 20, 23, 26) (28, 30, 32) sts on the US 10.5 / 6.5 mm circular needles.
Next row (WS): Rejoin MC yarn, p16 (18, 20, 23, 26) (28, 30, 32), turn work.
Next row (RS): K to 4 sts from end, k3tog, k1. (2 sts dec'd)
Next row (WS): P14 (16, 18, 21, 24) (26, 28, 30).

SEAM SHOULDERS

Return front right shoulder sts to a second spare circular needle. Using the other tip of the US 10.5 / 6.5 mm needles, RSs facing each other, seam the live sts of the right shoulder with the 3-Needle Bind-Off Method. Then return front and back left shoulder sts to two spare circular needles and seam the left shoulder together using a US 10.5 / 6.5 mm needle and the 3-Needle Bind-Off Method once more.

SLEEVES

Using desired US 10.5 / 6.5 mm needles for small circumference knitting and starting from just left of the centre of the underarm, join MC yarn and pick up and k 19 (20, 21, 24, 25) (27, 29, 30) sts along each side of the armhole. You should have 38 (40, 42, 48, 50) (54, 58, 60) sts. Join in the rnd and PM for the beginning of the rnd (BOR).

Work in Stockinette Stitch (k all sts) until the sleeve measures 9 (8.5, 8, 7.5, 6.75) (6, 5.25, 5)" / 23 (21.5, 20.5, 19, 17) (15, 13.5, 12.5) cm from underarm or until 8.5 (9, 9.5, 10, 11) (11.5, 12.5, 12.5)" / 21.5 (23, 24, 25.5, 28) (29, 31.5, 31.5) cm short of desired sleeve length.

Decrease rnd: K2, k2tog, k to last 4 sts, ssk, k2. (2 sts dec'd)
Continue in Stockinette Stitch (k all sts). Repeat the decrease rnd every 4th rnd 5 (6, 6, 5, 6) (6, 6, 5) more times, then repeat every 2nd rnd 3 (2, 3, 6, 6) (7, 9, 11) more times. [16 (16, 18, 22, 24) (26, 30, 32) sts dec'd]
You should have 20 (22, 22, 24, 24) (26, 26, 26) sts.

Next rnd: K to end.

Cuff

Change to desired US 9 / 5.5 mm needles for small circumference knitting. Switch to CC yarn.

Begin working the 1 x 1 Ribbing.
Next rnd: *K1, p1*, repeat *-* to end.
Continue in established 1 x 1 Ribbing until the cuff measures 1.5" / 4 cm.
Bind off loosely with preferred method.

NECKLINE

You will pick up the sts for the neckline and work a decorative slipped stitch pattern.

With US 9 / 5.5 mm circular needles and CC yarn, begin from right shoulder and pick up and knit 33 (35, 37, 35, 37) (39, 39, 41) sts along the back edge of the neckline, then pick up and knit 31 (33, 33, 35, 35) (37, 37, 39) stitches along the left side of the v-neck. Pick up and knit 1 st at the centre of the v-neck and place a removable marker on the centre st, then pick up an additional 31 (33, 33, 35, 35) (37, 37, 39) sts along the right side of the v-neck. Join to knit in the rnd and place marker for the BOR. You should have 96 (102, 104, 106, 108) (114, 114, 120) sts.

Note! Move stitch marker one row up each time after working centre st.

Next rnd: *K1, p1*, repeat *-* to end.
Dec rnd: *K1, p1*, repeat *-* to 2 sts before centre st, k1, s2kp, *k1, p1*, repeat *-* to end. (2 sts dec'd)
Next rnd: *K1, p1*, repeat *-* to 1 sts before centre st, k2, *k1, p1*, repeat *-* to end.

Dec rnd: *K1, slip 2 pwise wyif*, repeat *-* to 3 (1, 3, 3, 3) (3, 3, 1) st(s) from centre st, k1 (0, 1, 1, 1) (1, 1, 0), slip 1 (0, 1, 1, 0) (1, 1, 0) st(s) pwise wyif, s2kp, slip 1 (2, 1, 1, 0) (1, 1, 2) st(s) pwise wyif, *k1, slip 2 pwise wyif*, repeat *-* to 1 (2, 0, 2, 0) (1, 1, 2) st(s) from end of rnd, k1 (1, 0, 1, 0) (1, 1, 1), sl 0 (1, 0, 1, 0) (0, 0, 1) st(s) pwise wyif. (2 sts dec'd)

Next rnd: *K1, slip 2 pwise wyif*, repeat *-* to 2 (0, 2, 2, 1) (2, 2, 0) st(s) from centre st, k1 (0, 1, 1, 1) (1, 1, 0), slip 1 (0, 1, 1, 0) (1, 1, 0) st(s) pwise wyif, k centre st, slip 1 (2, 1, 1, 0) (1, 1, 2) st(s) pwise wyif, *k1, slip 2 pwise wyif*, repeat *-* to 1 (2, 0, 2, 0) (1, 1, 2) st(s) to end of rnd, k1 (1, 0, 1, 0) (1, 1, 1), slip 0 (1, 0, 1, 0) (0, 0, 1) st(s) pwise wyif.

Dec rnd: *K1, p1*, repeat *-* to 2 sts before centre st, k1, s2kp, *k1, p1*, repeat *-* to end. (2 sts dec'd)

Next rnd: *Slip 1 pwise wyif, k1, slip 1 pwise wyif*, repeat *-* until 1 (2, 1, 1, 0) (1, 1, 2) st(s) remain from centre st, slip 1 (1, 1, 1, 0) (1, 1, 1) st(s) pwise wyif, k0 (1, 0, 0, 0) (0, 0, 1), k centre st, k0 (1, 0, 0, 0) (0, 0, 1), slip 1 (1, 1, 1, 0) (1, 1, 1) st(s) pwise wyif, *slip 1 pwise wyif, k1, sl1 pwise wyif*, repeat *-* until 0 (1, 2, 1, 2) (0, 0, 1) st(s) remain to end of rnd, slip 0 (1, 1, 1, 1) (0, 0, 1) pwise wyif, k0 (0, 1, 0, 1) (0, 0, 0).

Dec rnd: *Slip 1 pwise wyif, k1, slip 1 pwise wyif*, repeat *-* until 1 (2, 1, 1, 3) (1, 1, 2) st(s) remain from centre st, slip 0 (1, 0, 0, 1) (0, 0, 1) st(s) pwise wyif, k0 (0, 0, 0, 1) (0, 0, 0), s2kp, k0 (0, 0, 0, 1) (0, 0, 0), slip 0 (1, 0, 0, 1) (0, 0, 1) st(s) pwise wyif, *slip 1 pwise wyif, k1, slip 1 pwise wyif*, repeat *-* until 0 (1, 2, 1, 2) (0, 0, 1) st(s) remain to end of rnd, slip 0 (1, 1, 1, 1) (0, 0, 1) pwise wyif, k0 (0, 1, 0, 1) (0, 0, 0). (2 sts dec'd)

Next rnd: *K1, p1*, repeat *-* to end.
Dec rnd: *K1, p1*, repeat *-* to 2 sts before centre st, k1, s2kp, *k1, p1*, repeat *-* to end.

Bind off with preferred bind-off method.

FINISHING

Weave in ends. Wet block to measurements.

Dami Hunter

30 Cresta

This triangular shawl features Garter Stitch and simple colour ridge sections. Cresta starts with just a few stitches and grows with increases – easy, once you learn the rhythm!

SIZES

1 (2)

FINISHED MEASUREMENTS

Wingspan: 44.25 (51.5)" / 110.5 (129) cm.
Centre Spine: 21.5 (25.5)" / 54 (63) cm.

MATERIALS

Yarn: Nest Worsted by Magpie Fibers (100% Corriedale Wool, 210 yds / 192 m – 100 g).
MC: 2 (3) skeins of colourway Marled Smoke (grey sample, p. 165) or Natural Marl (brown sample, p. 166).
CC: 1 (2) skein(s) of Midnight Velvet (grey sample) or colourway Natural Midnight (brown sample).
If you decide to use another yarn, you will need approx. 420 (630) yds / 384 (576) m of worsted-weight yarn in MC and approx.

180 (360) yds / 165 (329) m (CC) of worsted-weight yarn in CC.

Needles: US size 8 / 5 mm 32" / 80 cm circular needles.

Notions: Stitch markers.

GAUGE

20 sts x 28 rows to 4" / 10 cm in Stockinette Stitch, after blocking.

20 sts x 36 rows over 4" / 10 cm in Garter Stitch, after blocking.

NOTES

You can find the abbreviations and detailed instructions for techniques used in this pattern in the Abbreviations (pp. 20–23) and Techniques (pp. 15–19) sections.

Slip markers as you come across them.

You can carry your CC yarn up the side for the garter section. This way you will have fewer ends to weave in. Alternatively, cut the CC at the end of each ridge section if you prefer both outside edges to look identical.

CONSTRUCTION

This triangle shawl is knitted flat from top down in one piece: it starts with just 5 stitches and slowly grows into a generous piece. The increases are made on both edges and on either side of the central stitch. Garter Stitch and colour ridge sections vary throughout the shawl.

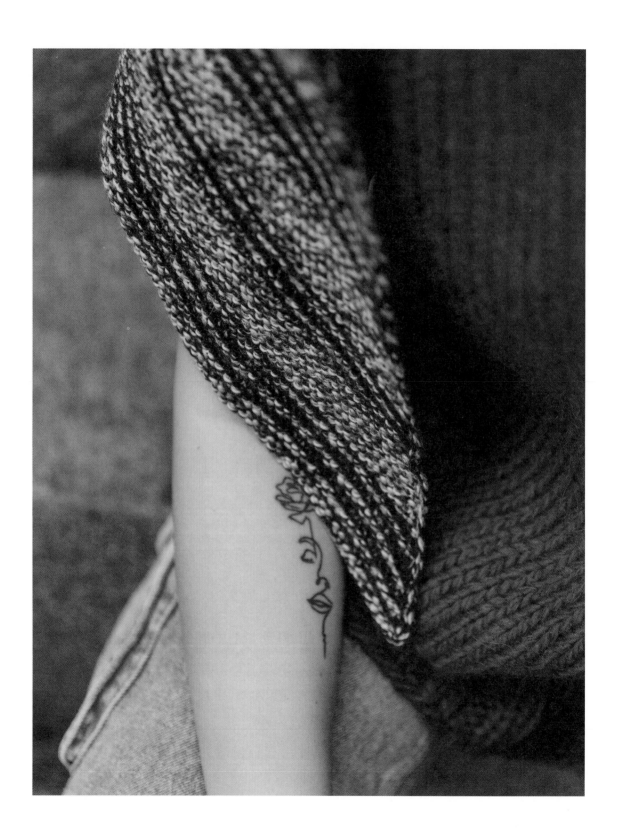

DIRECTIONS

SET-UP

With MC, cast on 5 sts with Long-Tail Cast-On Method or preferred method.

Note! Slip all sts purlwise throughout the pattern.

Row 1 (WS): Sl1 wyif, k1, PM, sl1 wyif, PM, k2.
Row 2 (RS): Sl1 wyif, kfb, SM, k1, SM, kfb, k1. (2 sts inc'd) (7 sts)
Row 3 (WS): Sl1 wyif, k to m, SM, sl1 wyif, SM, k3.

BODY

1. Garter Section

Continue working in MC.
Row 1 (RS): Sl1 wyif, kfb, k to 1 st before m, kfb, SM, k1, SM, kfb, k to the last 2 sts, kfb, k1. (4 sts inc'd)
Row 2 (WS): Sl1 wyif, k to m, SM, sl1 wyif, SM, k to end.
Repeat rows 1–2, 11 more times, ending on a WS row. 24 rows worked in total in this section.
You should have 55 sts.

2. Colour Ridge Section

Row 1 with CC
(RS): Sl1 wyif, kfb, k to 1 st before m, kfb, SM, sl1 wyib, SM, kfb, k to the last 2 sts, kfb, k1. (4 sts inc'd)
Slide sts to other end of the circular needles. Do not turn work, you will be working the RS again.

Row 2 with MC
(RS): Sl1 wyif, k to m, SM, k1, SM, k to end. Turn work.

Row 3 with CC
(WS): Sl1 wyif, kfb, k to 1 st before m, kfb, SM, sl1 wyif, SM, kfb, k to last 2 sts, kfb, k1. (4 sts inc'd)

Slide sts to other end of the circular needles. Do not turn work, you will be working the WS again.

Row 4 with MC
(WS): Sl1 wyif, k to m, SM, p1, SM, k to end.

One colour ridge completed.

Repeat rows 1–4 twice more. 12 rows worked in total in this section. You should have 79 sts.

Carry CC yarn up the sides for the Garter Section or cut. See Notes for more details.

Continue alternating Garter and Colour Ridge Sections in the following sequence:

3. Garter Section

Repeat rows 1–2, 5 times.
You should have 99 sts.

4. Colour Ridge Section w/CC

Repeat rows 1–4, 4 times.
You should have 131 sts.

5. Garter Section

Repeat rows 1–2, 5 times.
You should have 151 sts.

6. Colour Ridge Section w/CC

Repeat rows 1–4 twice.
You should have 167 sts.

7. Garter Section

Repeat rows 1–2, 5 times.
You should have 187 sts.

8. Colour Ridge Section w/CC

Repeat rows 1–4, 4 times.
You should have 219 sts.

9. Garter Section

Repeat rows 1–2, 5 times.
You should have 239 sts.

10. Colour Ridge Section w/CC

Repeat rows 1–4 twice.
You should have 255 sts.

11. Garter Section

Repeat rows 1–2, 5 times.
You should have 275 sts.

12. Colour Ridge Section w/CC

Repeat rows 1–4, 3 times.
You should have 299 sts.

Size 1 only
Continue to Bind Off.

13. Garter Section

Repeat rows 1–2, 5 times.
You should have 319 sts.

14. Colour Section Section w/CC

Repeat rows 1–4, 4 times.
You should have 351 sts.

Bind-Off

The following bind-off method is suggested for a loose bind-off.
With CC, *k2tog tbl, move remaining st back to left-hand needle*, repeat *–* to end. Thread tail through last st and gently pull tight.

FINISHING

Weave in ends. Wet block to measurements.

Tuuli Huhtala

31 Viikka

SUPER EASY!

Viikka is a visually stunning but easy-to-knit ribbed hat. The 3D look is created with changing ribbing sections. The brim can be folded once or twice, whichever you prefer.

SIZES

1 (2, 3)

To fit a head circumference of approx. 20–21 (21–23, 23–25)" / 51–53 (53–58.5, 58.5–63.5) cm.

FINISHED MEASUREMENTS

Circumference: 15 (15.5, 16.5)" / 37.5 (40, 42.5) cm in ribbing (unstretched). **Height:** 11 (12, 13)" / 28.5 (30.5, 32.5) cm.

MATERIALS

Yarn: 1 skein of Tandem by West Wool (90% Falkland merino, 10% Texel, 252 yds / 230 m – 100 g), colourway True Blue.

If you decide to use another yarn, you will need approx. 219 (230, 246) yds / 200 (210, 225) m DK-weight yarn.

Needles: US 2.5 / 3 mm DPNs. Alternatively, 16" / 40 cm or 32" / 80 cm circular needles if using the Magic-Loop Method.

Notions: Stitch marker.

GAUGE

32 sts x 30 rnds to 4" / 10 cm in 2 x 2 Ribbing (unstretched), after blocking.

NOTES

You can find the abbreviations and detailed instructions for techniques used in this pattern in the Abbreviations (pp. 20–23) and Techniques (pp. 15–19) sections.

Slip markers as you come across them.

CONSTRUCTION

This hat is knitted in 2 x 2 Ribbing in the rnd from the brim up. There are 4 horizontal sections and the crown decrease. Sections 1, 3 and the crown section begin with knit sts, sections 2 and 4 with purl sts.

DIRECTIONS

SECTION 1

Cast on 120 (128, 136) sts with preferred cast-on method, such as the German-Twisted Cast-On which creates a stretchy edge (you can find tutorials online). If you use DPNs, divide sts to needles as follows: 32+28+32+28 (32+32+32+32, 32+36+32+36) sts. Join to work in the rnd being careful not to twist sts. Place a marker for the beginning of the rnd (BOR).

Rnd 1: *K2, p2*, repeat *–* to end.
Repeat this rnd for 2 x 2 Ribbing until the work measures 2 (2, 2.5)" / 5 (5.5, 6) cm.

SECTION 2

Rnd 1: *P2, k2*, repeat *–* to end.
Repeat this rnd for 2 x 2 Ribbing until the work measures 4 (4.5, 4.5)" / 10 (11, 12) cm.

SECTION 3

Rnd 1: *K2, p2*, repeat *–* to end.
Repeat this rnd for 2 x 2 Ribbing until the work measures 6 (6.5, 7)" / 15 (16.5, 18) cm.

SECTION 4

Rnd 1: *P2, k2*, repeat *–* to end.
Repeat this rnd for 2 x 2 Ribbing until the work measures 8 (8.5, 9.5)" / 20 (22, 24) cm.

CROWN

Next, you will work the crown with decreases.

Size 1 only
Decreases begin on rnd 11 (6 decrease points).
Rnds 1–10: *K2, p2*, repeat *–* to end.
Rnd 11: *[K2, p2], repeat [–] twice more, k2, p 2 sts together (p2tog)*, repeat *–* twice more. *K2, p2*, repeat *–* twice more. Repeat from the beginning once more. (6 sts dec'd) (114 sts remain: 30+27+30+27 sts)
Rnd 12: *[K2, p2], repeat [–] twice more, k1, p2tog*, repeat *–* twice more. *K2, p2*, repeat *–* twice more. Repeat from the beginning once more. (6 sts dec'd) (108 sts remain: 28+26+28+26 sts)
Rnd 13: *[K2, p2], repeat [–] twice more, p2tog*, repeat *–* twice more. *K2, p2*, repeat *–* twice more. Repeat from the beginning once more. (6 sts dec'd) (102 sts remain: 26+25+26+25 sts)
Rnd 14: *[K2, p2], repeat [–] once more, k2, p1, p2tog*, repeat *–* twice more. *K2, p2*, repeat *–* twice more. Repeat from the beginning once more. (6 sts dec'd) (96 sts remain: 24+24+24+24 sts)

Size 2 only
Decreases begin on rnd 11 (8 decrease points).
Rnds 1–10: *K2, p2*, repeat *–* to end.
Rnd 11: *[K2, p2], repeat [–] twice more, k2, p2tog*, repeat *–* to end. (8 sts dec'd) (120 sts remain: 30+30+30+30 sts)
Rnd 12: *[K2, p2], repeat [–] twice more, k1, p2tog*, repeat *–* to end. (8 sts dec'd) (112 sts remain: 28+28+28+28 sts)
Rnd 13: *[K2, p2], repeat [–] twice more, p2tog*, repeat *–* to end. (8 sts dec'd) (104 sts remain: 26+26+26+26 sts)
Rnd 14: *[K2, p2], repeat [–] once more, k2, p1, p2tog*, repeat *–* to end. (8 sts dec'd) (96 sts remain: 24+24+24+24 sts)

Size 3 only
Decreases begin on rnd 7 (2 decrease points) and on rnd 11 (8 decrease points).
Rnds 1–6: *K2, p2*, repeat *–* to end.
Rnd 7: *[K2, p2], repeat [–] 15 times more, k2, p2tog*, repeat *–* once more. (2 sts dec'd) (134 sts remain: 32+35+32+35 sts)
Rnd 8: *[K2, p2], repeat [–] 15 times more, k1, p2tog*, repeat *–* once more. (2 sts dec'd) (132 sts remain: 32+34+32+34 sts)
Rnd 9: *[K2, p2], repeat [–] 15 times more, p2tog*, repeat *–* once more. (2 sts dec'd) (130 sts remain: 32+33+32+33 sts)
Rnd 10: *[K2, p2], repeat [–] 14 times more, k2, p1, p2tog*, repeat *–* once more. (2 sts dec'd) (128 sts remain: 32+32+32+32 sts)
Rnds 11–14: As size 2. (32 sts dec'd) (96 sts remain: 24+24+24+24 sts)

All sizes
(8 decrease points)
Rnds 15–25: Use DPNs or divide the sts with st markers into 4 sections with 24 sts in each (4 x 24 sts). Continue to work in 2 x 2 Ribbing. Decrease on every rnd working a p2tog in the middle (work decreases 2 sts before the middle) and at the end of every needle/section until 8 sts (4 x 2 sts) remain. Cut yarn. Thread the tail through the remaining sts. Pull tight to close the crown.

FINISHING

Weave in ends. Wet block or steam. The hat will get its final shape and look when worn.

Elena Solier Jansà

32 Brizna

This boxy sweater is comfortable to wear. The Slipped-Stitch Rib at the sweater's sides ensures an intuitive and engaging knit. Which is your favourite – the earthy green or the perky red?

SIZES

1 (2, 3, 4, 5) (6, 7, 8)

Recommended ease: 7.75–9.75" / 20–25 cm of positive ease.

FINISHED MEASUREMENTS

Chest Circumference: 42.25 (46, 50.75, 54.5, 61.25) (65, 68.75, 72.5)" / 106 (115.5, 127, 136.5, 153) (162.5, 172, 181) cm.
Upper Sleeve Circumference: 12.75 (14, 15, 16.5, 17.75) (18.75, 20.25, 20.75)" / 32 (35.5, 37.5, 41, 44.5) (47, 50.5, 52) cm.
Neck Width: 10.5 (10.5, 11, 11, 11.5) (11.5, 11.5, 11.5)" / 26.5 (26.5, 27.5, 27.5, 29) (29, 29, 29) cm.
Length from Underarm to Hem: 14.25" / 36 cm.

MATERIALS

Yarn:
Green sample
8 (9, 10, 11, 13) (14, 15, 16) skeins of Pastora by Xolla (100% Ripollesa Wool, 142 yds / 130 m – 50 g), colourway Molsa.

Red sample (without pockets)
4 (4, 5, 5, 6) (6, 7, 7) hanks of Corrie Worsted by La Bien Aimée (75% Falkland Corriedale, 25% Gotland wool, 250 yds / 230 m – 100 g), colourway Coquelicot.
2 (2, 2, 2, 3) (3, 3, 3) hanks of Mohair Silk by La Bien Aimée (70% mohair, 30% silk, 547 yds / 500 m – 50 g), colourway Aimée's Flashy Lipstick.
The red sample is worked with both yarns held together.

If you decide to use another yarn, you will need approx. 1140 (1280, 1420, 1560, 1850) (1990, 2130, 2270) yds / 1040 (1170, 1300, 1430, 1690) (1820, 1950, 2080) m of DK or worsted-weight yarn.

Needles: US 7 / 4.5 mm 32" or 40" / 80 or 100 cm circular needles (for body and sleeves), US 5 / 3.75 mm 32" or 40" / 80 or 100 cm circular needles (for hem, cuff and pockets) and an extra US 7 / 4.5 mm needle (for 3-Needle Bind-Off).

Notions: Two pieces of waste yarn of about 12" / 30 cm in a contrasting colour, stitch markers, stitch holders or waste yarn.

GAUGE

For Body

17 sts x 28 rds to 4" / 10 cm on US 7 / 4.5 mm needles in Stockinette Stitch in the rnd, after blocking.

For Pockets

19 sts x 32 rows to 4" / 10 cm on US 5 / 3.75 mm needles in Stockinette Stitch knitted flat, after blocking.

STITCH PATTERNS

Slipped-Stitch Ribbing

Worked in the rnd
Rnd 1: *P2, k1*, repeat *-* to 2 sts before end, p2.
Rnd 2: *P2, sl1 pwise wyib*, repeat *-* to 2 sts before end, p2.

Worked flat
Row 1 (WS): *K2, sl1 pwise wyif*, repeat *-* to 2 sts before end, k2.
Row 2 (RS): *P2, k1*, repeat *-* to 2 sts before end, p2.

NOTES

You can find the abbreviations and detailed instructions for techniques used in this pattern in the Abbreviations (pp. 20–23) and Techniques (pp. 15–19) sections.

Slip markers as you come across them.

CONSTRUCTION

This sweater is worked from bottom to top, first in the round and then flat for the front and back. A slipped-stitch rib runs up the sides of the sweater. The shoulders are joined with a 3-Needle Bind-Off. Patch pockets are knitted separately and attached using the Mattress Stitch Method. You can also leave out the pockets, as in the red sample.

DIRECTIONS

HEM

With US 5 / 3.75 mm needles, cast on 180 (196, 216, 232, 260) (276, 292, 308) sts using the Long-Tail Cast-On Method or method of choice. Place m for the beginning of rnd (BOR) and join to work in the rnd being careful not to twist sts.

Rnd 1: *K1, p1*, repeat *-* to end. Continue in the established 1 x 1 Ribbing for 8 rnds in total or until hem measures 1.25" / 3 cm.

BODY

Change to US 7 / 4.5 mm needles and start working the body. You will work a section of the Slipped-Stitch Rib at the sides and Stockinette Stitch for front and back.

On the next row, you will place a lifeline which is a piece of yarn that runs through every st of a row. In this pattern, the pocket placements are marked with it. Place the lifeline as follows: Thread your tapestry needle with a piece of yarn in a contrasting colour, then thread the tapestry needle through the live sts of your left-hand needle. Continue working normally, pretending that your lifeline is not there, but being careful not to knit it accidentally.

Set-up rnd: RM, k1, PM for new BOR, *add lifeline to the next k29 (29, 29, 29, 35) (35, 35, 35) sts, k29 (29, 29, 29, 35) (35, 35, 35) sts, PM, k61 (69, 79, 87, 95) (103, 111, 119) sts*, PM, repeat *-* to end.

Rnd 1: *[P2, k1] 9 (9, 9, 9, 11) (11, 11, 11) times, p2, SM, k to m, SM*, repeat *-* once more.
Rnd 2: *[P2, sl1 wyib] 9 (9, 9, 9, 11) (11, 11, 11) times, p2, SM, k to m, SM*, repeat *-* once more.

Repeat rnds 1–2 until work measures 14.25" / 36 cm from the cast-on edge.

SEPARATE FRONT AND BACK

You should have 29 (29, 29, 29, 35) (35, 35, 35) sts at the sides, 9 (9, 9, 9, 11) (11, 11, 11) of which are slipped sts. Now we are going to bind off the slipped st of the centre from every side panel, hold the back sts on a piece of waste yarn and continue knitting the front flat.

Set-up rnd: *P2, k1*, repeat *-* 4 (4, 4, 4, 5) (5, 5, 5) times, p2, bind off 1 st, *p2, k1* 4 (4, 4, 4, 5) (5, 5, 5) times, p2, SM, k to m, SM, *p2, k1*, repeat *-* 5 (5, 5, 5, 6) (6, 6, 6) times. Now transfer the next 89 (97, 107, 115, 129) (137, 145, 153) sts to a st holder or a piece of waste yarn and hold for back. Turn work.

FRONT

You will now work the front back and forth. The back will be worked later.
Row 1 (WS): Bind off 1 st, *k2, sl1 wyif*, repeat *-* 4 (4, 4, 4, 5) (5, 5, 5) times, k2, SM, p to m, SM, *k2, sl1 wyif*, repeat *-* 4 (4, 4, 4, 5) (5, 5, 5) times, k2.
Row 2 (RS): *P2, k1*, repeat *-* 4 (4, 4, 4, 5) (5, 5, 5) times, p2, SM, k to m, SM, *p2, k1* 4 (4, 4, 4, 5) (5, 5, 5) times, p2.
Row 3 (WS): *K2, sl1 wyif*, repeat *-* 4 (4, 4, 4, 5) (5, 5, 5) times, k2, SM, p to m, SM, *k2, sl1 wyif*, repeat *-* 4 (4, 4, 4, 5) (5, 5, 5) times, k2.
Repeat rows 2–3 until piece measures 6.25 (6.75, 7, 8, 8.75) (9.5, 10, 10.25)" / 16 (17, 18, 20.5, 22) (24, 25.5, 26) cm from underarm.

Repeat row 2 once more.

FRONT SHOULDER SHAPING

You will now be using short rows to shape the shoulders in order to get a more comfortable wear. Instructions for German Short Rows are given but you can use your preferred method. Keep working in pattern and in Stockinette Stitch, slipping markers as you encounter them.

At the end of the shoulder shaping you should work the double sts (DS) created with the short rows. If the double st is a knit st (or a slipped knit st), knit the double st. If the double st is a purl st, purl the double st.

Short row 1 (WS): Work in pattern until 1 (2, 2, 3, 4) (4, 5, 5) st(s) remain, turn work.
Short row 2 (RS): Make DS (MDS), work in pattern until 1 (2, 2, 3, 4) (4, 5, 5) st(s) remain, turn work.
Short row 3: MDS, work in pattern until 1 (2, 2, 3, 4) (4, 5, 5) st(s) remain before last DS, turn work.
Short row 4: MDS, work in pattern until 1 (2, 2, 3, 4) (4, 5, 5) st(s) remain before DS, turn work.
Short row 5: MDS, work in pattern until 2 (2, 3, 3, 4) (4, 5, 5) sts remain before DS, turn work.
Short row 6: MDS, knit to m, work in pattern until 2 (2, 3, 3, 4) (4, 5, 5) sts remain before last DS, turn work.
Repeat short rows 5–6 once more.

Short row 9: MDS, work in pattern until 2 (2, 3, 3, 4) (5, 5, 6) sts remain before last DS, turn work.
Short row 10: MDS, work in pattern until 2 (2, 3, 3, 4) (5, 5, 6) sts remain before last DS, turn work.
Repeat short rows 9–10 once more.

Short row 13: MDS, work in pattern until 2 (3, 3, 4, 4) (5, 5, 6) sts remain before last DS, turn work.
Short row 14: MDS, work in pattern until 2 (3, 3, 4, 4) (5, 5, 6) sts remain before last DS, turn work.
Repeat short rows 13–14 once more.

Next row (WS): MDS, work in pattern to the end of row, working DS as you encounter them.
Next row (RS): Work in pattern to the end of row, working DS and RM as you encounter them.

Cut yarn leaving a tail of about 50" / 127 cm. Place front sts to a st holder or a piece of waste yarn.

BACK

You will now work the back.
Transfer back sts to US 7 / 4.5 mm needles. You are going to start from the WS.

Row 1 (WS): *K2, sl1 wyif*, repeat *-* 4 (4, 4, 4, 5) (5, 5, 5) times, k2, SM, p to m, SM, *k2, sl1 wyif*, repeat *-* 4 (4, 4, 4, 5) (5, 5, 5) times, k2.
Row 2 (RS): *P2, k1*, repeat *-* 4 (4, 4, 4, 5) (5, 5, 5) times, p2, SM, k to m, SM, *p2, k1*, repeat *-* 4 (4, 4, 4, 5) (5, 5, 5) times, p2.
Repeat rows 1–2 until piece measures 6.25 (6.75, 7, 8, 8.75) (9.5, 10, 10.25)" / 16 (17, 18, 20.5, 22) (24, 25.5, 26) cm from underarm.

BACK SHOULDER SHAPING

Repeat front shoulder shaping instructions for back, keeping sts on the needles.

JOIN SHOULDERS

Place front sts onto a spare needle. With RS facing and attached yarn, bind off the first 22 (26, 30, 34, 40) (44, 48, 52) sts for front with corresponding sts for back using the 3-Needle Bind-Off Method. Pull and cut yarn leaving 6" / 15 cm tail.

Repeat instructions for second shoulder. You should have 45 (45, 47, 47, 49) (49, 49, 49) sts for neck on each needle.

NECK BIND-OFF

We now have two needles, one for the front and one for the back. We are going to bind off all sts. In order to close the gap that will naturally form between the two needles, we will pick up and knit two sts at each shoulder and bind them off as a normal st.

With RS facing, attach yarn and bind off all sts for front, working a regular bind-off. *Pick up and knit 1 st, bind off this st*, repeat *-*. Continue binding off for back. *Pick up and knit 1 st, bind off this st*, repeat *-* to end.

SLEEVES

Beginning at underarm and using US 7 / 4.5 mm needles, pick up and k 54 (60, 64, 70, 76) (80, 86, 88) sts around the armhole (approx. 2 sts in every 3 rows), PM for BOR and join to work in the rnd.

Work 4 rnds in Stockinette Stitch (k all sts).

Decrease rnd: K1, k2tog, k to last 3 sts, ssk, k1. (2 sts dec'd)

Repeat the decrease rnd every 12 (10, 8, 7, 6) (6, 5, 5) rnds 8 (10, 12, 14, 17) (17, 20, 20) more times. You should have 36 (38, 38, 40, 40) (44, 44, 46) sts.

Continue knitting until the sleeve measures 16" / 40.5 cm.

Cuff
Change to US 5 / 3.75 mm needles.

Rnd 1: *K1, p1*, repeat *-* to end.
Continue in the established 1x1 Ribbing for 8 rnds in total or until cuff measures 1.25" / 3 cm.

Repeat instructions for second sleeve.

PATCH POCKETS

Identify the 29 (29, 29, 29, 35) (35, 35, 35) sts from one of your life lines. With US 5 / 3.75 mm needles, pick up the right leg of every "v" of those 29 (29, 29, 29, 35) (35, 35, 35) sts plus one stitch at the right and one at the left. You should have 31 (31, 31, 31, 37) (37, 37, 37) sts. Remove the life line and attach yarn leaving 12" / 30 cm tail.

Row 1: K to end.
Row 2: P to end.
Repeat rows 1–2 a total of 16 times (32 rows worked) or until work measures 4" / 10 cm.

Bind off all sts using the 2-Stitch I-Cord Bind-Off. This method is suggested, as they give a neat and sturdy finish. Alternatively, you can bind off all sts using a regular bind-off method. If so, be sure to bind off tightly so the pockets do not turn out too roomy.

Work a 2-Stitch I-Cord Bind-Off as follows: Cast on 1 st using the Backwards Loop Cast-On Method. *K1, k2tog tbl. 2 sts on right-hand needle. Transfer those sts back to left-hand needle pwise*. Repeat *–*.

Next, seam the right side of the pocket using Mattress Stitch and the tail at the right bottom as follows: Identify the column of knit sts at the right of the textured section, align the pocket with the sweater. You are going to seam the first st of the pocket with that first column. If you gently tug on the right and left edge of your knit piece, you will see an horizontal bar between the two "v" legs; you will pick a bar from each piece and make it look like one knit piece. Thread yarn and draw the needle under the first bar from the sweater, right above the stitch where you started knitting the pocket.

Next, draw the needle under the first bar from the pocket, making sure it is the outermost column; it tends to curl. Continue working vertically, taking the needle back to each piece and drawing the needle under the bar just above the last one picked. Be sure to pull to close and the seam will be invisible.

Finally, when you encounter the i-cord, draw the needle under the two stitches from the cast-on / bind-off and lead the thread to the WS of the sweater.

Attach the yarn at the left bottom and seam the left side of the pocket using Mattress Stitch.

Repeat instructions for the second pocket.

FINISHING

Weave in ends. Wet block to measurements.

Jonna Hietala

33 Softie

Softie is Jonna Hietala's interpretation of the perfect hat. It's super warm, holds its shape and is firm enough for a good, long-lasting accessory. And best of all: it doesn't itch.

SIZE

1 (2, 3)

To fit a head circumference of approx. 20–21 (21–23, 23–25)" / 51–53 (53–58.5, 58.5–63.5) cm.

FINISHED MEASUREMENTS

Circumference (without stretching): 15 (15.75, 17.5)" / 38 (40, 44.5) cm.
Height (without brim folded): 13" / 32 cm.
Note! Because the hat stretches, its circumference is significantly smaller than your head's circumference.

MATERIALS

Yarn: 2 (2, 3) balls of Sandnes Garn Børstet Alpakka (96% alpaca, 4% nylon, 120 yds / 110 m – 50 g), colourways 5043 (lilac), 2112 (yellow), 4033 (dusty pink) and 9062 (green). You can also substitute one skein of Børstet Alpakka with Sandnes Garn Kos (9% wool, 62% baby alpaca, 29% nylon, 164 yds / 150 m – 50 g).

The hat is worked with two strands of yarn held together throughout the pattern.

If you decide to use another yarn, you will need approx. 229 (240, 267) yds / 210 (220, 244) m bulky-weight yarn.

Needles: US 8 / 5 mm 16" / 40 cm circular needles (or longer if you use the magic loop method) or DPNs.

Notions: Stitch marker.

GAUGE

18 sts x 18 rnds to 4" / 10 cm in 1 x 1 Ribbing, after blocking.

NOTES

You can find the abbreviations and detailed instructions for techniques used in this pattern in the Abbreviations (pp. 20–23) and Techniques (pp. 15–19) sections.

Slip markers as you come across them.

Knitted hats tend to stretch out and no one likes a hat that falls off one's head or doesn't stay in place. There are several reasons why a knitted hat doesn't hold its shape but the material is a big factor. Sheep's wool (particularly merino) is elastic and tends to hold its shape well, but for example silk mohair and 100% alpaca yarn are more prone to stretch with time. Thus, keep in mind the characteristics of the fibre when choosing yarn for your hat.

CONSTRUCTION

This hat is knitted seamlessly in the round from bottom to top. It is worked with two strands of yarn held together in 1 x 1 Ribbing and is designed with a foldable rib.

MODIFICATIONS

It is incredibly easy to adjust the hat size if needed: simply cast on a couple of stitches more or less. Just make sure to cast on a stitch count divisible by 4.

DIRECTIONS

Cast on 68 (72, 80) sts using the Long-Tail Cast-On or preferably the German Twisted Cast-On Method which creates a stretchy edge and is perfect for hats (you can find tutorials online).

Row 1: *K1, p1*, repeat *–* to end. PM and join to knit in the rnd being careful not to twist sts.
Continue in the established 1 x 1 Ribbing until the hat measures approx. 11" / 28 cm (approx. 52 rnds in total).

CROWN DECREASES

1st decrease rnd: *K3tog, p1*, repeat *–* to end. You should have 34 (36, 40) sts left on the needles.
Note! When doing the k3tog decreases, be careful not to drop the middle st.

Continue to work in 1 x 1 Ribbing for a total of 5 rnds.

2nd decrease rnd: *K2tog*, repeat *–* to the end. You should have 17 (18, 20) sts left on the needles.

Break yarn leaving a 8" / 20 cm long tail. Thread the tail through the remaining sts. Pull tight to close the crown.

At this point the hat may seem too tight and short but it will grow once soaked and blocked.

FINISHING

Weave in ends to the WS of the fabric. Wet block to measurements.

34 Cité

Cité is a modern, playful sweater with different textures and colours and an interesting construction. The pattern offers more of a challenge, but just take it one step at a time.

SIZES

1 (2, 3, 4, 5) (6, 7, 8)

Recommended ease: 13–15" / 33–38 cm of positive ease.

FINISHED MEASUREMENTS

Chest Circumference: 49 (53.5, 58, 60.25, 64.5) (67.75, 70, 74.5)" / 123 (134, 145, 150.5, 161.5) (169.5, 175, 186) cm.
Body Length: 19.75 (20, 20.75, 21, 21.75) (22.25, 22.75, 23.25)" / 50 (51, 52.5, 53.5, 55) (56.5, 58, 59) cm.
Sleeve Length: 9.5 (8.5, 7.75, 7.5, 6.5) (6, 5.75, 5)" / 23.5 (21.5, 19.5, 18.5, 16.5) (15, 14.5, 12.5) cm.
Sleeve Circumference: 14 (15, 15.5, 17.5, 18) (19.5, 21.5, 23)" / 36 (38, 39, 44, 46) (50, 55, 58) cm.

MATERIALS

Yarn: Cor by Olann (100% fine Merino, 142–197 yds / 130–180 m – 100 g)
Colour A: 3 (3, 3, 3, 3) (4, 4, 4) skeins of colourway Priestess.
Colour B: 4 (4, 4, 5, 5) (5, 5, 6) skeins of colourway Luna.
Colour C: 2 (2, 2, 2, 2) (3, 3, 3) skeins of colourway Froth.

Cloudy by Olann (74% Baby Suri Alpaca, 26% Mulberry Silk, 328 yds / 300 m – 50 g)
Colour D: 1 (1, 1, 1, 1) (2, 2, 2) skein(s) of colourway Atone.

If you decide to use another yarn, you will need approx.
Colour A: 347 (364, 380, 394, 412) (427, 443, 454) yds / 317 (333, 348, 360, 377) (390, 405, 415) m of aran-weight yarn.
Colour B: 487 (537, 595, 615, 675) (721, 743, 798) yds / 445 (491, 544, 562, 617) (659, 679, 730) m of aran-weight yarn.
Colour C: 286 (308, 328, 366, 390) (429, 473, 514) yds / 262 (282, 300, 335, 357) (392, 433, 470) m of aran-weight yarn.
Colour D: 224 (241, 257, 287, 306) (337, 371, 403) yds / 205 (220, 235, 262, 280) (308, 339, 369) m of lace-weight yarn.

Needles: US 9 / 5.5 mm 32" / 80 cm or longer circular needle (as main needle) and spare needles in the same size for the 3-Needle Bind-Off.
Note! Having to deal with 4 balls of yarn, you may find it more convenient to use two circular needles, switching from one to the other as you would with two straight needles.
US 10 / 6 mm 32" / 80 cm or longer circular needles (for the top band worked with 2 yarns held together).

Notions: 4 locking stitch markers, 2 stitch holders or waste yarn, blunt tapestry needle, a length of fingering yarn for seaming (in an approaching colour to Colour A or Colour B).

GAUGE

14.5 sts x 24 rows to 4" / 10 cm on US 9 / 5.5 mm needles in Stockinette Stitch, after blocking.

NOTES

You can find the abbreviations and detailed instructions for techniques used in this pattern in the Abbreviations (pp. 20–23) and Techniques (pp. 15–19) sections.

Slip markers as you come across them.

CONSTRUCTION

The lower part of the body and sleeves are worked in intarsia in colour A (sides) and colour B (centre). The top band is worked in a third colour with two yarns held together in slipped ribbing, giving a soft touch to this geometrical garment.

The body is worked flat from bottom to top in one piece with colours A and B. It is worked straight up to the underarm increases, then stitches are cast on for the front half of the sleeves. While the rest of the stitches are put on hold, the whole front body is worked straight and finished with the top band in slipped ribbing. The back panel is seamed to the left side. Stitches are picked up along the underarm cast-on and the complete back is worked in the same fashion as the front. The front and back are assembled at the shoulders with a 3-Needle Bind-Off in contrasting colour.

MODIFICATIONS

This sweater will also look fantastic when worked only in one yarn and colour.

DIRECTIONS

With US 9 / 5.5 mm needles and Colour A, cast on 25 (27, 31, 31, 33) (35, 37, 39) sts with the Long-Tail Cast-On Method or method of choice. Join Colour B and cast on 65 (71, 75, 79, 85) (89, 91, 97) sts. Join second ball of Colour A and cast on 24 (26, 30, 30, 32) (34, 36, 38) sts. Join second ball of Colour B and cast on 66 (72, 76, 80, 86) (90, 92, 98) sts. You should have 180 (196, 212, 220, 236) (248, 256, 272) sts on your needles.

Note! You will work the sts in the colour they were cast on in. At each colour change, cross working yarn over next thread on the WS to ensure a clean transition line. On the first and second rows, take care to interlock threads snuggly at each colour change to avoid a gap.

LOWER BODY

Next, you will work the hem.
Set-up row (WS): With Colour B, *p1, k1* to Colour A, switch to Colour A, p24 (26, 30, 30, 32) (34, 36, 38), switch to Colour B, p1, *k1, p1* to Colour A, switch to Colour A, p25 (27, 31, 31, 33) (35, 37, 39).
Row 1 (RS): K1, p all subsequent Colour A sts and k all Colour B sts.
Row 2 (WS): P all Colour B sts, k all Colour A sts to last st, p1.
Repeat rows 1–2 until body measures 11 (10.75, 11.25, 10.5, 11) (10.75, 10.25, 10)" / 28 (28, 29, 27.5, 28) (27.5, 26.5, 26) cm, or 8.75 (9.25, 9.5, 10.5, 10.75) (11.5, 12.5, 13.25)" / 22 (23, 23.5, 26, 27) (29, 31.5, 33) cm less than desired length, ending with a WS row.

UNDERARM INCREASES

Next row (WS) (placing the markers): With Colour B, p to Colour A, switch to Colour A, k12 (13, 15, 15, 16) (17, 18, 19), PM, 12 (13, 15, 15, 16) (17, 18, 19), switch to

Colour B, p to Colour A, switch to Colour A, k12 (13, 15, 15, 16) (17, 18, 19), PM, k to last st, p1.
Next row (RS) (increase row): With Colour A k1, p to 2 sts before side marker, pfb, p1, SM, p1, pfb, p to Colour B, k Colour B sts, with Colour A p to 2 sts before side marker, pfb, p1, SM, p1, pfb, p to Colour B, k Colour B sts to end. (4 sts inc'd)
Next row: Work as established to end.
Repeat these two rows 4 more times. You should have 200 (216, 232, 240, 256) (268, 276, 292) sts.

SLEEVES AND UPPER BODY

FRONT

Continue with working the front.
Next row (RS): K1, p to side m, RM, transfer 18 (19, 21, 21, 22) (23, 24, 25) sts just worked to stitch holder or waste yarn. With Colour A, cast on 29 (26, 23, 22, 19) (17, 16, 13) sts using the Purled Cast-On Method. [With yarn in front, insert the right-hand needle purlwise into the first st on the left-hand needle. Wrap and draw a loop as if to purl but instead of dropping the st off the left-hand needle, place the loop just created onto the left-hand needle. (1 st cast on)] K2, p next Colour A sts, k Colour B sts, p next Colour A sts to side m, RM, transfer all remaining sts to spare needle or waste yarn (keeping Colour B yarn attached), turn work.
Next row (WS): With Colour A, cast on 29 (26, 23, 22, 19) (17, 16, 13) sts using the Knitted Cast-On Method. P2, k next Colour A sts, p Colour B sts, k next Colour A sts to last 2 sts, sl1 wyif, p1.

You should have 157 (159, 161, 163, 165) (167, 169, 171) sts in total: 46 (44, 43, 42, 40) (39, 39, 37) Colour A sts, 65 (71, 75, 79, 85) (89, 91, 97) Colour B sts and 46 (44, 43, 42, 40) (39, 39, 37) Colour A sts.

Next row (RS): Sl1 wyib, k1, p Colour A sts, k Colour B sts, p Colour A sts to last 2 sts, sl1 wyib, k1.

Next row (WS): Sl1 wyif, p1, k Colour A sts, p Colour B sts, k Colour A sts to last 2 sts, sl1 wyif, p1.

Repeat these last two rows until piece measures 3.75 (4, 4.25, 4.5, 4.75) (5, 5.5, 6)" / 9.5 (10, 11, 11.5, 12) (12.5, 14, 15) cm from sleeve cast-on, ending with a RS row.

With WS facing, break first Colour A and Colour B yarn, leave last Colour A ball attached at the edge.

Front Top Band

The front top band will be worked with the aran yarn in Colour C held together with Colour D. The two selvedge sts in Colour A will be maintained on each side.

Switch to US 10 / 6 mm needles.

Note! In the subsequent rows, work selvedge sts between { } in Colour A.

Next row (WS): {Sl1 wyif, p1}, with Colours C+D p to last 2 sts, join Colour A, {sl1 wyif, p1}.

Next row (RS): {Sl1 wyib, k1}, with Colours C+D *p1, sl1*, repeat *–* to last 3 sts, p1, {sl1 wyib, k1}.

Next row (WS): {Sl1 wyif, p1}, with Colours C+D *k1, p1*, repeat *–* to last 3 sts, k1, {sl1 wyif, p1}.

Repeat last two rows until piece measures 7 (7.5, 7.75, 8.75, 9) (9.75, 10.75, 11.5)" / 18 (19, 19.5, 22, 23) (25, 27.5, 29) cm from sleeve cast-on, ending with a WS row. Cut Colour A yarn at the left side (with RS facing) and cut Colour C yarns. Colour A yarn remains attached at the RS.

Switch to US 9 / 5.5 mm needles.

Next row (RS): K all sts with Colour A.

Transfer all 157 (159, 161, 163, 165) (167, 169, 171) sts to spare needle or waste yarn, keeping Colour A yarn attached (to be used later for 3-Needle Bind-Off). The sts on hold are the shoulder and front neck sts.

BACK

Next, you will work the back.

Thread a tapestry needle with a length of fingering yarn. Seam the back Colour B panel to the side Colour A panel using the Mixed Mattress Stitch Method: *Insert the tapestry needle under the horizontal bar that runs between the first edge "V"s of the Stockinette panel and pull yarn through; insert needle under the first garter bar closest to the knit selvedge st of the Reversed Stockinette panel and pull yarn through.* Repeat *–*, working vertically along the two edges and progressing st by st. After a few inches / cms, gently pull the yarn to close the seam. Continue in this fashion to the end of the seam.

Return 101 (109, 117, 121, 129) (135, 139, 147) held back sts to main needle: 17 (18, 20, 20, 21) (22, 23, 24) Colour A sts, 66 (72, 76, 80, 86) (90, 92, 98) Colour B sts and 18 (19, 21, 21, 22) (23, 24, 25) Colour A sts. You have 2 sts in excess from the seam which will be decreased on the first row.

Set-up row (RS): Join Colour A. Starting at the right sleeve edge, pick up first selvedge st without knitting it, pick up and knit next selvedge st, pick up and p 27 (24, 21, 20, 17) (15, 14, 11) sts along cast-on right sleeve sts, insert the right-hand needle into garter bar between the right-hand needle and left-hand needle and purl it together with the next st, p next Colour A sts.

Working with attached Colour B, k Colour B sts to 2 sts before Colour A, k 2 sts together (k2tog).

Join new ball of Colour A. P 2 sts together (p2tog), p to last st, p2tog the last st with garter bar between the right-hand and left-hand needle, pick up and p 27 (24, 21, 20, 17) (15, 14, 11) sts along the cast-on left sleeve sts, pick up first selvedge st without knitting it, k last selvedge st.

You should have 157 (159, 161, 163, 165) (167, 169, 171) sts in total: 46 (44, 43, 42, 40) (39, 39, 37) Colour A sts, 65 (71, 75, 79, 85) (89, 91, 97) Colour B sts and 46 (44, 43, 42, 40) (39, 39, 37) Colour A sts.

Next row (WS): Sl1 wyif, p1, k Colour A sts, p Colour B sts, k Colour A sts to last 2 sts, sl1 wyif, p1.

Next row (RS): Sl1 wyib, k1, p Colour A sts, k Colour B sts, p Colour A sts to last 2 sts, sl1 wyib, k1.

Repeat these last two rows until piece measures 3.75 (4, 4.25, 4.5, 4.75) (5, 5.5, 6)" / 9.5 (10, 11, 11.5, 12) (12.5, 14, 15) cm from sleeve cast-on, ending with a RS row.

Break first Colour A and Colour B yarn, leave last Colour A ball attached at the edge.

Back Top Band

Switch to US 10 / 6 mm needles and work the back top band in the same fashion as for the front.

ASSEMBLE SHOULDERS AND SLEEVES

Return front sts to a spare needle. Place markers 60 (61, 61, 60, 61) (61, 61, 61) sts from each side edge of front and back [4 markers placed, 37 (37, 39, 43, 43) (45, 47, 49) sts between each pair of markers], WS of front and back are facing each other.

Shoulders

Assemble the sts for the left shoulder. With RS of front facing, starting at the left sleeve (at your right) and using Colour A yarn attached to back edge, bind off 59 (60, 60, 59, 60) (60, 60, 60) front and back sts using the 3-Needle Bind-Off Method. Remove the 2 markers you just reached. You have 1 st on the right-hand needle and 97 (98, 100, 103, 104) (106, 108, 110) sts left on both front and back needles. Transfer the st from the right-hand needle to a locking marker to keep it from unraveling.

Assemble the sts for the right shoulder. Now turn your work so that the back is facing. Starting at the right sleeve (at your right) and using Colour A yarn attached to front edge, bind off 59 (60, 60, 59, 60) (60, 60, 60) back and front sts using the Purled 3-Needle Bind-Off Method (worked like the regular 3-Needle Bind-Off but purl sts together instead of knitting them). Remove the 2 markers you just reached. You have 1 st on the right-hand needle and 37 (37, 39, 43, 43) (45, 47, 49) sts left on both front and back needles. Transfer the st from the right-hand needle to a locking marker to keep it from unraveling.

Neckline

At this point, try on the sweater to assess if you are happy with the fit of the neck opening. If needed, adjust it symmetrically.

Return the front live st from the locking marker to the right-hand needle and bind off all remaining front neck sts knitwise. Break yarn, pull the tail through the last st and fasten off. Proceed in the same fashion for the back. Thread tail to tapestry needle and close the neck opening neatly on both sides.

FINISHING

Weave in all ends. Wet block to measurements.

Natalya Berezynska

35 Knitword

This big, snuggly scarf features eye-catching KNIT letters. The repeated text is created with just knit and purl stitches, which means that the scarf is a great way to learn reading charts.

SIZE

One Size

FINAL MEASUREMENTS

Width: 12" / 30 cm.
Length: 98.5" / 246 cm.

MATERIALS

Yarn: 5 skeins of The Meri Wool by We Are Knitters (100% superwash merino, 149 yds / 136 m – 100 g), colourway Spotted Green.

If you decide to use another yarn, you will need approx. 740 yds / 677 m of chunky-weight yarn.

Needles: US 8 / 5 mm straight or circular needles.

Notions: Row counter (optional).

GAUGE

17 sts x 20 rows to 4" / 10 cm in Stockinette Stitch, after blocking.

NOTE

You can find the abbreviations and detailed instructions for techniques used in this pattern in the Abbreviations (pp. 20–23) and Techniques (pp. 15–19) sections.

Chart is read from bottom to top and from right to left on RS rows and from left to right on WS rows.

CONSTRUCTION

This scarf is worked from side to side from the bottom up. Letters are created with Stockinette Stitch on a Reverse Stockinette Stitch background. A border worked in Garter Stitch adds structure and prevents the edges from rolling.

MODIFICATIONS

The length is easily adjustable. Make fewer or more repeats to make the scarf shorter or longer. Make sure to always work a full 20-row repeat to keep the stitch pattern and text intact.

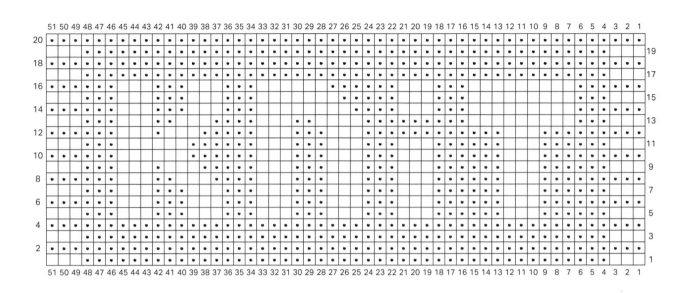

☐ RS: knit / WS: purl

• RS: purl / WS: knit

DIRECTIONS

Cast on 51 sts with Long-Tail Cast-On Method or method of choice.

GARTER BORDER 1

Knit 6 rows.

MAIN PART

You can work from written instructions below or from the chart.

Row 1 (RS): K3, p to last 3 sts, k3.
Row 2: K to end.
Rows 3–4: Repeat rows 1–2.
Row 5: K3, *p6, k3*, repeat *–* a total of 2 times, *p3, k3*, repeat *–* a total of 5 times.

Row 6: K6, *p3, k3*, repeat *–* a total of 4 times, *p3, k6*, repeat *–* a total of 2 times, k3.
Row 7: Repeat row 5.
Row 8: K6, p3, k2, p3, k1, *k3, p3*, repeat *–* a total of 3 times, k6, p3, k9.
Row 9: K3, *p6, k3*, repeat *–* a total of 2 times, *p3, k3*, repeat *–* a total of 2 times, p5, k3, p1, k3, p3, k3.
Row 10: K6, p6, k6, *p3, k3*, repeat *–* a total of 2 times, *p3, k6*, repeat *–* a total of 2 times, k3.
Row 11: K3, *p6, k3*, repeat *–* a total of 2 times, *p3, k3*, repeat *–* a total of 2 times, p6, k6, p3, k3.
Row 12: K6, p3, k1, p3, k5, *p3, k3*, repeat *–* a total of 2 times, k9, p3, k9.
Row 13: K3, p3, k9, p9, k4, p2, k3, p4, k3, p2, k3, p3, k3.
Row 14: K6, *p3, k3*, repeat *–* a total of 2 times, p8, k4, p3, k3, p9, k6.
Row 15: K3, p3, k9, p3, k3, p5, k7, *p3,

k3*, repeat *–* a total of 3 times.
Row 16: K6, *p3, k3*, repeat *–* a total of 2 times, p6, k6, p3, k3, p9, k6.
Rows 17–20: Repeat rows 1–2 twice. Repeat rows 1–20, 23 more times.

480 rows worked in total. The scarf measures approx. 97.25" / 243 cm.

GARTER BORDER 2

K 6 rows. Bind off all sts.

FINISHING

Weave in ends. Wet block to measurements.

Maija Kangasluoma

36 Elsa

The Elsa mittens feature a simple but beautiful check pattern. Thanks to a great fit, these are the perfect winter mittens – and when it gets really, really cold, wear two pairs!

SIZES

1 (2, 3)

To fit a hand circumference of approx. 7 (8, 8.5)" / 18 (20, 22) cm.

FINISHED MEASUREMENTS

Length from Cuff to Tip: 11 (11.5, 12)" / 28 (29, 30) cm.
Hand Circumference: 7 (8, 8.5)" / 18 (20, 22) cm.
Thumb Length: 3 (3, 3)" / 7 (7.5, 8) cm.

MATERIALS

Yarn: 2 skeins of Peer Gynt by Sandnes Garn (100% Norwegian wool, 100 yds / 91 m – 50 g), colourways 2122 Månestein (light yellow) and 3553 Stövet Plommerosa (pink).
Note! The largest size uses two full skeins of Peer Gynt. If you want to be extra sure

that you don't run out of yarn or want to make the cuff a bit longer, buy a third skein.

If you decide to use another yarn, you will need approx. 170 (184, 199) yds / 155 (168, 182) m of DK-weight yarn.

Needles: US 4 / 3.5 mm DPNs (set of 5). *Note!* The pattern is written for DPNs. You can also use circular needles but note that you need to take this into account when following the pattern.

Notions: A piece of waste yarn in a different colour.

GAUGE

22 sts x 40 rnds to 4" / 10 cm in Check Pattern, after blocking.

STITCH PATTERN

Check Pattern (in the rnd)
Knit and purl sts create a 2 x 2-st pattern.
Rnds 1 and 2: *P2, k2*, repeat *-* to end.
Rnds 3 and 4: *K2, p2*, repeat *-* to end.
Repeat rnds 1–4 for pattern.

NOTE

You can find the abbreviations and detailed instructions for techniques used in this pattern in the Abbreviations (pp. 20–23) and Techniques (pp. 15–19) sections.

CONSTRUCTION

These mittens are worked seamlessly in the round, beginning with the cuff. The cuff is in 2 x 2 Ribbing while the hand section features an all-over check pattern. The thumb opening is marked with waste yarn from which the stitches are picked up and knitted later.

DIRECTIONS

CUFF

Cast on 40 (44, 48) sts with the Long-Tail Cast-On Method or method of choice. Divide sts evenly on 4 DPNs, 10 (11, 12) sts on each. Join to knit in the rnd being careful not to twist sts. The beginning of the rnd (BOR) is between needle 1 and 4.

Work in 2 x 2 Ribbing as follows:
K2, p2, repeat *-* to end.
Continue to work in established ribbing until the cuff measures approx. 3.5" / 9 cm or desired length.

HAND

Work in Check Pattern for 20 (22, 24) rnds.

Create the thumb opening on rnd 21 (23, 25) as follows:

Left mitten
Work in established Check Pattern. Work sts on 1st needle. Work the first 2 sts of the 2nd needle. Work the next 7 (8, 9) sts with a waste yarn. Slip the waste yarn sts back onto the left-hand needle and work them again with the working yarn. Work the rnd to end in established Check Pattern.

Right mitten
Work in established Check Pattern. Work sts on 1st and 2nd needle. Work the first 2 sts of the 3rd needle. Work the next 7 (8, 9) sts with a waste yarn. Slip the waste yarn sts back onto the left-hand needle and work them again with the working yarn. Work the rnd to end in established Check Pattern.

Both mittens
Continue to work in established Check Pattern for 45 (47, 49) more rnds. The hand should now measure approx. 6.5 (7, 7)" / 16.5 (17.5, 18.5) cm or desired length.

DECREASES

Continue in established Check Pattern and start working decreases on the sides of the palm as follows: Work a k2tog tbl decrease (= k 2 sts together through the back loops) at the beginning of needles 1 and 3. Work a k2tog decrease (= k 2 sts together through the front loops) at the end of needles 2 and 4.

Note! Take the decreased sts into account when working the Check Pattern. Modify Check Pattern when necessary.

Work decreases on every rnd until 4 sts remain. Cut yarn, thread through remaining sts and pull to close. Pull the yarn end through the tip to the WS.

THUMB

Place the thumb sts from the waste yarn on 2 needles. Pick up additional sts around the thumb opening, so that you have 18 (20, 21) sts in total.

Divide sts evenly onto 3 needles, 6, 6, 6 (6, 7, 7; 7, 7, 7) sts on each. Begin working in Check Pattern from the lower right edge. Work the Check Pattern as established: be sure to check on which rnd of the pattern to start. It may be that the pattern doesn't continue in pattern at the upper edge but don't worry, you won't notice it later.

Note! On the 1st rnd, you can work the picked up sts through the back loops. This prevents holes.

Work in Check Pattern for a total of 22 (23, 24) rnds or until your thumb is covered when you try on the mittens.

Decreases

Continue in established Check Pattern and work a k2tog tbl decrease at the beginning of each needle until 3 sts remain. Cut yarn, thread through remaining sts and pull to close. Pull the yarn end through the tip to the WS.

FINISHING

Weave in ends. Wet block to measurements.

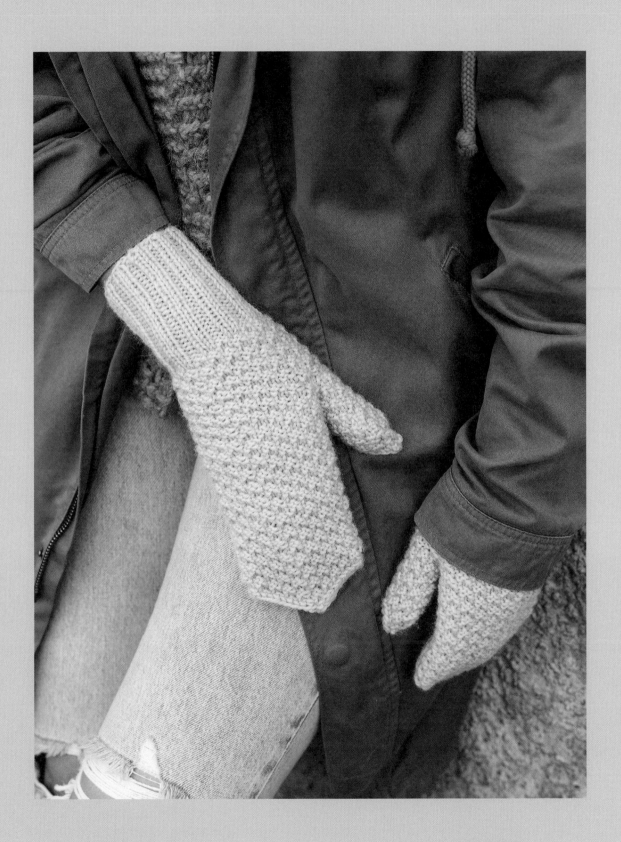

Jonna Hietala

37 Tivoli

Tivoli is an easy pattern that will keep you entertained and teach you a couple of fun new tricks. The addictive stripe pattern makes sure you will finish the sweater in no time.

SIZES

1 (2, 3, 4, 5) (6, 7, 8)

Recommended ease: 8–12" / 15–30 cm of positive ease.

FINISHED MEASUREMENTS

Chest Circumference: 44.75 (46.5, 52.75, 56, 62.5) (67.25, 70.5, 75.25)" / 112 (116, 132, 140, 156) (168, 176, 188) cm.
Collar Circumference: 19.25 (19.25, 20.75, 20.75, 22.5) (22.5, 24, 24)" / 48 (48, 52, 52, 56) (56, 60, 60) cm.
Upper Arm Circumference: 13.5 (14.5, 16, 16.75, 19.25) (20, 21.5, 23.25)" / 34 (36, 40, 42, 48) (50, 54, 58) cm.
Body Length: 13.5" / 34 cm.
Sleeve Length: 17.5" / 44 cm.

MATERIALS

Yarn: Hygge by Novita (100% wool, 66 yds / 60 m – 100 g).

C1 (lilac): 5 (6, 7, 7, 8) (9, 9, 10) balls, colourway 730 Blueberry Milk.
C2 (orange): 4 (4, 5, 5, 6) (6, 6, 7) balls, colourway 650 Waxcap.

If you decide to use another yarn, you will need approx. 331 (350, 405, 434, 505) (545, 590, 646) yds / 301 (318, 369, 394, 459) (496, 536, 587) m of bulky-weight yarn in C1 and approx. 221 (233, 270, 289, 337) (363, 393, 430) yds / 201 (202, 246, 263, 306) (330, 358, 391) m of bulky-weight yarn in C2.

Needles: US 15 / 10 mm 32–40" / 80–100 cm circular needles.

Notions: Stitch marker.

GAUGE

10 sts x 13 rnds to 4" / 10 cm in Stockinette Stitch, after blocking.

NOTES

You can find the abbreviations and detailed instructions for techniques used in this pattern in the Abbreviations (pp. 20–23) and Techniques (pp. 15–19) sections.

Slip stitch marker as you come across it.

CONSTRUCTION

This pullover is made mostly in the round. At first, you will work a couple of rows of the right back shoulder, then of the left. The shoulders are then joined together, after which you will continue in stockinette stitch until the back piece reaches the underarm. Next, it is time for the front piece. Once the front reaches the underarm, it is time to start working in the round. After the body, you pick up stitches for the sleeves and work them in the round.

DIRECTIONS

BACK

Right back shoulder

With C1, cast on 17 (18, 21, 23, 26) (29, 30, 33) sts using the Provisional Cast-On Method:

Step 1: Using waste yarn in a contrasting yarn, crochet a chain that is several sts longer than the number of sts you need to cast-on. Cut the yarn and pull it through the last loop.

Step 2: Turn the crochet chain over. Insert the tip of your knitting needle into the bump on the back of the first chain st. Using your working yarn, wrap yarn around the tip of your needle and pull a st through.

Repeat across the back of the crochet chain until you have cast on the number of sts needed.

Row 1 (RS): K to end.
Row 2 (WS): P to end, CO 2 sts using the Backwards Loop Cast-On Method. [19 (20, 23, 25, 28) (31, 32, 35) sts]
Row 3: K to end.
Row 4: P to end.
Cut yarn. Leave sts on hold.

Left back shoulder

With C1, cast on 17 (18, 21, 23, 26) (29, 30, 33) sts using the Provisional Cast-On Method.

Row 1 (RS): K to end.
Row 2 (WS): P to end.
Row 3: K to end, cast on 2 sts using the Backwards Loop Cast-On Method. [19 (20, 23, 25, 28) (31, 32, 35) sts]
Row 4: P to end.
Don't cut yarn.

Join back shoulders

Row 1 (RS): Continuing with the left back shoulder sts, k to end, cast on 18 (18, 20, 20, 22) (22, 24, 24) sts using the Backwards Loop Cast-On Method and k the right back shoulder sts from hold. [56 (58, 66, 70, 78) (84, 88, 94) sts]

Row 2 (WS): P to end.

Row 3: K to end.

Row 4: P to end.

Repeat rows 3–4, 3 more times. You will now have 14 rows in C1. Cut yarn. Leave sts on hold.

FRONT

Left front shoulder

With C1, cast on 17 (18, 21, 23, 26) (29, 30, 33) sts using the Provisional Cast-On Method.

Row 1 (RS): K to end.

Row 2 (WS): P to end.

Row 3: K to end.

Row 4: P to end.

Row 5: K2, m1l, k to end. [18 (19, 22, 24, 27) (30, 31, 34) sts]

Row 6: P to end.

Row 7: K2, m1l, k to end. [19 (20, 23, 25, 28) (31, 32, 35) sts]

Row 8: P to end.

Row 9: K2, m1l, k to end. [20 (21, 24, 26, 29) (32, 33, 36) sts]

Row 10: P to end.

Row 11: K2, m1l, k to end. [21 (22, 25, 27, 30) (33, 34, 37) sts]

Row 12: P to end.

Cut yarn and place sts on hold.

Right front shoulder

With C1, cast on 17 (18, 21, 23, 26) (29, 30, 33) sts using the Provisional Cast-On Method.

Row 1 (RS): K to end.

Row 2 (WS): P to end.

Row 3: K to end.

Row 4: P to end.

Row 5: K to 2 sts before end, m1r, k2. [18 (19, 22, 24, 27) (30, 31, 34) sts]

Row 6: P to end.

Row 7: K to 2 sts before end, m1r, k2. [19 (20, 23, 25, 28) (31, 32, 35) sts]

Row 8: P to end.

Row 9: K to 2 sts before end, m1r, k2. [20 (21, 24, 26, 29) (32, 33, 36) sts]

Row 10: P to end.

Row 11: K to 2 sts before end, m1r, k2. [21 (22, 25, 27, 30) (33, 34, 37) sts]

Don't cut yarn.

Join front shoulders

Row 1: Continuing with the right front sts, k to end, cast on 14 (14, 16, 16, 18) (18, 20, 20) sts using the Backwards Loop Cast-On Method, and k the left front sts from hold. [56 (58, 66, 70, 78) (84, 88, 94) sts]

Row 2: P to end.

The front now has 14 rows in C1. Cut yarn.

At this point, join the shoulders of the back and front pieces by using the 3-Needle Bind-Off Method. This way, it will be easier to knit the rest of the pullover. Unravel the crochet chain and pick up the live sts on the needle from each shoulder, then work a 3-Needle Bind-Off.

Continue working on the body in the stripe pattern (14 rows or rnds first in C2 and then C1). Work the front sts first. When you have worked a total of 25 (26, 28, 29, 30) (31, 32, 33) rows from the cast-on, work the back piece to same length and then join back and front pieces together (instructions below). After joining, continue to work in Stockinette Stitch in the rnd (k all sts), keeping the stripe pattern intact.

JOIN BACK AND FRONT

Continue from the right side of the front piece. K the front piece sts, then the back piece sts. Join to work in the round. You should now have 112 (116, 132, 140, 156) (168, 176, 188) sts in total. Place stitch marker for the beginning of the rnd (BOR).

BODY

Once you have completed the 14 rnds of the C1 stripe (from the cast-on, the sweater now has two C1 stripes), k one more stripe with C2. Cut C2.

Ribbing

Change to C1 and k 4 rnds.

Next rnd: *K1tbl, p1*, repeat *–* to end. Continue to work in the established Twisted 1 x 1 Ribbing for 9 more rnds. Bind off loosely in pattern.

SLEEVES

Starting from the underarm and with C1, pick up and k 34 (36, 40, 42, 48) (50, 54, 58) sts. The amount of sts is not crucial, as long as it is an even amount. Both sides of the sleeve should hold the same number of sts. Place BOR marker.

K 13 more rnds in C1.

Change to C2 and k 14 rnds,
Change to C1 and k 14 rnds. Cut C1
Change to C2 and k 8 rnds.

Next rnd: *K1tbl, p1*, repeat *–* to end. Continue to work in the established Twisted 1 x 1 Ribbing for 5 more rnds. Bind off loosely in pattern.

NECKLINE

With C1, pick up and knit 48 (48, 52, 52, 56) (56, 60, 60) sts. Place BOR m.

Rnd 1: *K1tbl, p1*, repeat *–* to end. Continue to work in the established Twisted 1 x 1 Ribbing for 5 more rnds.

FINISHING

Weave in the ends and wet block to measurements.

Maaike van Geijn

38 Koket

A beret is the chicest hat there is! The shape is created with increases and decreases, but there are also sections where you can relax by knitting Stockinette Stitch.

SIZES

1 (2, 3)

For a head circumference of approx. 20–21 (21–23, 23–25)" / 51–53 (53–58.5, 58.5–63.5) cm.

Recommended ease: 1.5" / 4 cm of negative ease at the brim (worn around the forehead).

FINISHED MEASUREMENTS

Brim Circumference (smallest point): 17 (18.25, 19.25)" / 42.5 (45.5, 48) cm.
Circumference (widest point): 29.5 (33, 35.5)" / 75 (85, 90) cm.
Brim to Crown (excluding stalk): 7.5 (8, 9)" / 19 (20, 23) cm.

MATERIALS

Yarn: 1 skein of Ovis et Cetera Corriedale Mohair (50% corriedale, 50% mohair, 437 yds / 400 m – 100 g), colourway Charcoal.

The yarn is held double throughout the pattern.

If you decide to use another yarn, you will need approx. 437 yds / 400 m of light fingering-weight yarn held double. You can also use light fingering-weight yarn held together with brushed (silk) mohair: you will need approx. 175 (195, 230) yds / 160 (178, 210) m of light-fingering-weight yarn and 175 (195, 230) yds / 160 (178, 210) m of brushed (silk) mohair.

Alternatively, you can use approx. 274 yds / 250 m of heavier fingering or sport-weight yarn held single. Make sure to swatch for gauge and adapt pattern if necessary.

Needles: US 2 / 2.75 mm (for brim and start of beret) and US 2.5 / 3 mm (for body) 16" / 40 cm circular needles. US 2.5 / 3 mm 32" / 80 cm circular needles or a set of DPNs (for crown and i-cord stalk).

Notions: Stitch markers.

GAUGE

30 sts x 36 rnds to 4" / 10 cm on US 2.5 / 3 mm needles in Stockinette Stitch, after blocking.

NOTES

You can find the abbreviations and detailed instructions for techniques used in this pattern in the Abbreviations (pp. 20–23) and Techniques (pp. 15–19) sections.

Slip markers as you come across them.

You want to obtain a nice, dense fabric that gives the beret some firmness. Thus, make sure to choose a yarn, which contains wool and not a 100% alpaca or mohair yarn. Rustic 100% natural yarns work best for this design.

You can also wear the beret inside out with the Reverse Stockinette Stitch as the right side. Knit the beret and stalk normally in Stockinette Stitch as described below. After blocking, turn your beret inside out. Do not forget to turn the stalk as well, using a needle or pencil to pop it out.

CONSTRUCTION

This beret is worked seamlessly in the round from the brim to the crown and finished with a neat i-cord stalk.

DIRECTIONS

With US 2 / 2.75 mm needles holding two strands of yarn together, cast on 128 (136, 144) sts using the Long-Tail Cast-On Method or method of choice. Be careful not to cast on too tightly.

Place m for the beginning of rnd (BOR) and join to work in the rnd being careful not to twist sts.

BRIM

Set-up rnd: *K2, p2*, repeat *–* to end. Work in the established 2 x 2 Ribbing 9 (11, 13) rnds in total.

BODY

Work 6 (7, 8) rnds in Stockinette Stitch (k all sts).

Change to US 2.5 / 3 mm needles and work 2 (3, 4) rnds in Stockinette Stitch (k all sts).

Increase rnd: *K3, m1r*, repeat *–* to 2 (4, 6) sts before end, k2 (4, 6). [42 (44, 46) st inc'd]
You should have 170 (180, 190) sts.

Continue working 14 (16, 18) rows in Stockinette Stitch (k all sts).

Decrease rnd: *K15 (16, 17), k2tog*, repeat *–* to end. (10 sts dec'd)
You should have 160 (170, 180) sts.

Continue knitting 17 (19, 21) rnds in Stockinette Stitch (k all sts).

CROWN

Set-up rnd: *K16 (17, 18), PM*, repeat *–* to end.

Rnd 1 (dec): *K to 2 sts before m, k2tog, SM*, repeat *–* to end. (10 sts dec'd)
Rnd 2: K to end.
Repeat rnds 1–2 until 20 sts remain. While knitting the crown, the number of sts will gradually decrease. When necessary, switch to longer needles if using the Magic Loop Technique or to DPNs.

Next rnd: *K2tog*, repeat *–* 10 times. Remove markers while knitting, except BOR m. (10 sts dec'd)

STALK

Prepare for i-cord stalk: *K1, k2tog*, repeat *–* 3 times, k1. (3 sts dec'd) (7 sts remain)

I-Cord Stalk
Slide the 7 remaining live sts onto a DPN or keep them on your circular needle. K 7 sts from left-hand needle to right-hand needle. Do not turn work. Note that, because you did not turn your work, the working yarn is still on the left edge of your work, rather than on the right edge. *Slide these 7 sts all the way to your other needle tip. Pull the working yarn tightly across the back from left to right and k7 again*. Work *–* for 5 rows, or until you have a little stalk of 0.5" / 1.5 cm.

Break yarn, leaving at least a 6" / 15 cm long tail. Draw the tail twice through the remaining sts and secure on the inside of the beret.

FINISHING

Weave in ends.

Block the finished piece to measurements. To achieve the unique beret shape, blocking requires a special blocking technique. Block the beret to measurements by using a suitable-sized plate with a circumference corresponding to the widest point of the beret (29.5, 33, 35.5" / 75, 85, 90 cm). The beret should be fully stretched on the plate, like a ufo. Make sure not to overstretch the wet beret. You can put the plate upside down on a smaller bowl where you place the brim, making sure not to overstretch the brim. Leave to dry completely.

Rebekka Mauser

39 Kreuzberg

The Kreuzberg slipover features wide stripes in seven colours. It is named after a Berlin neighbourhood where Rebekka Mauser stumbled upon a 1970s slipover that inspired this modern knit.

SIZES

1 (2, 3, 4, 5) (6, 7, 8)

Recommended ease: 3–5" / 7.5–12.5 cm of positive ease.

FINISHED MEASUREMENTS

Chest Circumference: 38.25 (41.75, 45.25, 50.75, 56) (59.5, 64, 68.5)" / 95.5 (104, 113, 127, 140) (149, 160, 171) cm.
Total Length from Middle of Back Neck to Hem: 21.5 (23, 24.25, 24.25, 25.75) (27, 27, 28.5)" / 54 (57, 60.5, 60.5, 64) (67.5, 67.5, 71) cm.
Armhole Depth: 8.5 (9.25, 9.75, 10, 11) (11.5, 12, 12.5)" / 21 (23.5, 24.5, 25.5, 27.5) (29, 30.5, 32) cm.
Front Neck Depth: 3.25" / 8.5 cm.
Neck Width: 7.75 (7.75, 8.25, 8.75, 8.75) (8.75, 9.25, 9.5)" / 19.5 (19.5, 20.5, 21.5, 21.5) (21.5, 23, 24) cm.
Shoulder Width (excluding edging): 2.25 (2.75, 3, 3.25, 3.75) (4.25, 4.5, 5)" / 5.5 (6.5, 7, 8.5, 9.5) (10.5, 11, 12) cm.

MATERIALS

Yarn: Gilliatt by De Rerum Natura (100% wool, 273 yds / 250 m – 100 g).
C1: 1 skein of colourway L'Heure Bleu.
C2: 1 skein of colourway Genêt.
C3: 1 skein of colourway Bouleau.
C4: 1 skein of colourway Iroise.
C5: 1 (1, 1, 2, 2) (2, 2, 2) skein(s) of colourway Bruyère.
C6: 1 skein of colourway Lagon.
C7: 1 skein of colourway Argile.

If you decide to use another yarn, you will need approx.
C1: 85 (141, 153, 170, 189) (203, 216, 230) yds / 78 (129, 140, 155, 173) (186, 198, 210) m of worsted-weight yarn.
C2: 85 (94, 153, 170, 189) (203, 216, 230) yds / 78 (86, 140, 155, 173) (186, 198, 210) m of worsted-weight yarn.
C3: 85 (94, 102, 113, 189) (203, 216, 230) yds / 78 (86, 93, 103, 173) (186, 198, 210) m of worsted-weight yarn.
C4: 85 (94, 102, 113, 126) (203, 216, 230) yds / 78 (86, 93, 103, 115) (186, 198, 210) m of worsted-weight yarn.
C5: 224 (245, 263, 287, 316) (335, 356, 453) yds / 205 (224, 241, 262, 289) (306, 326, 414) m of worsted-weight yarn.
C6: 85 (94, 102, 113, 126) (135, 144, 153) yds / 78 (86, 93, 103, 115) (123, 132, 140) m of worsted weight yarn.
C7: 85 (94, 102, 113, 126) (135, 144, 153) yds / 78 (86, 93, 103, 115) (123, 132, 140) m of worsted-weight yarn.

Needles: US 4 / 3.5 mm 16" / 40 cm and 32" / 80 cm needles (for ribbing), US 7 / 4.5 mm 32" / 80 cm circular needles (for body). US 8 / 5 mm crochet hook for the Provisional Crochet Cast-On.

Notions: Stitch markers, stitch holders or waste yarn, tapestry needle, spare US 7 / 4.5 mm circular needles in any length.

GAUGE

18 sts x 29 rows to 4" / 10 cm on US 7 / 4.5 mm needles in Stockinette Stitch, after blocking.

NOTES

You can find the abbreviations and detailed instructions for techniques used in this pattern in the Abbreviations (pp. 20–23) and Techniques (pp. 15–19) sections.

Slip markers as you come across them.

CONSTRUCTION

This completely seamless slipover is worked top down, beginning with a Provisional Cast-On. The shoulders are shaped with short rows. After the back is completed, the fronts are worked separately (each knitted flat) and the crewneck is shaped with increases. Both sides of the front are then joined and the front is knitted top down flat to the underarm while the armhole is shaped with increases. The back and front are joined in the round for the lower body, which is worked top down in the round to the ribbed hem. Stitches are picked up around the armhole and a ribbed edging is worked in the round. In the same way the ribbed neck edging is worked.

MODIFICATIONS

Both ease and length can be adjusted. For example, choose a size with more ease for a more relaxed fit or go down a size for a fitted look. Work more or less stripes to adjust the body length (each stripe is 1.4" / 3.5 cm wide) to your personal preferences.

DIRECTIONS

BACK

The back is worked flat. With C1 and US 7 / 4.5 mm circular needles, cast on 63 (67, 71, 77, 81) (85, 89, 95) sts using the Provisional Crochet Cast-On Method. A provisional cast-on has the advantage that it's possible to work from the live sts of both sides of the cast-on and no new sts have to be picked up. Cast on as follows:
Step 1: Using waste yarn in a contrasting colour, crochet a chain that is several stitches longer than the number of sts you need to cast-on. Cut the yarn and pull it through the last loop.
Step 2: Turn the crochet chain over. Insert the tip of your knitting needle into the bump on the back of the first chain st. Using your working yarn, wrap yarn around the tip of your needle and pull a st through.
Repeat across the back of the crochet chain until you have cast on the number of sts needed.

Next row (WS): K1, p9 (11, 12, 14, 16) (18, 19, 21), PM, p43 (43, 45, 47, 47) (47, 49, 51), PM, p to 1 st before end, k1. You should have 10 (12, 13, 15, 17) (19, 20, 22) sts for each shoulder and 43 (43, 45, 47, 47) (47, 49, 51) sts for the back neck.

SHAPE SHOULDERS

The shoulder slope is shaped with short rows. For this purpose, German Short Rows are worked to create double stitches (DS) at the turning points of the short rows. When working across the entire row again, both legs of the respective double stitch are knitted (respectively purled on WS rows) together as a single st (kDS and pDS).
Short row 1 (RS): K to 2nd m, SM, k1, make DS (mDS), turn work.
Short row 2 (WS): SM, p to m, SM, p1, mDS, turn work.

Short row 3 (RS): SM, k to DS, kDS, k3 (4, 5, 6, 7) (8, 8, 9), mDS, turn work.
Short row 4 (WS): P to DS, pDS, p3 (4, 5, 6, 7) (8, 8, 9), mDS, turn work
Short rows 5–6: Repeat short rows 3–4 once.
Short row 7 (RS): K to DS, kDS, k to end.
Next row (WS): K1, p to DS while removing both markers, pDS, p to 1 st before end, k1.
Cut C1.

UPPER BACK

Join C2 and start working in rows back and forth across all sts.
Row 1 (RS): K to end.
Row 2 (WS): K1, p to 1 st before end, k1.
Rows 3–10: Repeat rows 1–2 another 4 times.
Change to next colour and continue working in 10-Row Stripe Pattern (5 repeats of rows 1 and 2 for each stripe) until back measures 6.75 (7.25, 7.25, 7, 7) (7, 7, 7)" / 17 (18.5, 18.5, 18, 18) (18, 18, 18) cm from cast-on along armhole edge.

SHAPE ARMHOLES

The armholes are shaped with increases on both sides on every RS row while working the 10-Row Stripe Pattern. Take care to follow the directions for your size and do not forget to alternate colours in the striping sequence.
Row 1 (RS): K2, m1r, k to 2 sts before end, m1l, k2. (2 sts inc'd)
Row 2 (WS): K1, p to 1 st before end, k1.
Repeat rows 1–2 another 4 (5, 7, 9, 12) (14, 16, 18) times. You should have 73 (79, 87, 97, 107) (115, 123, 133) sts for the back.
Row 3 (RS): Turn work to the WS, cast on 3 sts using the Backwards Loop Cast-On Method or method of choice, turn work back to the RS, k to end, cast on 3 sts using the Backwards Loop Cast-On Method or method of choice. (6 sts inc'd)

Row 4 (WS): P to end.

You should have 79 (85, 93, 103, 113) (121, 129, 139) sts for the back.

Cut yarn. Place back sts on waste yarn to be worked later for the lower body.

LEFT FRONT

With RS facing and beginning at the left (as worn) neck edge, unravel the last 11 (13, 14, 16, 18) (20, 21, 23) sts of the Provisional Cast-On for left shoulder and place live sts on US 7 / 4.5 mm circular needles. Leave remaining sts of the Provisional Cast-On to be worked later for right front and neckband.

Join C1.

Set-up row 1 (RS): K to end.

Set-up row 2 (WS): K1, p to 1 st before end, k1.

Shape Left Shoulder and Left Side of Neck

The slope of the left shoulder is shaped using short rows while the shaping of the left side of the neck with increases begins.

Short row 1 (RS): K to 3 (3, 2, 2, 2) (2, 3, 3) sts before end, mDS, turn work.

Short row 2 (WS): P to 1 st before end, k1.

Short row 3 (RS): K2, m1r, k until 2 (3, 4, 5, 6) (7, 7, 8) sts before previous DS, mDS, turn work. (1 st inc'd)

Short row 4 (WS): P to 1 st before end, k1.

Short row 5 (RS): K3, mDS, turn work.

Short row 6 (WS): P1, k1.

Next row (RS): K2, m1r, k to end working all DS by knitting through both loops as a single st as you pass them. (1 st inc'd)

Next row (WS): K1, p to 1 st before end, k1.

You should have 13 (15, 16, 18, 20) (22, 23, 25) sts for the left shoulder.

Cut C1.

Shape Left Front and Left Side of Neck

Front neck shaping continues with increases.

Join C2.

Row 1 (RS): K to end.

Row 2 (WS): K1, p to 1 st before end, k1.

Row 3 (RS): K2, m1r, k to end. (1 st inc'd)

Row 4 (WS): Repeat row 2.

Rows 5–8: Repeat rows 3 and 4 another 2 times.

Row 9 (RS): Turn work to WS, cast on 2 sts using the Backwards Loop Cast-On Method or method of choice, turn work back to RS, k to end. (2 sts inc'd)

Row 10 (WS): K1, p to end.

You should have 18 (20, 21, 23, 25) (27, 28, 30) sts for the left front.

Cut C2 and join C3.

Rows 11–12: Repeat rows 9 and 10 once.

Row 13 (RS): Turn work to WS, cast on 3 sts using the Backwards Loop Cast-On Method, turn work back to RS, k to end. (3 sts inc'd)

Row 14 (WS): Repeat row 6.

You should have 23 (25, 26, 28, 30) (32, 33, 35) sts for the left front.

Cut yarn. Place sts on waste yarn to be worked later for lower body.

RIGHT FRONT

With RS facing and beginning at the right (as worn) armhole edge, unravel the first 11 (13, 14, 16, 18) (20, 21, 23) sts of the Provisional Cast-On for right shoulder and place the live stitches on US 7 / 4.5 mm circular needles. Leave the remaining sts of the Provisional Cast-On to be worked later for the neckband.

Join C1.

Set-up row 1 (RS): K to end.

Set-up row 2 (WS): K1, p to 1 st before end, k1.

Set-up row 3 (RS): K to end.

Shape Right Shoulder and Right Side of Neck

The slope of the right shoulder is shaped using short rows while the shaping of the right side of the neck with increases begins.

Short row 1 (WS): K1, p until 3 (3, 2, 2, 2) (2, 3, 3) sts before end, mDS, turn work.

Short row 2 (RS): K to 2 sts before end, m1l, k2. (1 st inc'd)

Short row 3 (WS): K1, p until 2 (3, 4, 5, 6) (7, 7, 8) sts before previous DS, mDS, turn work.

Short row 4 (RS): K to end.

Short row 5 (WS): K1, p2, mDS, turn work.

Short row 6 (RS): M1l, k2. (1 st inc'd)

Next row (WS): K1, p to 1 st before end working all DSs by purling through both loops as a single st as you pass them, k1.

You should have 13 (15, 16, 18, 20) (22, 23, 25) sts for the right shoulder.

Cut C1.

Shape Right Front and Right Side of Neck

Front neck shaping continues with increases.

Join C2.

Row 1 (RS): K to end.

Row 2 (WS): K1, p to 1 st before end, k1.

Row 3 (RS): K to 2 sts before end, m1l, k2. (1 st inc'd)

Row 4 (WS): Repeat row 2.

Rows 5–8: Repeat rows 3 and 4 another 2 times.

Row 9 (RS): K to end, cast on 2 sts using the Backwards Loop Cast-On Method. (2 sts inc'd)

Row 10 (WS): P to 1 st before end, k1.

You should have 18 (20, 21, 23, 25) (27, 28, 30) sts for the right front.

Cut C2 and join C3.

Rows 11 and 12: Repeat rows 9 and 10 once.

Row 13 (RS): K to end, cast on 3 sts using the Backwards Loop Cast-On Method. (3 sts inc'd)

Row 14 (WS): Repeat row 6.

You should have 23 (25, 26, 28, 30) (32, 33, 35) sts for the right front.

Do not cut the yarn.

JOINING FRONTS

Next, new sts are cast on to join the right and left front. With the RS facing and C3 yarn, knit across right front sts and cast on 17 (17, 19, 21, 21) (21, 23, 25) sts using the Backwards Loop Cast-On Method or method of choice. Transfer left front sts to a second needle (in larger size) and still with RS facing, knit across left front sts to end. You should have 63 (67, 71, 77, 81) (85, 89, 95) sts for the front.

FRONT

Start working in rows back and forth across the complete front.
Row 1 (WS): K1, p to 1 st before end, k1.
Row 2 (RS): K to end.
Repeat rows 1–2 once, followed by row 1 once again.
Cut C3 and join C4.

Row 3 (RS): K to end.
Row 4 (WS): K1, p to 1 st before end, k1.
Rows 5–10: Repeat rows 3 and 4 another 4 times.
Change to next colour and continue working in the 10-Row Stripe Pattern (5 repeats of rows 1 and 2 for each stripe) until front measures 6.75 (7.25, 7.25, 7, 7) (7, 7, 7)" / 17 (18.5, 18.5, 18, 18) (18, 18, 18) cm, measured from top of the shoulder along armhole edge. Make sure to work the same number of rows as for back.

Shape Armholes

Proceed with armhole shaping as described for the back section.
You should have 79 (85, 93, 103, 113) (121, 129, 139) sts for the front.
Do not cut the yarn.

BODY JOINING

Transfer the back sts from the waste yarn to a second pair of needles (in US 7 / 4.5 mm size). Cast on sts using the Backwards Loop Cast-On Method or method of choice.
With the RS facing, starting at the right side where working yarn is attached, k across the front sts, cast on 3 (4, 4, 5, 6) (6, 7, 7) sts, PM, cast on 4 (5, 5, 6, 7) (7, 8, 8) sts, k across back sts, cast on 3 (4, 4, 5, 6) (6, 7, 7) sts, PM, cast on 4 (5, 5, 6, 7) (7, 8, 8) sts, PM to mark the beginning of the rnd (BOR) and join for working in the rnd. You should have 172 (188, 204, 228, 252) (268, 288, 308) sts for the body.

BODY

From this point the body is worked in the rnd down to the hem while working in the 10-Round Stripe Pattern. Under each arm a "fake seam" – a column of reverse Stockinette Stitch – is worked where colour changes blend nicely.
Body rnd 1: K to m, SM, p1, k to m, SM, p1, k to end.
Repeat the previous rnd until the current stripe is completed. Cut yarn.
Transfer of BOR: Remove BOR m, slip the previous 4 (5, 5, 6, 7) (7, 8, 8) sts from the right-hand needle back to the left-hand needle until m, RM and place new BOR m. The beginning of the rnd is now directly under the right arm.
Body rnd 2: P1, k to m, SM, p1, k to end. Continue repeating the previous rnd and working in the 10-Round Stripe Pattern (10 repeats of Body Rnd for each stripe) until a total of 14 (15, 16, 16, 17) (18, 18, 19) stripes have been worked and the slipover measures approx. 19.25 (20.75, 22, 22, 23.5) (24.75, 24.75, 26.25)" / 48.5 (51.5, 55, 55, 58.5) (62, 62, 65.5) cm from back neck to hem or work measures approx. 2.25" / 5.5 cm less than total desired length. Make sure to end after a full stripe.
Cut yarn.

HEM

Change to US 4 / 3.5 mm needles (32" / 80 cm length) and join C5.
Set-up rnd: P1, k to m, RM, p1, k to end.
Hem rnd: *P1, k1*, repeat *–* to end.
Continue to work in established 1 x 1 Ribbing for 2.25" / 5.5 cm.

Remove BOR m and bind off sts loosely. If you wish, you can for e.g. try the Sewn Tubular Bind-Off Method which gives the garment a very neat look and a flexible edge. Tutorials can be found online.

NECK EDGING

Carefully unravel the Provisional Cast-On and place live sts onto US 4 / 3.5 mm needles (16" / 40 cm length). With RS facing and starting at the right side of the back neck as worn, join C5 and knit across back neck sts. Pick up and k 59 (59, 61, 63, 63) (63, 65, 67) sts along the front neck opening edge (approx. 3 sts to 4 rows and 1 st in each cast-on st) in a nice rounded curve. Make sure to get an even number of sts. Place BOR m and join for working in the rnd. You should have 100 (100, 104, 108, 108) (108, 112, 116) sts for the neck.
Neck rnd: *P1, k1*, repeat *–* to end.
Continue to work in established 1 x 1 Ribbing another 7 rnds. Remove BOR m and bind off loosely.

ARMHOLE EDGING

With RS facing and US 4 / 3.5 mm needles (16" / 40 cm length), join C5. Beginning at the centre of underarm where the purl stitch column is, pick up and k 4 (5, 5, 6, 7) (7, 8, 8) sts along the cast-on edge. Then pick up and k 83 (91, 95, 99, 107) (111, 117, 123) sts evenly spaced (approx. 2 sts to 3 rows) along the armhole, followed by 3 (4, 4, 5, 6) (6, 7, 7) sts along the cast-on edge. Make sure to get an even number of sts.

Place BOR m and join for working in the rnd. You should have 90 (100, 104, 110, 120) (124, 132, 138) sts for the armhole edging. **Edging rnd:** *P1, k1*, repeat *–* to end. Continue to work in established 1 x 1 Ribbing another 7 times.

Remove BOR m and bind off loosely.

Repeat the instructions for the second armhole edging.

FINISHING

Weave in ends. Wash and block to measurements.

40

52

Renate Kamm — Veera Jussila — Erin Jensen — Miriam Walchshäusl

Lærke Boelt Back — George Cullen — Pauliina Kuunsola — Jonna Hietala

Aatu Äikiä — Teti Lutsak — Isabell Kraemer

Renate Kamm

40 Capreoli

This scarf is a great way to explore knitting with two strands of yarn held together and play with colour combinations. The fabric is sturdy and fully reversible.

SIZES

1 (2)

FINISHED MEASUREMENTS

Length: 66.5 (88.5)" / 166 (221.5) cm.
Width: 11.5 (14.25)" / 30 (36) cm.

MATERIALS

Yarn: Loft by Brooklyn Tweed (100% American Targhee-Columbia wool, 275 yds / 251 m – 50 g).
MC: 2 (4) skeins of colourway Soot.
CC1: 2 (4) skeins of colourway Embers.
CC2: 2 (4) skeins colourway Fossil.

Two strands of yarn are held together throughout the pattern to create the marled look.

If you decide to use another yarn, you will need approx. 550 (880) yds / 503 (805) m of fingering-weight yarn in MC, 525 (840) yds / 480 (768) m in CC1 and 525 (840) yds / 480 (768) m in CC2.

Needles: US 8 / 5 mm straight or 32" / 80 cm circular needles.

Notions: Stitch markers, removable marker or safety pin.

GAUGE

17 sts x 26 rows to 4" / 10 cm with 2 strands of yarn held together in Chevron Pattern, after blocking.

STITCH PATTERN

Modified Garter Stitch (2 strands of different colour)

Row 1 (RS): K to end.
Row 2 (WS): K1, *k5, DK2 (WS), k6*, repeat *–* to end.
Row 3: *K6, DK2 (RS), k5*, repeat *–* to last st, k1.
Rows 4–7: Repeat rows 2–3 twice.
Row 8: Repeat row 2.

DK2: The two loops of a marled stitch are worked separately, one loop at a time as follows:

WS row: (1) Move both strands of working yarn between the needles to the front, towards you; (2) with the single strand of working yarn, matching newly added colour, purl same coloured loop of the double stitch, drop the loop off the needle and the working strand in the back; (3) then, using the 2nd strand of working yarn (colour of previously worked solid section), knit the remaining same colour loop of the double stitch, drop the loop off the needle.

RS row: (1) Move both strands of working yarn between the needles to the front; (2) with the single strand of working yarn matching the colour of prev worked solid section, purl same coloured loop of the double stitch, drop the loop off the needle and the working strand in the back; (3) then, using the 2nd strand of working yarn (newly added colour), knit the remaining same colour loop of the double stitch, drop the loop off the needle.

Note! After all 8 rows of the Modified Garter Stitch have been completed both loops of the DK2 stitch are again worked as one stitch.

WRITTEN INSTRUCTIONS FOR CHART

Chevron Pattern (a repeat of 12 sts + 1 last st)

Row 1 (RS): *P2, k2, p2, k1, p2, k2, p1*, repeat *–* to last st, p1.

Row 2 (WS): K1, *k1, p2, k2, p1, k2, p2, k2*, repeat *–* to end.

Row 3: *P1, k2, p2, k3, p2, k2*, repeat *–* to last st, p1.

Row 4: K1, *p2, k2, p3, k2, p2, k1*, repeat *–* to end.

Row 5: *K2, p2, k2, p1, k2, p2, k1*, repeat *–* to last st, k1.

Row 6: P1, *p1, k2, p2, k1, p2, k2, p2*, repeat *–* to end.

Row 7: *K1, p2, k2, p3, k2, p2*, repeat *–* to last st, k1.

Row 8: P1, *k2, p2, k3, p2, k2, p1*, repeat *–* to end.

Rows 9–16: Repeat rows 1–8.

NOTES

You can find the abbreviations and detailed instructions for techniques used in this pattern in the Abbreviations (pp. 20–23) and Techniques (pp. 15–19) sections.

Choose three coordinating colourways (1 dark, 1 medium and 1 light colour). For the marl-colour combinations consider a neutral (e.g. black, dark grey, dark brown) as the dark colour, a strong medium base (e.g. green, blue, violet, red, or orange) as the medium colour, and a light neutral (e.g. white, beige, cream, light grey) as the light colour.

Chart is read from bottom to top and from right to left on RS rows and from left to right on WS rows. The 12 stitches within the red border are repeated, the last stitch is worked at the end. On WS rows the chart begins with one stitch, then the stitches within the red border are repeated to the end. The chart symbols show the stitches as they appear on the RS of fabric.

Markers are placed at the beginning of every repeat to help easily track the 12-stitch repeat. Slip markers as you come to them throughout the pattern. A marker, or safety pin is attached to the right side of the fabric to help identify right side rows from wrong side rows.

CONSTRUCTION

This long scarf is worked flat in one piece. The fabric is sturdy and fully reversible. It is knitted with two strands of yarn held together throughout the pattern, except for the DK2 stitch where each of the 2 strands is worked separately with its corresponding-coloured loop.

DIRECTIONS

With 2 strands of MC held together, cast on 49 (61) sts using your preferred stretchy cast-on method. For example the Backwards Loop Cast-On is an easy cast-on method to achieve a stretchy cast-on edge. Cast on sts as follows: cast on 13 sts, PM, *cast on 12 sts, PM*, repeat *–* 1 (2) more time(s), cast on 12 sts, turn work.

Before working the first RS row, attach a removable marker or safety pin into the first loop to mark the RS of fabric. Continue with 2 strands of MC held together.

Same-Colour Panel

Work 8 rows in Garter Stitch (2 strands of same colour) as follows beginning on the RS:

Rows 1–8: K to end.

Work next 16 rows in Chevron Pattern as follows:

Row 9 (RS): *P2, k2, p2, k1, p2, k2, p1*, repeat *–* 3 (4) more times, p1.

Row 10 (WS): K1, *k1, p2, k2, p1, k2, p2, k2*, repeat *–* 3 (4) more times.

Row 11: *P1, k2, p2, k3, p2, k2*, repeat *–* 3 (4) more times, p1.

Row 12: K1, *p2, k2, p3, k2, p2, k1*, repeat *–* 3 (4) more times.

Row 13: *K2, p2, k2, p1, k2, p2, k1*, repeat *–* 3 (4) more times, k1.

Row 14: P1, *p1, k2, p2, k1, p2, k2, p2*, repeat *–* 3 (4) more times.

Row 15: *K1, p2, k2, p3, k2, p2*, repeat *–* 3 (4) more times, k1.

Row 16: P1, *k2, p2, k3, p2, k2, p1*, repeat *–* 3 (4) more times.

Row 17–24: Repeat row 9–16 once more.

Cut 1 strand of MC.

Attach 1 strand of CC1. Continue with 1 strand MC and 1 strand CC1 held together.

CHEVRON CHART

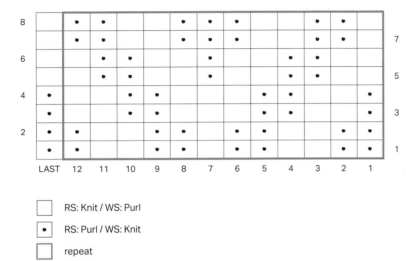

RS: Knit / WS: Purl

RS: Purl / WS: Knit

repeat

Different-Colour Panel

Work 8 rows in Modified Garter Stitch with 2 strands of different colour as follows:

Row 1 (RS): K to end.

Row 2 (WS): K6, DK2 (WS), k6, *k5, DK2 (WS), k6*, repeat *–* 2 (3) more times.

Row 3: *K6, DK2 (RS), k5*, repeat *–* 3 (4) more times, k1.

Rows 4–8: Repeat rows 2–3 twice more, then row 2 once.

Rows 9–24: Work next 16 rows of Chevron Pattern same as previous section.

Cut 2nd strand of MC.

Attach another strand of CC1. With both strands of CC1, work 24 rows following Same Colour Panel directions. Cut 1 strand of CC1.

Attach 1 strand of CC2. With both strands (1 strand CC1 and 1 strand CC2) work 24 rows following Different Colour Panel directions. Cut 2nd strand of CC1.

Attach another strand of CC2. With both strands of CC2 work 24 rows following Same Colour Panel directions. Cut 1 strand of CC2.

Attach 1 strand of MC. With both strands (1 strand CC2 and 1 strand MC) work 24 rows following Different Colour Panel directions. Cut 2nd strand of CC2.

Attach another strand of MC.

Repeat the entire sequence of 144 rows from the beginning 2 (3) more times. A total of 432 (576) rows have been worked. With 2 strands of MC held together work all 24 rows of the Same Colour Panel directions, then work 8 rows of Garter Stitch (k every row).

Bind off all sts and remove markers.

FINISHING

Weave in ends. Wet block the scarf to measurements.

Veera Jussila

41 Viimein

Viimein is a boxy sweater with a slightly cropped hem. You can knit it in a single colour – like the grey version on the next spread – or use scrap yarns and make it as colourful as you want.

SIZES

1 (2, 3, 4, 5) (6, 7, 8)

Recommended ease: 6–8" / 15–20 cm of positive ease.

FINISHED MEASUREMENTS

Chest Circumference: 38.25 (42.25, 47.25, 51.25, 57) (61, 65, 69)" / 97.5 (107.5, 120, 130, 145) (155, 165, 175) cm.
Waist Circumference: 35.5 (39.5, 44.25, 48.25, 54.25) (58, 62, 66)" / 90 (100, 112.5, 122.5, 137.5) (147.5, 157.5, 167.5) cm.
Length from Underarm to Hem: 11" / 28 cm.
Sleeve Length from Underarm to Cuff: 16.5 (17, 17.25, 17.25, 17.75) (18, 18.5, 19)" / 42 (43, 44, 44, 45) (46, 47, 48) cm.

MATERIALS

Yarn

The sweater can be knitted entirely with scrap yarn, but you can also acquire yarn just for this project. You will need two yarns or sets of yarn (one as the main colour and the other for striping):

MC: Yarn in similar shades (the sample sweater has white as MC), approx. DK-weight or slightly heavier (273 yds / 250 m – 100 g). For example Sandness Garn Merinoull, Retrosaria Mungo and BC Garn Semilla Melange are great options.
CC: Yarn in other colours for striping, approx. fingering-weight or thinner (437 yds / 400 m – 100 g).
The sweater is worked with two yarns held together.

The grey sweater was knitted with the following yarns held together:
Tukuwool DK (100% Finnish wool, 273 yds / 250 m – 100 g), colourway 03 Auri.
Sandnes Garn Tynn Silk Mohair (57% mohair, 28% silk, 15% wool, 232 yds / 212 m – 25 g), colourway 1022.

If you want to knit the sweater with one single yarn, choose an aran-weight yarn (164 yds / 150 m – 100 g). For example, De Rerum Natura Cyrano, BC Garn Northern Lights and Isager Alpaca 3 work well held single.
You will need approx. 655 (670, 830, 980, 1230) (1420, 1613, 1820) g in total or 1072 (1105, 1367, 1608, 2023) (2329, 2647, 2986) yds / 980 (1010, 1250, 1470, 1850) (2130, 2420, 2730) m.

Needles: US 7 / 4.5 mm and US 8 / 5 mm 32" / 80 cm circular needles.

Notions: 5 stitch markers.

GAUGE

16 sts x 24 rnds = 4" / 10 cm on US 8 / 5 mm needles in Stockinette Stitch, after blocking.

TECHNIQUES

Striping

The stripes in the sample sweater are 3 rnds each.

When changing yarns, change either the MC or the CC, not both at the same time. When changing yarns, knit with both old and new yarn for approx. 6" / 15 cm holding all yarns together. This way, the tails will already be woven in.

NOTES

You can find the abbreviations and detailed instructions for techniques used in this pattern in the Abbreviations (pp. 20–23) and Techniques (pp. 15–19) sections.

Slip stitch markers as you come across them.

CONSTRUCTION

This boxy sweater is knitted top down in the round holding two yarns together. The shoulderlines are shaped while working German Short Rows at the neckline. After working the shoulder section with increases, the front and back pieces are worked flat, separately, to equal lengths. After this they are again worked in the round.

DIRECTIONS

NECKLINE

With just MC and US 7 / 4.5 mm needles, cast on 76 (76, 80, 80, 80) (88, 88, 88) sts. Join to work in the rnd and PM for the beginning of rnd (BOR).

Work in 1 x 1 Ribbing as follows:
K1, p1, repeat *–* to end of rnd.
Work in established 1 x 1 Ribbing for 8 rnds in total.

Attach CC and continue to work with both MC and CC while striping the CC yarns. Change to US 8 / 5 mm needles and k 1 rnd adding markers as follows: K1, PM, k36 (36, 38, 38, 38) (42, 42, 42) (front), PM, k2 (sleeve), PM, k36 (36, 38, 38, 38) (42, 42, 42) (back), PM, k1. The BOR marker is on the other shoulder.

SHORT ROWS

Next, you work German Short Rows, so that the back sits a little higher than the front. At the same time, you work increases on the shoulders, next to the sleeve sts. You can stripe during the short rows or begin after completing them.

RS: K1, SM, m1l, k1, turn work. (1 st inc'd)
WS: MDS. *P to marker, m1rp, SM, p2, SM, m1lp*. Repeat *–* once, and then p1. Turn work. (4 sts inc'd)
RS: MDS. *K to marker, m1r, SM, k2, SM, m1l*, repeat *–*. K to DS, kDS, k1, turn work. (4 sts inc'd)
WS: MDS. *P to marker, m1rp, SM, p2, SM, m1lp*, repeat *–*. P to DS, pDS, p1, turn work. (4 sts inc'd)
Repeat the previous 2 rows (RS and WS) 5 more times. Both shoulders now have 7 DSs. MDS and k to BOR making the RS increases as before. During the next rnd, work remaining DSs as 1 st.

SHOULDER INCREASES

Increase rnd: K1, SM, m1l, k to marker, m1r, SM, k2, m1l, k to marker, m1r, SM, k1. (4 sts inc'd)
Continue working the increase rnd until the back piece (between the markers) has 76 (84, 94, 102, 114) (122, 130, 138) sts. Continue to stripe as before.

You have worked shoulder increases 20 (24, 28, 32, 38) (40, 44, 48) times, including the increases in the short rows.

FRONT

Next, separate the front and back pieces: K1, RM, k to next marker, RM, k1, turn work.

Leave the 76 (84, 94, 102, 114) (122, 130, 138) back sts on hold on the cable of the circular needle or place them on scrap yarn, and continue to work the front. The front piece has 76 (84, 94, 102, 114) (122, 130, 138) sts.

Row 1 (WS): P to end.
Row 2 (RS): K to end.
Continue to work in Stockinette Stitch (k all sts on RS, p all sts on WS) while continuing to stripe, until piece measures approx. 6.75 (7, 7.5, 8.25, 9.5) (9.75, 10.75, 11.5)" / 17 (18, 19, 21, 24) (25, 27, 29) cm measured from the edge of the armhole. Cut yarns and leave front sts on hold on the cable of the circular needle or place them on scrap yarn.

BACK

Move the back sts back to the needle. With RS facing you, join new lengths of MC and CC and begin to work the back sts as follows:
K1, RM, k to next marker, RM, k1, turn work.

Row 1 (WS): P to end.

Row 2 (RS): K to end.

Continue to work in Stockinette Stitch (k all sts on RS, p all sts on WS) while continuing to stripe, until piece measures approx. 6.75 (7, 7.5, 8.25, 9.5) (9.75, 10.75, 11.5)" / 17 (18, 19, 21, 24) (25, 27, 29) cm measured from the edge of the armhole. The front and back piece are now of the same length.

JOIN THE PIECES

Knit the back sts (RS row), PM (BOR marker). Continue by knitting the front sts and place another marker (side marker). K the back sts to BOR. You should now have 156 (172, 192, 208, 232) (248, 264, 280) sts.

Decrease rnd: *K1, ssk, k to last 3 sts before the marker, k2tog, k1, SM*, repeat *–*. (4 sts dec'd)

Non-decrease rnd: K to end.

Repeat the decrease and non-decrease rnds a total of 3 times. You should now have 144 (160, 180, 196, 220) (236, 252, 268) sts. Remove the side marker.

Continue working in Stockinette Stitch (k all sts) while striping at the same time, until the body measures, 9" / 23 cm from the underarm (or 2" / 5 cm less than desired length).

Cut CC and continue with MC only. Change to US 7 / 4.5 mm needles and begin to work in *k1, p1* rib for 2" / 5 cm. BO all sts loosely or use a stretchy bind-off technique.

SLEEVES

For the sleeves, you will pick up sts from the underarm and stripe holding the yarns together as you did for the body.

With US 8 / 5 mm needles and both MC and CC, from the centre of the underarm, pick up and k 26 (28, 30, 33, 37) (40, 43, 45) sts from the underarm to the shoulder. Then pick up and k 26 (28, 30, 33, 37) (40, 43, 45) sts from the other side of the armhole. Join to work in the rnd and PM for BOR. Pick up 2 sts for every 3 rows.

You should now have 52 (56, 60, 66, 74) (80, 86, 90) sts.

Decreases

Non-decrease rnds: K 12 (10, 9, 8, 6) (6, 5, 5) rnds.

Decrease rnd: K1, k2tog, k to last 3 sts, ssk, k1. (2 sts dec'd)

Repeat the non-decrease rnds and decrease rnd a total of 6 (7, 8, 9, 11) (12, 14, 14) times while striping at the same time. You should now have 40 (42, 44, 48, 52) (56, 58, 62) sts.

Work in Stockinette Stitch until the sleeve measures 14.5 (15, 15.25, 15.25, 15.75) (16, 16.5, 17)" / 37 (38, 39, 39, 40) (41, 42, 43) cm, or 2" / 5 cm less than desired length.

Cut CC and continue with MC only.

Change to US 7 / 4.5 mm needles and work *k1, p1* -ribbing for 2" / 5 cm.

Bind off all sts loosely or with a stretchy bind-off technique. If the cuff feels loose, you can also use a tight bind-off.

Work the other sleeve the same. You can choose to match the stripes in the first sleeve or use a different order.

FINISHING

Weave in all ends on the WS. Steam or wet block to measurements.

Erin Jensen

42 Poseidon Ridge

Poseidon Ridge is a classic triangle shawl that's engaging and easily memorised – but with a twist. It looks like brioche, but it's much easier!

SIZE

One Size

FINISHED MEASUREMENTS

Length: 66" / 167 cm.
Depth: 33" / 83 cm.

MATERIALS

Yarn: 3 skeins of Studio DK by Neighborhood Fiber Co. (100% organic Merino, 275 yds / 251 m – 113 g), colourway Woodberry.

2 skeins of Loft by Neighborhood Fiber Co. (70% mohair, 30% silk, 459 yds / 420 m – 50 g), colourway Woodberry.

Both yarns are held together throughout the pattern.

If you decide to use another yarn, you will need approx. 825 yds / 755 m of DK-weight yarn and approx. 750 yds / 686 m of lace-weight yarn.

Needles: US 10 / 6 mm and US 10.5 / 7 mm 32" / 80 cm circular needles.

Notions: Stitch markers.

GAUGE

14.5 sts x 24 rows to 4" / 10 cm on US 10 / 6 mm in Half Twisted Rib, after blocking.

STITCH PATTERNS

Half Twisted Rib
for swatching
Row 1 (RS): *K1tbl, p*, repeat *–* to end.
Row 2 (WS): *K, p1tbl*, repeat *–* to end.

NOTES

You can find the abbreviations and detailed instructions for techniques used in this pattern in the Abbreviations (pp. 20–23) and Techniques (pp. 15–19) sections.

Slip markers as you come across them.

Note the RS of your shawl with a removable marker. It is easy to mix up the RS and WS while knitting.

Bind off with a needle 1–2 sizes larger than your gauge needle. All knitting, but especially rib pattern knitting, blooms when blocked. You do not want your bind-off to be a hindrance to your shawl reaching its full size.

If working the optional i-cord edging: On every RS row, knit the first two and last two stitches loosely. On the WS, do not pull your working yarn too tightly after slipping the first two stitches and working the third stitch.

CONSTRUCTION

This triangle shawl is knitted from top to bottom, beginning from the centre of the long edge and making increases on both edges and on both sides of the central stitch. It is worked flat in one piece with an optional i-cord that you will continue to work for the top edge.

Upon cast-on choose either a beginner-friendly Garter Tab Cast-On or the more advanced I-Cord Tab Cast-On (pictured in sample). From there, both sides are worked in a Half Twisted Rib and Eyelet pattern, while increasing on each right side.

DIRECTIONS

Using the Long-Tail Cast-On Method or method of choice, cast on 2 sts.
Continue by choosing either the Garter Tab Set-Up or the I-Cord Tab Set-Up.

If working the Garter Tab/Edge, turn work.
If working the I-Cord Tab/Edge, do not turn work.

GARTER TAB SET-UP

Rows 1–6: K to end.
Do not turn work after working row 6.
Turn work 90 degrees clockwise.
Pick up 3 sts, 1 in each of the garter ridges. (3 sts inc'd) (5 sts in total)
Turn work 90 degrees clockwise again.
Pick up 2 sts from the 2-stitch cast-on edge. (2 sts inc'd) (7 sts in total)
Turn work.
Continue to Shawl Body Set-Up.

I-CORD TAB SET-UP

Row 1 (RS): Slip both sts to the left-hand needle.
Row 2 (RS): K to end.
Repeat rows 1–2, 3 more times. Do not turn work.
Turn work 90 degrees clockwise.
Pick up 3 sts along the newly created i-cord. (3 sts inc'd) (5 sts in total)
Turn work 90 degrees clockwise again.
Pick up 2 sts from the 2-stitch cast-on edge. (2 sts inc'd) (7 sts in total)

Note! When using the I-Cord Tab Set-Up omit the k2 on the first and last sts of each WS row. Instead, with yarn in front, slip the first and last 2 sts purlwise on the WS.

Turn work and continue to Shawl Body Set-Up.

SHAWL BODY SET-UP

Row 1 (WS): K2, PM, p1tbl, PM, p1, PM, p1tbl, PM, k2.
Row 2 (RS): K2, SM, m1l, k1tbl, m1r, SM, k1, SM, m1l, k1tbl, m1r, SM, k2. (4 sts inc'd) (11 sts)
Row 3 (WS): K2, SM, k1, p1tbl, k1, SM, p1, SM, k1, p1tbl, k1, SM, k2.

SHAWL BODY

Row 1 (RS): K2, SM, m1l, *p1, k1tbl*, repeat *–* to 1 st before m, p1, m1r, SM, k1, SM, m1l, p1, *k1tbl, p1*, repeat *–* to m, m1r, SM, k2. (4 sts inc'd)

Row 2 (WS): K2, SM, *p1tbl, k1*, repeat *–* to 1 st before m, p1tbl, SM, p1, SM, p1tbl, *k1, p1tbl*, repeat *–* to m, SM, k2.

Row 3 (RS): K2, SM, m1l, *k1tbl, p1*, repeat *–* to 1 st before m, k1tbl, m1r, SM, k1, SM, m1l, k1tbl, *p1, k1tbl*, repeat *–* to m, m1r, SM, k2. (4 sts inc'd)

Row 4 (WS): K2, SM, *k1, p1tbl*, repeat *–* to 1 st before m, k1, SM, p1, SM, k1, *p1tbl, k1*, repeat *–* to m, SM, k2.

Rows 5–20: Repeat rows 1–4, 4 more times. (32 sts inc'd in total) (51 sts)
Your st count should be as follows: 2 sts – 23 sts – 1 st – 23 sts – 2 sts.

Rows 21–22: Repeat rows 1–2 once more. (4 sts inc'd) (55 sts)
Your st count should be as follows: 2 sts – 25 sts – 1 st – 25 sts – 2 sts.

EYELET RIB

In this section, a couple of special abbreviations will be used.
sl1tbl: Slip st through back loop. Put the right needle through the back loop of the st from left to right and slip the st off the left needle. This will cause the st to twist.

sl1kw: Slip 1 st knitwise from left-hand needle to right-hand needle with yarn in back (when working RS) and with yarn in front (when working WS).

sl1pw: Slip 1 st purlwise from left-hand needle to right-hand needle with yarn in back (when working RS) and with yarn in front (if working WS).

Start working the eyelet rib section as follows:

Row 23 (RS): K2, SM, m1l, k1tbl, *yo, sl1kw, sl1tbl, sl 2 sts from right-hand needle to left-hand needle, k2tog*, repeat *–* to m, yo, SM, k to m, SM, yo, *sl1pw, sl1kw, sl 2 sts from right-hand needle to left-hand needle, k2tog tbl, yo*, repeat *–* to 1 st before m, k1tbl, m1r, SM, k2. (4 sts inc'd) (59 sts)

Row 24 (WS): K2, SM, *k1, p1tbl*, repeat *–* to 1 st before m, k1, SM, p1, SM, k1, *p1tbl, k1*, repeat *–* to m, SM, k2.

Rows 25–32: Repeat rows 1–4 of Shawl Body twice. (16 sts inc'd) (75 sts)
Your st count should be as follows: 2 sts – 35 sts – 1 st – 35 sts – 2 sts.

Rows 33–34: Repeat rows 1–2 of Shawl Body once. (4 sts inc'd) (79 sts)
Your st count should be as follows: 2 sts – 37 sts – 1 st – 37 sts – 2 sts.

Rows 35–36: Repeat rows 1–2 of Eyelet Rib once. (4 sts inc'd) (83 sts)
Your st count should be as follows: 2 sts – 39 sts – 1 st – 39 sts – 2 sts.

Rows 37–52: Repeat rows 1–4 of Shawl Body 4 times. (32 sts inc'd) (115 sts)
Your st count should be as follows: 2 sts – 55 sts – 1 st – 55 sts – 2 sts.

Rows 53–54: Repeat rows 1–2 of Shawl Body once. (4 sts inc'd) (119 sts)
Your st count should be as follows: 2 sts – 57 sts – 1 st – 57 sts – 2 sts

Rows 55–56: Repeat rows 1–2 of Eyelet Rib once. (4 sts inc'd) (123 sts)
Your st count should be as follows: 2 sts – 59 sts – 1 st – 59 sts – 2 sts.

Rows 57–64: Repeat rows 1–4 of Shawl Body twice. (16 sts inc'd) (139 sts)
Your st count should be as follows: 2 sts – 67 sts – 1 st – 67 sts – 2 sts.

Rows 65–66: Repeat rows 1–2 of Shawl Body once. (4 sts inc'd) (143 sts)
Your st count should be as follows: 2 sts – 69 sts – 1 st – 69 sts – 2 sts.

Rows 67–68: Repeat rows 1–2 of Eyelet Rib one time. (4 sts inc'd) (147 sts)
Your st count should be as follows: 2 sts – 71 sts – 1 st – 71 sts – 2 sts.

Rows 69–84: Repeat rows 1–4 of Shawl Body 4 times. (32 sts inc'd) (179 sts)
Your st count should be as follows: 2 sts – 87 sts – 1 st – 87 sts – 2 sts.

Rows 85–86: Repeat rows 1–2 of Shawl Body once. (4 sts inc'd) (183 sts)
Your st count should be as follows: 2 sts – 89 sts – 1 st – 89 sts – 2 sts.

Rows 87–88: Repeat rows 1–2 of Eyelet Rib once. (4 sts inc'd) (187 sts)
Your st count should be as follows: 2 sts – 91 sts – 1 st – 91 sts – 2 sts.

Rows 89–96: Repeat rows 1–4 of Shawl Body twice. (16 sts inc'd) (203 sts)
Your st count should be as follows: 2 sts – 99 sts – 1 st – 99 sts – 2 sts.

Rows 97–98: Repeat rows 1–2 of Shawl Body once. (4 sts inc'd) (207 sts)
Your st count should be as follows: 2 sts – 101 sts – 1 st – 101 sts – 2 sts.

Row 99–100: Repeat rows 1–2 of Eyelet Rib once. (4 sts inc'd) (211 sts)

Your st count should be as follows: 2 sts – 103 sts – 1 st – 103 sts – 2 sts.

Rows 101–116: Repeat rows 1–4 of Shawl Body 4 times. (32 sts inc'd) (243 sts)
Your st count should be as follows: 2 sts – 119 sts – 1 st – 119 sts – 2 sts.

Rows 117–118: Repeat rows 1–2 of Shawl Body once. (4 sts inc'd) (247 sts)
Your st count should be as follows: 2 sts – 121 sts – 1 st – 121 sts – 2 sts.

Rows 119–120: Repeat rows 1–2 of Eyelet Rib once. (4 sts inc'd) (251 sts)
Your st count should be as follows: 2 sts – 123 sts – 1 st – 123 sts – 2 sts.

Rows 121–128: Repeat rows 1–4 of Shawl Body twice. (16 sts inc'd) (267 sts)
Your st count should be as follows: 2 sts – 131 sts – 1 st – 131 sts – 2 sts.

Rows 129–130: Repeat rows 1–2 of Shawl Body once. (4 sts inc'd) (271 sts)
Your st count should be as follows: 2 sts – 133 sts – 1 st – 133 sts – 2 sts.

Rows 131–132: Repeat rows 1–2 of Eyelet Rib once. (4 sts inc'd) (275 sts)
Your st count should be as follows: 2 sts – 135 sts – 1 st – 135 sts – 2 sts.

Rows 133–148: Repeat rows 1–4 of Shawl Body 4 times. (32 sts inc'd) (307 sts)
Your st count should be as follows: 2 sts – 151 sts – 1 st – 151 sts – 2 sts.

BIND–OFF

Row 149 (RS): Bind off loosely in pattern across all sts.

FINISHING

Weave in all ends. Block the shawl aggressively to measurements.

Miriam Walchshäusl

43–45 Joyce

This set consists of a hat, a scarf and a pair of fingerless mitts. With large needles and DK-weight yarn, these accessories knit up fast. The stitch pattern is rewarding but not too hard to create.

SIZES

Hat & Fingerless Mitts
1 (2, 3)

Recommended ease: Approx. 5" / 7.5 cm (for hat) and 0.5–1" / 1.5–2.5 cm of negative ease (for mitts) for a snug fit.

Scarf
One Size

FINISHED MEASUREMENTS

Hat
Circumference: 19.25 (20.75, 22.5)" / 48 (52, 56.5) cm.
Height: 8 (8, 8.25)" / 20 (20, 21) cm.

Mitts
Length: 8.25 (8.75, 9)" / 21 (21.5, 22.5) cm.
Palm Circumference: 5.75 (6.5, 7.5)" / 14 (16.5, 19) cm.

Scarf
Length: 86.5" / 216 cm.
Width: 12.25" / 30.5 cm.

MATERIALS

Hat
Yarn: C1: 2 balls of Heavy Merino by Knitting for Olive (100% wool, 137 yds / 125 m – 50 g), colourway Rust.
C2: 2 balls of Soft Silk Mohair by Knitting for Olive (70% mohair, 30% silk, 246 yds / 225 m – 25 g), colourway Rust.
C3: 1 ball of Shio by Ito Yarn (100% wool, 525 yds / 480 m – 40 g), colourway Hydrangea.
You will be knitting with 1 strand of C1 and 2 strands of C2 held together throughout the pattern, 4 strands of C3 held together will be used for embroidering.
If you decide to use another yarn, you will need approx. 153 (164, 175) yds / 140 (150, 160) m of worsted-weight yarn in C1, 306 (328) 350 yds / 280 (300, 320) m of lace-weight yarn in C2 and 22 yds / 20 m of lace-weight yarn in C3 for contrast stitching, preferably in bright contrast colour.

Mitts
Yarn: C1: 1 ball of Heavy Merino by Knitting for Olive (100% wool, 137 yds / 125 m – 50g), colourway Rust.
C2: 1 ball of Soft Silk Mohair by Knitting for Olive (70% mohair, 30% silk, 246 yds / 225 m – 25 g), colourway Rust.
C3: 1 ball of Shio by Ito Yarn (100% wool, 525 yds / 480 m – 40 g), colourway Hydrangea.
You will be knitting with 1 strand of C1 and 2 strands of C2 held together throughout the pattern, 4 strands of C3 held together will be used for embroidering.
If you decide to use another yarn, you will need approx. 95 (106, 112) yds / 87 (97, 102) m of worsted-weight yarn in C1, 190 (212, 224) yds / 174 (194, 205) m of lace-weight yarn in C2 and 22 yds / 20 m of lace-weight yarn in C3 for contrast stitching, preferably in bright contrast colour.

Scarf
Yarn: C1: 5 balls of Heavy Merino by Knitting for Olive (100% wool, 137 yds / 125 m – 50 g), colourway Rust.
C2: 6 balls of Soft Silk Mohair by Knitting

for Olive (70% mohair, 30% silk, 246 yds / 225 m – 25 g), colourway Rust.
C3: 1 ball of Shio by Ito Yarn (100% wool, 525 yds / 480 m – 40 g), colourway Hydrangea.

You will be knitting with 1 strand of C1 and 2 strands of C2 held together throughout the pattern, 4 strands of C3 held together will be used for embroidering.

If you decide to use another yarn, you will need approx. 656 yds / 600 m of worsted-weight yarn in C1, 1312 yds / 1200 m of lace-weight yarn in C2 and 220 yds / 201 m of lace-weight yarn in C3 or contrast stitching, preferably in bright contrast colour.

Full Set

Yarn: C1: 7 balls of Heavy Merino by Knitting for Olive (100% wool, 137 yds / 125 m – 50 g), colourway Rust.
C2: 8 balls of Soft Silk Mohair by Knitting for Olive (70% mohair, 30% silk, 246 yds / 225 m – 25 g), colourway Rust.
C3: 1 ball of Shio by Ito Yarn (100% wool, 525 yds / 480 m – 40 g), colourway Hydrangea.

You will be knitting with 1 strand of C1 and 2 strands of C2 held together throughout the pattern, 4 strands of C3 held together will be used for embroidering.

If you decide to use another yarn, you will need approx. 904 (926, 943) yds / 827 (847, 862) m of worsted-weight yarn in C1, 1808 (1852, 1886) yds / 1654 (1694, 1725) m of lace-weight yarn in C2 and 264 yds / 241 m of lace-weight yarn in C3 for contrast stitching, preferably in bright contrast colour.

Needles: US 8 / 5 mm 24" / 60 cm circular or straight needles.

Notions: Stitch markers, tapestry needle, scrap cardboard for making pompoms.

GAUGE

17 sts x 25 rows to 4" / 10 cm in Stockinette Stitch, after blocking.

STITCH PATTERNS

Joyce Pattern (in the rnd)

Rnds 1–5: K to end.
Rnd 6: *P1, k1*, repeat *–* to end.

Joyce Pattern (flat)

Rows 1, 3 and 5 (RS): K to end.
Rows 2 and 4 (WS): K1, p to 1 st before end, k1.
Row 6: K1, *k1, p1*, repeat *–* to 1 st before end, k1.

NOTES

You can find the abbreviations and detailed instructions for techniques used in this pattern in the Abbreviations (pp. 20–23) and Techniques (pp. 15–19) sections.

Slip stitch markers as you come across them.

You can use circular needles or DPNs, depending on your favourite method for small circumference knitting.

CONSTRUCTION

The scarf is worked flat in the main pattern, while the mitts as well as the hat are both worked bottom up in the round. The scarf and mitts both feature a 1 x 1 Ribbing at the start and then change into the main Joyce pattern.

The garments receive their finishing touches afterwards by lightly threading a contrast colour through the knitted piece. This creates an overall fun and pleasing look, while staying highly versatile and opening space for your own creativity. Play with colour and make the unisex set yours.

MODIFICATIONS

These pieces are great for using up stash and left-over yarn from other projects!

DIRECTIONS: HAT

With 1 strand of C1 and 2 strands of C2 held together, cast on 82 (88, 96) sts using the Long-Tail Cast-On Method or method of choice.

Set-up row: Place marker for the beginning of rnd (BOR), *k1, p1*, repeat *–* to end.
Join sts to knit in the rnd being careful not to twist sts.

BODY

Rnd 1: *K1, p1*, repeat *–* to end.
Continue to work in established 1 x 1 Ribbing for 18 rnds in total.

Knit 1 rnd (k all sts).
Work another 18 rnds of 1 x 1 Ribbing.

Start working the Joyce pattern as follows:
Rnds 1–5: K to end.
Rnd 6: *P1, k1*, repeat *–* to end.
Repeat previous 6 rnds once more.

CROWN

Next, you will work the crown decreases. You will work decreases according to your size in some rnds, while at the same time continuing to follow the established Joyce pattern.

Knit 1 rnd.

Size 1 only
Decrease rnd 1: K2, *k2tog, k4*, repeat *–* 6 times, k2tog, k3, *k2tog, k4*, repeat *–* 6 times, k2tog, k1. (14 sts dec'd) (68 sts)

Size 2 only
Decrease rnd 1: K2, *k2tog, k4*, repeat *–* 4 times, *k2tog, k3*, repeat *–* 7 times, *k2tog, k4*, repeat *–* 4 times, k2tog, k1. (16 sts dec'd) (72 sts)

Size 3 only
Decrease rnd 1: K3, *k2tog, k6*, repeat *–* 11 times, k2tog, k3. (12 sts dec'd) (84 sts)

All sizes
Knit 3 rnds.
Next rnd: *P1, k1*, repeat *–* to end.
Knit 1 rnd.

Size 1 only
Decrease rnd 2: K2, k2tog, k2, *k2tog, k3*, repeat *–* 11 times, k2tog, k2, k2tog, k1. (14 sts dec'd) (54 sts)

Size 2 only
Decrease rnd 2: K2, *k2tog, k2*, repeat *–* 4 times, *k2tog, k3*, repeat *–* 7 times, *k2tog, k2*, repeat *–* 4 times, k2tog, k1. (16 sts dec'd) (56 sts)

Size 3 only
Decrease rnd 2: K3, *k2tog, k5*, repeat *–* 11 times, k2tog, k2. (12 sts dec'd) (72 sts)

All sizes
Knit 3 rnds.
Next rnd: *P1, k1*, repeat *–* to end.
Knit 1 rnd.

Size 1 only
Decrease rnd 3: K1, *k2tog, k2*, repeat *–* 6 times, k2tog, k1, *k2tog, k2*, repeat *–* 6 times, k2tog. (14 sts dec'd) (40 sts)

Size 2 only
Decrease rnd 3: K1, *k2tog, k2*, repeat *–* 4 times, *k2tog, k1*, repeat *–* 7 times, *k2tog, k2*, repeat *–* 4 times, k2tog. (16 sts dec'd) (40 sts)

Size 3 only
Decrease rnd 3: K2, *k2tog, k4*, repeat *–* 11 times, k2tog, k2. (12 sts dec'd) (60 sts)

All sizes
Knit 1 rnd.

Size 1 only
Decrease rnd 4: K1, k2tog, *k2tog, k1*, repeat *–* 11 times, *k2tog*, repeat *–* twice. (14 sts dec'd) (26 sts)

Size 2 only
Decrease rnd 4: K1, *k2tog*, repeat *–* 4 times, *k2tog, k1*, repeat *–* 7 times, *k2tog*, repeat *–* 4 times, k2tog. (16 sts dec'd) (24 sts)

Size 3 only
Decrease rnd 4: K2, *k2tog, k3*, repeat *–* 11 times, k2tog, k1. (12 sts dec'd) (48 sts)

All sizes
Knit 1 rnd.
Next rnd: *P1, k1*, repeat *–* to end.
Knit 1 rnd.

Size 1 only
Decrease rnd 5: Work k3tog decrease twice, work k2tog decrease to end. (14 sts dec'd) (12 sts)

Size 2 only
Decrease rnd 5: Work k3tog decrease twice, work k2tog decrease to end. (13 sts dec'd) (11 sts)

Size 3 only
Decrease rnd 5: K1, *k2tog, k2*, repeat *–* 11 times, k2tog, k1. (12 sts dec'd) (36 sts)
Decrease rnd 6: K1, *k2tog, k1*, repeat *–* 11 times, k2tog. (12 sts dec'd) (24 sts)
Decrease rnd 7: Work k2tog decrease 12 times. (12 sts dec'd) (12 sts)

Cut yarn leaving a long tail, thread through remaining 12 (11, 12) sts and secure.

FINISHING

Weave in ends. Wet block to measurements.

Work one pompom and sew onto the top of your hat.

Embroidery

Work embroidery with C3. From yarn C3, cut 4 strands of approx. 35" / 89 cm and thread them through a tapestry needle. *Work 3 rows of narrow spaced stitching, 3 rows of wide spaced stitching, 3 rows of narrow spaced stitching*, repeat *–* after leaving a few Joyce pattern repeats without embroidery.

Narrow spaced stitching: Start in Joyce pattern rnd/row 2 and, from back to front, work over and then under every stitch leg in this rnd/row, pulling the thread carefully (not too tight). At the end of the rnd/row stitch from back into rnd/row 3 and continue in established pattern while making sure to use every other leg in up/down motion than in previous rnd/row. Continue same pattern for rnd/row 4. 3 total embroidery rnds/rows worked.

Wide spaced stitching: Start in Joyce pattern rnd/row 2 and, from back to front, work over and then under every full stitch (2 stitch legs) in this rnd/row, pulling the thread carefully (not too tight). At the end of the rnd/row stitch from back into rnd/row 3 and continue in established pattern while making sure to use every other leg in up/down motion than in previous rnd/row. Continue same pattern for rnd/row 4. 3 total embroidery rnds/rows worked.

DIRECTIONS: MITTS

With 1 strand of C1 and 2 strands of C2 held together, cast on 24 (28, 32) sts using your elastic cast-on method of choice, such as the German Twist Cast-On Method.

Set-up row: Place marker for the beginning of the rnd (BOR), *k1, p1*, repeat *–* across all sts. Join sts to knit in the rnd being careful not to twist sts.

BODY

Continue in 1 x 1 Ribbing for 25 (27, 29) rnds total, or until desired ribbing length.

Note! The work will now be split in two in order to work the thumb hole. You are working flat, back and forth, from this point onwards.

Row 1 (RS): K to end of row, turn work.
Row 2 (WS): K1, p to 1 st before end, k1, turn work.
Continue working the Joyce Pattern (rows 1–6) as described a total of 2 times, ending with a row 6.

Note! You will now join your work again to the rnd and knit the remaining part in the rnd.
Rnd 1: K all sts, join to continue working in the rnd.
Rnd 2: K to end.
Continue working the Joyce Pattern (rnds 1–6) once.
Work another 5 rnds in Joyce Pattern (or until you reach desired length), remove BOR marker and bind off loosely.

FINISHING

Weave in ends. Wet block to measurements.

With C3 work embroidery as instructed for the hat.

DIRECTIONS: SCARF

With 1 strand of C1 and 2 strands of C2 held together, cast on 52 sts using the Long-Tail Cast-On Method or method of choice.

Set-up Row (WS): K1, p until 1 st before end, k1.

BODY

Note! Start and end all rows with a knit st as indicated in Stitch Patterns.
Start with row 1 of the Joyce Pattern (flat) and continue knitting in pattern.

Work the pattern repeat (rows 1–6) 89 more times, ending after a row 6. Your work should now measure 86.5" / 216 cm measured from the cast-on edge. If desired, you can also knit the scarf longer.

Bind off loosely.

FINISHING

Weave in ends. Wet block to measurements.

Create 10 pompoms, 5 each on every short side of the scarf.

With C3 work embroidery as instructed for the hat.

46 Glow

Glow is a simple but fun headband. It's knitted in the round with two strands of yarn together. Make it either classic or bold, depending on the colours you choose.

SIZES

1 (2, 3)

Recommended ease: 4.5–6" / 11.5–15 cm of negative ease.

To fit a head circumference of 20–21 (21–23, 23–25)" / 51–53.5 cm (53.5–58.5, 58.5–63.5) cm.

FINISHED MEASUREMENTS

Circumference: 16 (17.25, 18.75)" / 40 (43.5, 46.5) cm.

MATERIALS

Yarn: 1 skein of Peruvian Highland Wool by Filcolana (100% new wool, 109 yds / 100 m – 50 g), colourway 255 Limelight.

1 skein of Tilia by Filcolana (70% super kid mohair, 30% mulberry silk, 230 yds / 210 m – 25 g), colourway 101 Offwhite.

In addition, the sample features stripes made in various scraps of silk mohair yarn.

Both yarns – one strand of each – are held together throughout the pattern.

If you decide to use another yarn, you will need approx. 55 (65, 71) yds / 50 (60, 65) m of DK-weight yarn and approx. 55 (65, 71) yds / 50 (60, 65) m of lace-weight yarn.

Needles: US 6 / 4 mm 16" / 40 cm circular needles.

Notions: 1 stitch marker.

GAUGE

18 sts x 28 rows to 4" / 10 cm in Twisted Ribbing, after blocking.

NOTES

You can find the abbreviations and detailed instructions for techniques used in this pattern in the Abbreviations (pp. 20–23) and Techniques (pp. 15–19) sections.

Slip stitch marker as you come across it.

CONSTRUCTION

This headband is knitted seamlessly in the round with two strands of yarn held together.

MODIFICATIONS

If you want a multicoloured, striped version, you can use different strands of left-over silk mohair instead. You will need approx. 230 yds / 210 m / 25 g of lace weight silk mohair. Knit with each colour for about 0.2–1.2" / 0.5–3 cm, or to liking. You can choose as many or as few colours as you want to, depending on your preferences. The sample features stripes made in various scraps of silk mohair yarn.

DIRECTIONS

Cast on 72 (78, 84) sts using the Long-Tail Cast-On Method or method of choice. Place marker for the beginning of the rnd (BOR) and join to work in the rnd being careful not to twist sts.

Rnd 1: *K1tbl, p1*, repeat *–* to end. Continue in established 1 x 1 Twisted Ribbing until the work measures 6.5 (7, 7)" / 16.5 (18, 18) cm.

FINISHING

Fold the knitted piece down with the WSs facing each other. Then, attach the two edges (cast-on and live sts) together, while at the same time binding off the live sts loosely. Pick up one st from the cast-on edge, place the st on the left-hand needle and knit the two sts together in ribbing (make sure to match the established rib pattern). At the same time, bind off using a stretchy bind-off method. This means you will always have a maximum of two sts on the right-hand needle. Continue until you have picked up all sts from the cast-on edge and bound the sts off.

Weave in all ends. Wet block to measurements.

George Cullen

47 Colour Field

Colour Field is a fun scarf with diagonal edges. Because it is knitted in simple Garter Stitch, you can concentrate on the shaping. Marling offers a great opportunity to play with colours.

SIZE

One Size

FINISHED MEASUREMENTS

Length: 60" / 150 cm.
Width: 11.75" / 29.5 cm.

MATERIALS

Yarn: MC: 2 skeins of Cirro by The Fibre Co. (40% alpaca, 40% cotton, 20% merino, 246 yds / 225 m – 50 g), colourway Graceful.
CC: 7 balls (1 in each colour) of Lore Minis by The Fibre Co. (100% Romney wool, 68 yds / 62 m – 25 g), colourways Gentle, Passionate, Sensitive, Courage, Stable, Caring and Pensive.
If you decide to use another yarn, you will need approx. 487 yds / 445 m of sport-weight yarn in MC and a total of approx. 322 yds / 294 m of DK-weight yarn in CC.

Needles: US 10 / 6 mm straight or 24–40" / 60–100 cm long circular needles.

Notions: 3 stitch markers.

GAUGE

15 sts x 28 rows to 4" / 10 cm in Garter Stitch with MC and CC held together, after blocking.

SPECIAL TECHNIQUES

Marling

Marling refers to the technique of knitting two strands of yarn together at the same time as if they were a single strand. In the pattern where it reads 'with MC + CC' knit with both a strand of the MC and a strand of the CC to create a marled fabric. When switching from double-stranded (marled) sections to single-stranded (un-marled) sections, the CC should be left at the front of the work ready to knit the next row.

NOTES

You can find the abbreviations and detailed instructions for techniques used in this pattern in the Abbreviations (pp. 20–23) and Techniques (pp. 15–19) sections.

This scarf can be knitted with lots of small fragments of leftover DK-weight yarns in place of the CC Lore Minis for the marled sections. Each marled shape takes approx. 23 yds / 21 m (approx. 9 g) of DK-weight yarn.

Two strands of a lace-weight mohair can be used instead of the proposed MC. However, please note that this will increase meterage requirements. When holding several strands together, be careful that none of the strands are dropped.
When adding in a new CC, there is no need to tie it in as it is held in place as if it is knitted, just leave a long enough tail to weave in at the end.

Half of the row is knitted with a single strand of the MC and the other half is knitted with both the MC and CC held together. The point at which you move from knitting single-stranded to double-stranded is marked by a central stitch marker. The CC changes with each new block and alternates throughout the project for a total of 14 blocks consisting of 7 different colours used twice.

Diagonal edges are created by increasing or decreasing on either side of some RS rows and an edge is created by slipping stitches. These edge stitches are marked by stitch markers.

Slip markers as you come across them.

CONSTRUCTION

This scarf is knitted from end to end and consists of alternating marled and un-marled sections.

MODIFICATIONS

The length of the scarf can be lengthened or shortened by adding or taking away blocks.

DIRECTIONS

With MC, cast on 44 sts using the Long-Tail Cast-On Method or method of choice.

SET-UP SECTION

Row 1 (RS): With MC k2, PM, k25, PM, with MC+CC k15, PM, sl2 pwise wyif.
Row 2 (WS): With MC + CC k2, SM, k to marker, bring CC to the front, SM, with MC k to marker, SM, sl2 pwise wyif.
Row 3 (RS): With MC k2, SM, ssk, k to marker, SM, with MC + CC k to 1 st before marker, k into the front and back of the same st (kfb), SM, sl2 pwise wyif.
Row 4 (WS): Repeat row 2.
Row 5 (RS): Repeat row 3.
Row 6 (WS): Repeat row 2.
Row 7 (RS): With MC k2, SM, k to marker, SM, with MC+CC k to marker, SM, sl2 pwise wyif.
Repeat rows 2–7, 3 times and then rows 2–6 once more. Break CC.

You should have 27 double-stranded sts to the left of the central marker (including the slipped edge sts) and 17 single-stranded sts to the right of the central marker (including the slipped edge sts). You should have 44 sts in total.

RIGHT-LEANING BLOCK

Row 1 (RS): With MC + new CC k2, SM, k to marker, bring CC to the front, SM, with MC k to marker, SM, sl2 pwise wyif.
Row 2 (WS): With MC k2, SM, k to marker, SM, with MC + CC k to m, SM, sl2 pwise wyif.
Row 3 (RS): With MC + CC k2, SM, kfb, k to marker, bring CC to the front, SM, with MC k to 2 st before marker, k2tog, SM, sl2 pwise wyif.
Row 4 (WS): Repeat row 2.
Row 5 (RS): Repeat row 3.
Row 6 (WS): Repeat row 2.
Repeat rows 1–6, 4 more times. Break CC.

You should have 27 double-stranded sts to the right of the central marker (including the slipped edge sts) and 17 single-stranded sts to the left (including the slipped edge sts). You should have 44 sts in total.

LEFT-LEANING BLOCK

Row 1 (RS): With MC k2, SM, k to marker, SM, with MC + new CC k to marker, SM, sl2 pwise wyif.
Row 2 (WS): With MC + CC k2, SM, k to marker, bring CC to the front, SM, with MC k to marker, SM, sl2 pwise wyif.
Row 3 (RS): With MC k2, SM, ssk, k to marker, SM, with MC + CC k to 1 st before marker, kfb, SM, sl2 pwise wyif.
Row 4 (WS): Repeat row 2.
Row 5 (RS): Repeat row 3.
Row 6 (WS): Repeat row 2.
Repeat rows 1–6, 4 times. Break CC. You should have 27 double-stranded sts to the left of the central marker (including the slipped edge sts) and 17 single-stranded sts to the right of the central marker (including the slipped edge sts). You should have 44 sts in total.

Repeat instructions for the right leaning blocks and left leaning blocks another 5 times and then the right leaning block once more alternating between the CC colours.

With MC bind off all sts being careful not to pull sts too tightly. Remove stitch markers as you reach them.

FINISHING

Weave in ends. Wet block lightly to measurements.

Pauliina Kuunsola

48 Vaapukka

These cosy mitts are engaging to knit, featuring different textured patterns that are created with just knit and purl stitches. The length of the mitts is easy to alter.

SIZES

1 (2, 3)

Recommended ease: Approx. 0.5–1" / 1.5–2.5 cm of negative ease for a snug fit.

To fit a hand circumference of approx. 6.5 (7, 7.5)" / 16.5 (18, 19) cm.

FINISHED MEASUREMENTS

Hand Circumference: 6 (6.5, 7)" / 15 (16.5, 17.5) cm.
Height: Approx. 6.25" / 15.5 cm.

MATERIALS

Yarn: 1 skein of Lalland Aran by Di Gilpin (100% lambswool, 164 yds / 150 m – 100 g), colourway Firebird.
If you decide to use another yarn, you will need approx. 66 (82, 99) yds / 61 (75, 91) m of aran-weight yarn.

Needles: US 6 / 4 mm DPNs or circular needles suitable for knitting small circumferences in the rnd (16" / 40 cm needles or 32" / 80 cm needles, if using the Magic-Loop Method).

Notions: Stitch holder or scrap yarn, stitch marker.

GAUGE

16 sts x 30 rnds to 4" / 10 cm in textured pattern, after blocking.

NOTES

You can find the abbreviations and detailed instructions for techniques used in this pattern in the Abbreviations (pp. 20–23) and Techniques (pp. 15–19) sections.

Chart is read from bottom to top and from right to left.

Slip markers as you come across them.

You can alter the length by working extra repeats of the chart before the thumb.

It is best to use a yarn with good stitch definition, so that the different stitch patterns will be well defined.

CONSTRUCTION

These mitts are worked from the bottom up in the round. You first work a rib, then work the textured pattern by following the chart, and finish with a top rib. The thumb is worked last.

DIRECTIONS

Cast on 24 (26, 28) sts with the Long-Tail Cast-On or a stretchy cast-on method of choice. Place a marker for the beginning of rnd (BOR) and join for working in the rnd. Be careful not to twist sts.

BOTTOM RIB

Start to work the cuff in 1 x 1 Ribbing as follows:
Rib rnd: *K1, p1*, repeat *–* to end.
Work in established ribbing for a total of 14 rnds.

TEXTURED PATTERN

Next, you will start working the textured pattern. Start working from the chart. Repeat rnds 1–4 a total of 4 times. Note the size-specific instructions below (also marked in the chart).

Size 1
Work sts 3–14 and 17–28.

Size 2
Work sts 1–14 and 17–28.

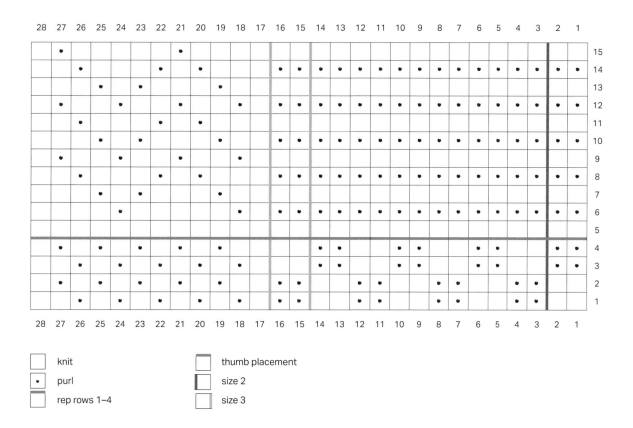

knit

• purl

rep rows 1–4

thumb placement

size 2

size 3

Size 3
Work sts 1–28.

On the next rnd (rnd 5), k all sts until you reach st number 6 (8, 8). Place that st and the next 3 sts (4 sts in total) to a stitch holder or waste yarn. These sts will later be worked for the thumb. Cast on 4 sts (either the Backwards Loop Cast-On Method or the Knitted Cast-On Method is recommended). Continue to work in the rnd by knitting all sts to BOR marker.

Continue to work according to the chart, until all rnds have been worked.

TOP RIBBING

K 1 rnd. Then begin to work the 1 x 1 Ribbing as follows:
Rib rnd: *K1, p1*, repeat *–* to end.
Work in established ribbing for a total of 5 rnds.

Bind off all sts using your preferred method.

THUMB

Move the 4 sts from the holder onto your needles and pick up and k 8 more sts from around the thumb hole. You should have 12 sts on your needles. Place a marker for BOR and join for working in the rnd.

Work thumb in 1 x 1 Ribbing as follows:
Rib rnd: *K1, p1*, repeat *–* to end.
Work in established ribbing for a total of 5 rnds.

Bind off all sts using your preferred method.

FINISHING

Weave in all ends. Gently wet block to smooth the sts, but avoid stretching too much to keep the texture.

Jonna Hietala

49 Ernest

This super-soft balaclava is perfect for pairing with your winter coat. If you have never tried Fisherman's Rib, now is the time – it's fun and simple!

SIZE

One Size

FINISHED MEASUREMENTS

Width (measured with the balaclava lying flat): 8.5" / 22 cm.
Height: 13.25" / 34 cm.

MATERIALS

Yarn: 3 balls of Børstet Alpakka by Sandnes Garn (96% alpaca, 4% polyester, 120 yds / 110 m – 50 m), colourway 8532. If you decide to use another yarn, you will need approx. 310 yds / 284 m of bulky-weight yarn.

The balaclava is worked holding the yarn double.

Note! Even though Børstet Alpakka is categorised as a bulky weight yarn, it is rather light and airy. Should you wish to substitute it, try to find a similar yarn, i.e. Fashion Light Luxury by Rico Design, Luxair by Schulana or Painted Suri by Araucania. If using a different kind of yarn, swatching is highly recommended. Also note that this may affect the yardage.

Needles: US 6 / 4 mm 16–24" / 40–60 cm for the ribbing that frames the face and US 10.5 / 6.5 mm, 16–24" / 40–60 cm.

Notions: Stitch marker.

GAUGE

12 sts x 12 rnds to 4" / 10 cm on US 10.5 / 6.5 mm needles in Fisherman's Rib after blocking.

NOTES

You can find the abbreviations and detailed instructions for techniques used in this pattern in the Abbreviations (pp. 20–23) and Techniques (pp. 15–19) sections.

Slip stitch marker when you come across it.

CONSTRUCTION

At first, this balaclava is worked in the round from the bottom up. After the neck ribbing, it is time to bind off some stitches to work the rest of the balaclava flat and switch to Fisherman's Rib, in which the knit stitches are worked into the stitch below. This creates a stretchy, fluffy fabric. The crown is created in the same way as the basic heel of a wool sock.

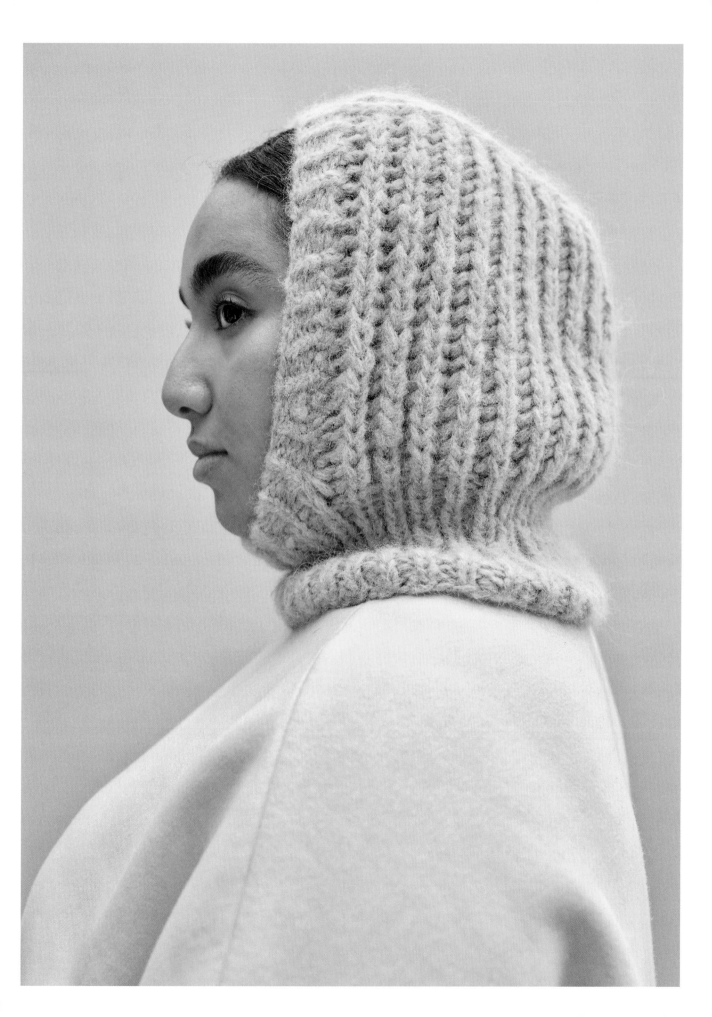

DIRECTIONS

NECK RIBBING

With two strands held together and US 10.5 / 6.5 mm, cast on 60 sts using the German Twisted Cast-On Method that creates a stretchy edge (you can find tutorials online). Join for working in the rnd and place a marker for the beginning of the rnd (BOR).

Rnd 1: *K1, p1*, repeat *–* to end. Repeat rnd 1, 19 more times (= 20 rnds in total).

Next: Remove BOR. Bind off the first 11 sts very loosely in pattern. (49 sts)

HOOD

From now on, the balaclava is worked flat.

Row 1 (RS): *K1b (= knit into the st on the row below the st on the needle), p1*, repeat *–* to end. *Note!* From now on (depending on the row: RS or WS), the first and the last sts are plain knit or purl sts.
Row 2 (WS): K1, p1, *k1b, p1*, repeat *–* to last st, k1.
Row 3: P1, *k1b, p1*, repeat *–* to end. Repeat rows 2–3, 19 more times (ending with a RS row).

CROWN

Row 1 (WS): K1, *p1, k1b*, repeat *–* 14 more times, p2tog, turn work. (16 unworked sts remain)
Row 2 (RS): Sl1 pwise wyib, *p1, k1b*, repeat *–* 5 more times, p1, sl1 pwise wyib, p1, psso, turn work. (16 unworked sts remain)
Row 3: Sl1 pwise wyif, continue in Fisherman's Rib until 1 st before the hole, p2tog, turn work.
Row 4: Sl1 pwise wyib, continue in Fisherman's Rib until 1 st before the hole,

sl1 pwise wyib, k1, psso. *Note!* From now on, the st that follows the slipped st is either a plain knit or purl st (according to the pattern).
Repeat rows 3–4 until there are no side sts left. BO in pattern.

FRONT RIBBING

Change to smaller needles and pick up and knit 68 sts in total (15 sts from the forehead, 20 sts from the left side, 13 sts from the chin, 20 sts from the right side). The amount of sts isn't crucial, as long as it is an even number close to the original amount. Place BOR marker.

Rnd 1: Work with the smaller needle (working the sts from the larger needle onto it). *K1tbl, p1*, repeat to BOR m. Repeat rnd 1, 5 more times.

Bind off loosely or using a stretchy bind-off of your choice (for example Jeny's Surprisingly Stretchy Bind-Off method for which you can find tutorials online). If you wish to use a regular bind-off method, it's recommended to change to the larger needle and still bind off very loosely in pattern.

FINISHING

Weave in ends and steam block to measurements. Steaming keeps the fabric fluffier with this kind of yarn.

Aatu Äikiä

50 Syyskuu

Syyskuu is a cosy hat with a folded, contrast-colour brim. The fun pompom on top adds a bit of playfulness. This pattern is suitable for beginners, as it features basic stitches only.

SIZES

1 (2, 3)

For a head circumference of approx. 20–21 (21–23, 23–25)" / 51–53 (53–58.5, 58.5–63.5) cm.

FINISHED MEASUREMENTS

Brim Circumference: 16.5 (18.5, 20)" / 42.5 (47, 51) cm.
Height: 10.5 (11.25, 11.5)" / 27 (28.5, 29.5) cm.

MATERIALS

Yarn: C1: 1 skein of Semilla Melange by BC Garn (100% wool, 191 yds / 175 m – 50 g), colourway 12.
C2: 1 skein of Lammull by Vänö Ull (100% wool, 164 yds / 150 m – 50 g), colourway black-white.
If you decide to use another yarn, you will need approx. 104 (115, 127) yds / 95 (105, 115) m of sport-weight yarn in C1 and 100 (111, 122) yds / 92 (102, 112) m of sport-weight yarn in C2.

Needles: US 1.5 / 2.5 mm and US 4 / 3.5 mm 16" / 40 cm circular needles and DPNs of the same size for small circumference knitting, if not using the Magic Loop Method.

Notions: Stitch markers, cardboard (if you don't have a pompom maker).

GAUGE

23 sts x 34 rows to 4" / 10 cm on US 4 / 3.5 mm needles in Stockinette Stitch, after blocking.

NOTES

You can find the abbreviations and detailed instructions for techniques used in this pattern in the Abbreviations (pp. 20–23) and Techniques (pp. 15–19) sections.

Slip markers as you come across them.

CONSTRUCTION

This hat is knitted seamlessly in the rnd from the brim to the crown. It features a deep brim in 2 x 2 Ribbing worn folded double, a stockinette body in a contrasting colour and a fun pompom on top.

DIRECTIONS

BRIM

With C1 and US 1.5 / 2.5 mm needles, cast on 96 (108, 116) sts using the Long-Tail Cast-On Method or a method of choice. Place marker for the beginning of the rnd (BOR) and join to work in the rnd. Be careful not to twist sts.

Start to work in ribbing:
Rnd 1: *K2, p2*, repeat *–* to end.
Work in established 2 x 2 Ribbing for 44 (49, 54) more rnds, or until your work measures 5.5 (6, 6.5)" / 14 (15, 16) cm from the cast-on edge. Cut C1.

BODY

Change to C2 and US 4 / 3.5 mm needles.

Sizes 1 and 3 only
Rnd 1: K48 (–, 58), m1l, k to marker, m1l.
You should now have 98 (108, 118) sts.

All sizes
Work in Stockinette Stitch until the hat measures 11.5 (12, 12.25)" / 29 (30, 31) cm from cast-on.

CROWN

Change to US 4 / 3.5 mm DPNs.

Next rnd: *K11 (12, 13), PM*, repeat *–*
a total of 8 times, k10 (12, 14).

Decrease rnd: *K to m, k2tog, SM*,
repeat *–* to end.

Next rnd: K to end.

Repeat the last 2 rnds until you have 17 (18, 19) sts remaining. Cut yarn, leaving at least a 6" / 15 cm tail. With a tapestry needle, thread the yarn through the remaining sts (remove markers as you come across them), closing the gap.

FINISHING

Weave in the cast-on yarn tail to the RS of the unfolded brim. Weave in all other ends to the WS of the hat.

Wet block to measurements.

Make the pompom. Attach the pompom to the crown using the two long ends. Thread both of the ends through the crown and weave them onto the WS.

Teti Lutsak

51 Funky Turtle

Funky Turtle is a relaxed, cute pullover that is worked seamlessly from the top down. Teti Lutsak wanted to make it a simple knit that is still truly unique.

SIZES

1 (2, 3, 4, 5) (6, 7, 8)

Recommended ease: 4–5" / 10–13 cm of positive ease.

FINISHED MEASUREMENTS

Chest Circumference: 39.5 (43, 47.25, 50.5, 54.75) (58, 62.25, 65.75)" / 99 (107.5, 118, 126.5, 138) (145.5, 156, 164) cm.

Turtleneck Circumference (unstretched): 13.75 (14.75, 15.75, 16.5, 17.5) (18.5, 19.5, 20.25)" / 34.5 (37, 39, 41.5, 44) (46, 48.5, 51) cm.

Yoke Depth (middle of the front, excl. turtleneck): 9.5 (9.5, 9.75, 10.5, 11) (11.25, 12, 12.25)" / 23.5 (23.5, 24.5, 26.5, 27.5) (28, 30, 31) cm.

Body Length from Underarm to Hem: 15.25" / 39 cm.

Hem Circumference: 36 (39, 43, 46.25, 49.75) (53, 57, 60)" / 90 (97.5, 107.5, 115.5, 124.5) (132.5, 142.5, 150) cm.

Upper Arm Circumference: 12.75 (13.5, 14.25, 16, 17.75) (19.25, 21, 22)" / 31.5 (33.5, 36, 40, 44) (48.5, 52.5, 54.5) cm.

Cuff Circumference (unstretched): 7 (7.5, 8, 9, 9.75) (10.75, 11.75, 12)" / 17.5 (18.5, 20, 22.5, 24.5) (27, 29, 30) cm.

Sleeve Length (excl. ribbing on the cuff): 19.25" / 49 cm.

MATERIALS

Yarn: Highland DK by LITLG (100% untreated highland wool, 246 yds / 225 m — 100 g).

C1: 2 (2, 2, 2, 2) (3, 3, 3) skeins of colourway Oast.

C2: 2 (2, 2, 3, 3) (3, 3, 3) skeins of colourway Camel.

C3: 2 (2, 2, 2, 2) (2, 3, 3) skeins of colourway Thistle.

C4: 1 skein of colourway Nut.

If you decide to use another yarn, you will need approx.

C1: 357 (381, 406, 431, 480) (517, 554, 578) yds / 326 (348, 371, 394, 439) (473, 507, 529) m of DK-weight yarn.

C2: 394 (431, 455, 504, 541) (578, 627, 652) yds / 360 (394, 416, 461, 495) (529, 573, 596) m of DK-weight yarn.

C3: 344 (369, 406, 431, 455) (492, 517, 541) yds / 315 (338, 371, 394, 416) (450, 473, 495) m of DK-weight yarn.

C4: 49 (54, 62, 62, 66) (74, 74, 74) yds / 45 (49, 57, 57, 60) (68, 68, 68) m of DK-weight yarn.

Or a total of approx. 1144 (1235, 1329, 1428, 1542) (1661, 1772, 1845) yds / 1046 (1129, 1215, 1306, 1410) (1520, 1621, 1688) m of DK-weight yarn.

Needles: US 4 / 3.5 mm 24–32" / 60–80 cm circular needles (for the ribbing) and US 6 / 4 mm 24–32" / 60–80 cm circular needles (for everything else).

Notions: At least 3 stitch markers, stitch holders or waste yarn.

GAUGE

19 sts x 22 rnds to 4" / 10 cm on US 6 / 4 mm needles in Stockinette Stitch, after blocking.

26 sts x 32 rnds to 4" / 10 cm on US 4 / 3.5 mm needles in Modified Half-Twisted Ribbing, after blocking (unstretched).

NOTES

You can find the abbreviations and detailed instructions for techniques used in this pattern in the Abbreviations (pp. 20–23) and Techniques (pp. 15–19) sections.

Slip markers as you come across them.

Charts are read from bottom to top and from right to left.

The bottom of the round yoke is shaped with Wrap&Turn Short Rows which make the back of the yoke longer and give the garment an overall better fit. They can, however, be omitted if you do not feel comfortable with a new technique.

CONSTRUCTION

This pullover is knitted seamlessly from the top down in the round. The turtleneck, hem and cuffs are worked in a modified half-twisted ribbing. The rest of the garment is worked in Stockinette Stitch. A simple stranded colourwork pattern highlights the transition between sections. The body and sleeves are worked straight with increases before the hem ribbing on the body and decreases before the cuffs.

DIRECTIONS

NECK

Begin with the turtleneck. With C1 and US 4 / 3.5 mm needles, cast on 90 (96, 102, 108, 114) (120, 126, 132) sts using a method of choice. (If you wish, you can try the Tubular Cast-On Method which provides a perfectly rounded, stretchy edge. Tutorials can be found online.) Join to work in the rnd and place a marker for the beginning of the rnd (BOR).

Begin working the Modified Half-Twisted Ribbing as follows:
Rnd 1: *K1tbl, p1*, repeat *–* to end.
Rnd 2: *K1, p1*, repeat *–* to end.
Continue working rnds 1–2 for approx. 2.75" / 7 cm finishing with a rnd 1.

Double Band
Break the C1 yarn and change to C2.
Rnd 1: *K1, yo*, repeat *–* to end. The st count has doubled. You should have 180 (192, 204, 216, 228) (240, 252, 264) sts.
Rnd 2: *Sl1 wyib, p1*, repeat *–* to end.
Rnd 3: *K1, sl1 wyif*, repeat *–* to end.
Rnd 4: *Sl1 wyib, p1*, repeat *–* to end.
Rnd 5: *K1, sl1 wyif*, repeat *–* to end.
Rnd 6: *Sl1 wyib, p1*, repeat *–* to end.
Rnd 7: *P2tog*, repeat *–* to end. The st count has returned to its original number. You should have 90 (96, 102, 108, 114) (120, 126, 132) sts.

YOKE

You will start to work the yoke. Break the C2 yarn and change to C3 and US 6 / 4 mm needles.
Rnds 1–4: K to end.
Rnd 5: *K3, make a left lifted increase (LLI)*, repeat *–* to end. You should have 120 (128, 136, 144, 152) (160, 168, 176) sts.
Rnd 6: K to end.
Rnd 7: *Yo, k2, pull yo over the 2 knit sts*, repeat *–* to end.

Rnds 8–13: K to end.
Rnd 14: *K4, LLI*, repeat *–* to end. You should have 150 (160, 170, 180, 190) (200, 210, 220) sts.
Rnds 15–17: K to end.
Rnd 18: *Yo, k2, pull yo over the 2 knit sts*, repeat *–* to end.

Rnds 19–22: K to end.
Rnd 23: *K5, LLI*, repeat *–* to end. You should have 180 (192, 204, 216, 228) (240, 252, 264) sts.
Rnds 24–28: K to end.
Rnd 29: *K6, LLI*, repeat *–* to end. You should have 210 (224, 238, 252, 266) (280, 294, 308) sts.
Rnd 30: K to end.
Rnd 31: *Yo, k2, pull yo over the 2 knit sts*, repeat *–* to end.

Rnds 32–35: K to end.
Rnd 36: *K7, LLI*, repeat *–* to end. You should have 240 (256, 272, 288, 304) (320, 336, 352) sts.
Rnds 37–41: K to end.
Rnd 42: *K8, LLI*, repeat *–* to end. You should have 270 (288, 306, 324, 342) (360, 378, 396) sts.

Size 1 only
Rnd 43: K to end.

All other sizes
Rnds 43–45: K to end.

All sizes resume
Next rnd: *Yo, k2, pull yo over the 2 k sts*, repeat *–* to end.

Work in Stockinette Stitch (k all sts) a total of 2 (2, 4, 8, 10) (12, 16, 18) rnds. On the last rnd, prepare to work short rows and place a marker to mark the middle of the rnd (MOF) as follows: k135 (144, 153, 162, 171) (180, 189, 198), place MOF, k135 (144, 153, 162, 171) (180, 189, 198).
Short Row Shaping of the Back
The back of the yoke is shaped with a total of 9 (9, 11, 11, 11) (13, 13, 13) short rows. Working short rows means working a fraction of sts flat on the RS, turning

the work around and on the next row working a fraction of sts flat on the WS. The Wrap&Turn Short Row Technique is recommended for this pattern. Use German Short Rows if preferred but make sure to adjust the instructions where necessary. *Note!* You can also skip this section if you prefer and move on to Yoke.

Short row 1 (RS): K to 20 sts before MOF m, w&t.
Short row 2 (WS): P to 20 sts before MOF m, w&t.
Short rows 3, 5 and 7 (RS): K to 24 sts before previous wrap, w&t.
Short rows 4, 6 and 8 (WS): P to 24 sts before previous wrap, w&t.

Sizes 3, 4 and 5: Repeat short rows 3–4 once more.
Sizes 6, 7 and 8: Repeat short rows 3–4 twice more.

Next row: K to BOR m.

Yoke (continued)

Sizes 1 (3, 5, 7) only
Next rnd: K67 (76, 85, 94), LLI, k136 (154, 172, 190), LLI, k67 (76, 85, 94), remove MOF marker and at the same time pick up wraps and k2tog with their corresponding sts. You should have 272 (308, 344, 380) sts.

Sizes 2 (4, 6, 8) only
Next rnd: K all sts, remove MOF m and at the same time pick up wraps and k2tog with their corresponding sts.

All sizes resume
Pick up C4 and work according to the Separation of Body and Sleeves Chart and written instructions.
Rnds 1–2: *K2 with C3, k1 with C4, k1 with C3*, repeat *–* to end. Break the C3 yarn.
Rnd 3: *Sl1 wyib, k3 with C4*, repeat *–* to end.
Without breaking the yarn move on to the next section.

SEPARATION OF BODY AND SLEEVES

Rnd 1: With C4, k43 (46, 50, 52, 55) (57, 60, 63) sts of the back, temporarily bind off or place on hold the next 50 (52, 54, 58, 62) (66, 70, 72) sts for the right sleeve, cast on 8 (10, 12, 16, 20) (24, 28, 30) sts for the underarm using the Backwards Loop Cast-On Method or method of choice, k86 (92, 100, 104, 110) (114, 120, 126) sts of the front, temporarily bind off or place on hold the next 50 (52, 54, 58, 62) (66, 70, 72) sts for the left sleeve, cast on 8 (10, 12, 16, 20) (24, 28, 30) sts for the underarm using the Backwards Loop Cast-On Method or method of choice and k the remaining 43 (46, 50, 52, 55) (57, 60, 63) sts of the back to the end of rnd.

Break the C4 yarn and pick up C2. You should have 188 (204, 224, 240, 260) (276, 296, 312) sts for the body.

Rnd 2: *K2 with C2, sl1 wyib, k1 with C2*, repeat *–* to underarm (*Note!* Not a full pattern repeat), k8 (10, 12, 16, 20) (24, 28, 30) (*Note!* There is no pattern on the underarms), then work the front sts according to the previously established pattern to underarm, k8 (10, 12, 16, 20) (24, 28, 30) and continue colourwork to end.

Work with C2 in Stockinette Stitch (k all sts) until desired length or until the body measures approx. 11.75" / 30 cm from the underarms. Then pick up C4 and follow the Transition into the Hem/Cuff Chart and written instructions.
Rnds 1–2: *K2 with C2, k1 with C4, k1 with C2*, repeat *–* to end. Break the C2 yarn.
Rnd 3: *Sl1 wyib, k3 with C4*, repeat *–* to end.
Rnd 4: K all sts with C4. Break the C4 yarn and pick up C3.
Rnd 5: *K2 with C3, sl1 wyib, k1 with C3*, repeat *–* to end.

Rnds 6–9: K to end.

Switch to US 4 / 3.5 mm needles and increase for the hem ribbing as follows:
Sizes 1 (2, 5, 6) only
Rnd 10: *K1, p1, k1, p1, LLI, p1, k1, p1, k1, m1lp*, repeat *–* to 4 sts before end, k1, p1, k1, p1. You should have 234 (254, 324, 344) sts.

Sizes 3 (4, 7, 8) only
Rnd 10: *K1, p1, k1, p1, LLI, p1, k1, p1, k1, m1lp*, repeat *–* to the end. You should have 280 (300, 370, 390) sts.

HEM RIBBING

Finish the hem with working a section of the Modified Half-Twisted Ribbing as follows:
Rnd 1: *K1tbl, p1*, repeat *–* to end.
Rnd 2: *K1, p1*, repeat *–* to end.
Repeat rnds 1–2 for approx. 1.75" / 4.5 cm finishing with rnd 2. Bind off all sts loosely. (If you wish, you can try the Tubular Bind-Off Method which gives the garment a very neat look and a flexible edge. Tutorials can be found online.)

SLEEVES

Return to the sts left on hold for the sleeves.

Rnd 1: With C4 starting in the middle of the underarm with US 6 / 4 mm needles, pick up and k4 (5, 6, 8, 10) (12, 14, 15) sts of the underarm, pick up and k1 extra st to avoid a hole, k50 (52, 54, 58, 62) (66, 70, 72) sts of the sleeve, pick up and k1 extra st and k the remaining 4 (5, 6, 8, 10) (12, 14, 15) sts of the underarm.

Join to work in the rnd and place a marker for the beginning of the rnd (BOR). Break the C4 yarn and pick up C1. You should have 60 (64, 68, 76, 84) (92, 100, 104) sts.

Rnd 2: With C1, k5 (6, 7, 9, 11) (13, 15, 16), then work the sleeve sts according to the previously established pattern and

SEPARATION OF BODY AND SLEEVES CHART

rnd 2 body
rnd 1 body/sleeve
rnd 3 yoke
rnd 2 yoke
rnd 1 yoke

☐ C2/C1
▨ C3
▨ C4
√ Slip 1 st with yarn in back of the work

TRANSITION INTO THE HEM/CUFF CHART

rnd 5
rnd 4
rnd 3
rnd 2
rnd 1

☐ C2/C1
▨ C3/C2
▨ C4
√ Slip 1 st with yarn in back of the work

Separation of Body and Sleeves Chart to 5 (6, 7, 9, 11) (13, 15, 16) sts before the end of rnd, k5 (6, 7, 9, 11) (13, 15, 16).

Work with C1 in Stockinette Stitch (k all sts) until desired length or until the sleeve measures approx. 15.75" / 40 cm from the underarm.

Pick up the C4 yarn and follow the Transition into the Hem/Cuff Chart and written instructions.
Rnds 1–2: *K2 with C1, k1 with C4, k1 with C1*, repeat *–* to end. Break the C1 yarn.
Rnd 3: *Sl1 wyib, k3 with C4*, repeat *–* to end.
Rnd 4: K to end with C4. Break the C4 yarn and pick up C2.
Rnd 5: *K2 with C2, sl1 wyib, k1 with C2*, repeat *–* to end.
Rnds 6–9: K to end.

Change to US 4 / 3.5 mm needles and decrease for the cuff ribbing as follows:
Sizes 1 (3, 4, 5, 6, 7) only

Rnd 10: *K2tog, k2*, repeat *–* to 4 sts before end, k4. You should have 46 (52, 58, 64, 70, 76) sts.

Sizes 2 (8) only
Rnd 10: *K2tog, k2*, repeat *–* to end. You should have 48 (78) sts.

Cuffs
Work the cuff in Modified Half-Twisted Ribbing as follows:
Rnd 1: *K1, p1*, repeat *–* to end.
Rnd 2: *K1tbl, p1*, repeat *–* to end.
Repeat rnds 1–2 for approx. 1.75" / 4.5 cm finishing with rnd 1. Bind off all sts loosely.

Repeat the instructions for the second sleeve.

FINISHING

Weave in ends. Wet block to measurements.

Isabell Kraemer

52 Juttu

Juttu is your new favourite cardigan! Thanks to its top-down construction, it's easy to try on as you go. The stitch patterns may look long – but it's all knits, purls and slipped stitches.

SIZES

1 (2, 3, 4, 5) (6, 7, 8)

Recommended ease: 10–12" / 25.5–30.5 cm of positive ease.

FINISHED MEASUREMENTS

Chest Circumference (based on back width doubled): 44.5 (48.5, 53.25, 57.25, 62.75) (66.75, 70.75, 74.75)" / 111 (121, 133, 143, 157) (167, 177, 187) cm.
Front Width (each): 11 (12.25, 13.5, 14.25, 15.75) (16.5, 17.75, 18.5)" / 27.5 (30.5, 33.5, 35.5, 39.5) (41.5, 44.5, 46.5) cm.
Yoke Depth (measured along arm opening): 7 (7.25, 8, 9, 9.5) (9.75, 10.5, 10.75)" / 17 (18, 20, 22.5, 23.5) (24.5, 26, 27) cm.
Upper Arm Circumference: 14.5 (15.25, 16.5, 17.5, 19.5) (20.75, 22, 22.5)" / 36 (38, 41, 44, 49) (52, 55, 56) cm.
Body Length from Underarm (adjustable): 14.75 (14.75, 14.75, 14.25, 13.75) (13.5, 13.5, 13.25)" / 37.5 (37.5, 37.5, 36, 35) (34, 34, 33.5) cm.

Sleeve Length from Underarm (adjustable): 16.75 (16.75, 16.75, 15.5, 15.25) (15, 15, 14.25)" / 42.5 (42.5, 42.5, 39.5, 38.5) (38, 38, 36) cm.
Total Length (measured at centre of back): 21.75 (22, 22.75, 23.25, 23.25) (23.25, 24, 24)" / 54.5 (55.5, 57.5, 58.5, 58.5) (58.5, 60, 60.5) cm.

MATERIALS

Yarn: 8 (9, 10, 10, 11) (12, 13, 13) skeins of Brusca by Rosa Pomar (100% wool, 137 yds / 125 m – 50 g), colourway B (beige version) or colourway 6B (orange version). If you decide to use another yarn, you will need approx. 1068 (1162, 1289, 1348, 1493) (1593, 1701, 1759) yds / 977 (1063, 1179, 1233, 1365) (1457, 1555, 1608) m of DK or worsted-weight yarn.

Needles: US 6 / 4 mm 40" / 100 cm circular needles and DPNs (for body and sleeves), US 5 / 3.75 mm 40" / 100 cm circular needles and DPNs (for ribbings).

Notions: Stitch holders or waste yarn, stitch markers.

GAUGE

20 sts x 28 rows to 4" / 10 cm on US 6 / 4 mm needles in Stockinette Stitch, after blocking.
20 sts x 31 rows to 4" / 10 cm on US 6 / 4 mm needles in texture pattern, after blocking.
Please use instructions for back pattern for your gauge swatch.
Note! Row gauge is important. Armhole length is determined by the number of rows. Please take the time to check both stitch and row gauge.

STITCH PATTERNS

RFP (Right Front Pattern)
Worked over a multiple of 2 + 1

Row 1 (RS): K to m, SM, *k1, p1*, repeat *–* to 6 sts before end, k1, p3, sl1 wyif, k1.
Row 2 (WS): Sl1 wyif, k4, p1, *k1, p1*, repeat *–* to m, SM, k to 2 sts before end, p2.
Row 3 (RS): Repeat row 1.
Row 4 (WS): Sl1 wyif, k4, p1, *k1, p1*, repeat *–* to m, SM, p to end.

Row 5 (RS): Repeat row 1.
Row 6 (WS): Sl1 wyif, k4, p1, *k1, p1*, repeat *–* to m, SM, k1, *sl1 with yarn in back (wyib), k1*, rep *–* to 2 sts before end, p2.
Row 7 (RS): K2, *sl1 wyif, p1* to 1 st before m, sl1 wyif, SM, *k1, p1*, repeat *–* to 6 sts before end, k1, p3, sl1 wyif, k1.
Row 8 (WS): Repeat row 6.
Row 9 (RS): Repeat row 1.
Row 10 (WS): Repeat row 4.
Row 11 (RS): Repeat row 1.
Row 12 (WS): Repeat row 2.

Row 13 (RS): Repeat row 1.
Row 14 (WS): Sl1 wyif, k4, p1, *k1, p1*, repeat *–* to m, SM, p1, *k1, p1*, repeat *–* to 2 sts before end, p2.
Row 15 (RS): Repeat row 1.
Row 16 (WS): Sl1 wyif, k4, p1, *k1, p1*, repeat *–* to m, SM, k1, *p1, k1*, repeat *–* to 2 sts before end, p2.
Row 17 (RS): Repeat row 1.
Row 18 (WS): Repeat row 14.
Row 19 (RS): Repeat row 1.
Row 20 (WS): Repeat row 16.
Row 21 (RS): Repeat row 1.
Row 22 (WS): Repeat row 14.

Rows 23–34: Repeat rows 1–12.

Row 35 (RS): Repeat row 1.
Row 36 (WS): Repeat row 4.
Rows 37–44: Repeat rows 35–36, 4 more times.

Repeat rows 1–44 for pattern.

LFP (Left Front Pattern)
Worked over a multiple of 2 + 1

Row 1 (RS): K1, sl1 wyif, p3, k1, *p1, k1*, repeat *–* to m, SM, k to end.
Row 2 (WS): P2, k to m, SM, *p1, k1*, repeat *–* to 6 sts before end, p1, k4, sl1 wyif.
Row 3 (RS): Repeat row 1.
Row 4 (WS): P to m, SM, *p1, k1*, repeat *–* to 6 sts before end, p1, k4, sl1 wyif.
Row 5 (RS): Repeat row 1.
Row 6 (WS): P2, k1, *sl1 wyib, k1*, repeat

– to m, SM, *p1, k1*, repeat *–* to 6 sts before end, p1, k4, sl1 wyif.
Row 7 (RS): K1, sl1 wyif, p3, k1, *p1, k1*, repeat *–* to m, SM, *sl1 wyif, p1*, repeat *–* to 3 sts before end, sl1 wyif, k2.
Row 8 (WS): Repeat row 6.
Row 9 (RS): Repeat row 1.
Row 10 (WS): Repeat row 4.
Row 11 (RS): Repeat row 1.
Row 12 (WS): Repeat row 2.

Row 13 (RS): Repeat row 1.
Row 14 (WS): P3, *k1, p1*, repeat *–* to m, SM, *p1, k1*, repeat *–* to 6 sts before end, p1, k4, sl1 wyif.
Row 15 (RS): Repeat row 1.
Row 16 (WS): P2, k1, *p1, k1*, repeat *–* to m, SM, *p1, k1*, repeat *–* to 6 sts before end, p1, k4, sl1 wyif.
Row 17 (RS): Repeat row 1.
Row 18 (WS): Repeat row 14.
Row 19 (RS): Repeat row 1.
Row 20 (WS): Repeat row 16.
Row 21 (RS): Repeat row 1.
Row 22 (WS): Repeat row 14.

Rows 23–34: Repeat rows 1–12.

Row 35 (RS): Repeat row 1.
Row 36 (WS): Repeat row 4.
Rows 37–44: Repeat rows 35–36, 4 more times.

Repeat rows 1–44 for pattern.

BP (Back Pattern)
Worked over a multiple of 2 + 1
Row 1 (RS): K to end.
Row 2 (WS): P2, k to 2 sts before end, p2.
Row 3 (RS): K to end.
Row 4 (WS): P to end.
Row 5 (RS): K to end.
Row 6 (WS): P2, k1, *sl1 wyib, k1*, repeat *–* to 2 sts before end, p2.
Row 7 (RS): K2, *sl1 wyif, p1*, repeat *–* to 3 sts before end, sl1 wyif, k2.
Row 8 (WS): Repeat row 6.
Row 9 (RS): K to end.
Row 10 (WS): P to end.
Row 11 (RS): K to end.
Row 12 (WS): Repeat row 2.

Row 13 (RS): K to end.
Row 14 (WS): P3, *k1, p1*, repeat *–* to 2 sts before end, p2.
Row 15 (RS): K to end.
Row 16 (WS): P2, k1, *p1, k1*, repeat *–* to 2 sts before end, p2.
Row 17 (RS): K to end.
Row 18 (WS): Repeat row 14.
Row 19 (RS): K to end.
Row 20 (WS): Repeat row 16.
Row 21 (RS): K to end.
Row 22 (WS): Repeat row 14.

Rows 23–34: Repeat rows 1–12.

Row 35 (RS): Repeat row 1.
Row 36 (WS): Repeat row 4.
Rows 37–44: Repeat rows 35–36, 4 more times.

Repeat rows 1–44 for pattern.

Body Pattern
Worked over a multiple of 2 + 1
Row 1 (RS): K1, sl1 wyif, p3, k1, *p1, k1*, repeat *–* to m, SM, k to m, SM, *k1, p1*, repeat *–* to 6 sts before end, k1, p3, sl1 wyif, k1.
Row 2 (WS): Sl1 wyif, k4, p1, *k1, p1*, repeat *–* to m, SM, k to m, SM, *p1, k1*, repeat *–* to 6 sts before end, p1, k4, sl1 wyif.
Row 3 (RS): Repeat row 1.
Row 4 (WS): Sl1 wyif, k4, p1, *k1, p1*, repeat *–* to m, SM, p to m, SM, *p1, k1*, repeat *–* to 6 sts before end, p1, k4, sl1 wyif.
Row 5 (RS): Repeat row 1.
Row 6 (WS): Sl1 wyif, k4, p1, *k1, p1*, repeat *–* to m, SM, *k1, sl1 wyib*, repeat *–* to 1 st before m, k1, SM, *p1, k1*, rep *–* to 6 sts before end, p1, k4, sl1 wyif.
Row 7 (RS): K1, sl1 wyif, p3, k1, *p1, k1*, repeat *–* to m, SM, sl1 wyif, *p1, sl1 wyif*, repeat *–* to m, SM, *k1, p1*, repeat *–* to 6 sts before end, k1, p3, sl1 wyif, k1.
Row 8 (WS): Repeat row 6.
Row 9 (RS): Repeat row 1.
Row 10 (WS): Repeat row 4.
Row 11 (RS): Repeat row 1.
Row 12 (WS): Repeat row 2.

Row 13 (RS): Repeat row 1.

Row 14 (WS): Sl1 wyif, k4, p1, *k1, p1*, repeat *-* to m, SM, *p1, k1*, repeat *-* to 1 st before m, p1, SM, *p1, k1*, repeat *-* to 6 sts before end, p1, k4, sl1 wyif.

Row 15 (RS): Repeat row 1.

Row 16 (WS): Sl1 wyif, k4, p1, *k1, p1*, repeat *-* to m, SM, *k1, p1*, repeat *-* to 1 st before m, k1, SM, *p1, k1*, repeat *-* to 6 sts before end, p1, k4, sl1 wyif.

Row 17 (RS): Repeat row 1.

Row 18 (WS): Repeat row 14.

Row 19 (RS): Repeat row 1.

Row 20 (WS): Repeat row 16.

Row 21 (RS): Repeat row 1.

Row 22 (WS): Repeat row 14.

Rows 23–34: Repeat rows 1–12.

Row 35 (RS): Repeat row 1.

Row 36 (WS): Repeat row 4.

Rows 37–44: Repeat rows 35–36, 4 more times.

Repeat rows 1–44 for pattern.

NOTES

You can find the abbreviations and detailed instructions for techniques used in this pattern in the Abbreviations (pp. 20–23) and Techniques (pp. 15–19) sections.

Slip markers as you come across them.

CONSTRUCTION

This open cardigan is worked seamlessly from the top down. Starting with the right front, German Short Rows are worked back and forth to shape the shoulder slope. After completing the short row shaping, the right front is worked in pattern to the final length of the arm opening. It is then placed on hold to work the left front to match. Stitches for the back are picked up from the cast-on edges of both the right and left front and worked in pattern to match the length of the fronts.

Fronts and back are then joined at the underarm to work the body in one piece to the bottom ribbing. Sleeve stitches are picked up around the arm opening to work the sleeves top down in the round in plain Stockinette Stitch to the cuffs. No additional finishing is required.

MODIFICATIONS

Body and sleeves can be lengthened or shortened by working more or less rows/ rounds before starting the ribbing. Size can be adjusted by working widthwise from the size you need for your chest, and lengthwise from the size you need for your upper arms. Upper arm circumference is determined by the armhole length – work more or less rows for both fronts and back (follow instructions for a smaller/ bigger size) to adjust armhole length.

DIRECTIONS

RIGHT FRONT

Using US 6 / 4 mm circular needles, cast on 56 (61, 67, 72, 79) (84, 89, 94) sts using the Long-Tail Cast-On Method or method of choice.

Sizes 1, 4, 6 and 8 only

Row 1 (WS): Sl1 wyif, k4, p1, *k1, p1*, repeat *-* a total of 5 (–, –, 6, –) (7, –, 7) times, PM, p to 3 sts before end, p2tog, p1. You should have 55 (–, –, 71, –) (83, –, 93) sts: 16 (–, –, 18, –) (20, -, 20) sts for collar and 39 (–, –, 53, –) (63, –, 73) sts for right front.

Sizes 2, 3, 5 and 7 only

Row 1 (WS): Sl1 wyif, k4, p1, *k1, p1*, repeat *-* a total of – (5, 5,–, 6) (–, 7, –) times, PM, p to end. You should have – (61, 67, –, 79) (–, 89, –) sts: – (16, 16, –, 18) (–, 20, –) sts for collar and – (45, 51, –, 61) (–, 69, –) sts for right front.

All sizes

Next, you will shape the shoulder slopes using German Short Rows.

Row 2 (RS): K to m, SM, *k1, p1*, repeat *-* to 6 sts before end, k1, p3, sl1 wyif, k1.

Short row 1 (WS): Sl1 wyif, k4, p1, *k1, p1*, repeat *-* to m, SM, p1, turn.

Short row 2 (RS): Make double stitch (MDS), SM, *k1, p1*, repeat *-* to 6 sts before end, k1, p3, sl1 wyif, k1.

Short row 3 (WS): Sl1 wyif, k4, p1, *k1, p1*, repeat *-* to m, SM, purl double stitch (pDS), p4 (4, 4, 5, 5) (6, 6, 7), turn.

Short row 4 (RS): MDS, k to m, SM, *k1, p1*, repeat *-* to 6 sts before end, k1, p3, sl1 wyif, k1.

Short row 5 (WS): Sl1 wyif, k4, p1, *k1, p1*, repeat *-* to m, SM, p to DS, pDS, p4 (4, 4, 5, 5) (6, 6, 7), turn.

Short row 6 (RS): MDS, k to m, SM, *k1, p1*, repeat *-* to 6 sts before end, k1, p3, sl1 wyif, k1.

Repeat short rows 5–6, 7 (8, 8, 8, 8) (8, 8, 8) more times.

Next row (WS): Sl1 wyif, k4, p1, *k1, p1*, repeat *–* to m, SM, p to DS, pDS, p to end.

START RIGHT FRONT PATTERN (RFP)

Note! Each size starts with a different row of the pattern, which results in slightly different looks for the top part of the cardigan but makes the joining of fronts and back smooth and easy.

Size 1 only
Work rows 39–44, then rows 1–44 of RFP.

Size 2 only
Work rows 37–44, then rows 1–44 of RFP.

Size 3 only
Work rows 31–44, then rows 1–44 of RFP.

Size 4 only
Work rows 23–44, then rows 1–40 of RFP.

Size 5 only
Next row (RS): K to m, SM, *k1, p1*, repeat *–* to 6 sts before end, k1, p3, sl1 wyif, k1.
Next row (WS): Sl1 wyif, k4, p1, *k1, p1, repeat *–* to m, SM, p to end.
Repeat last two rows once more.
Work rows 23–44, then rows 1–44 of RFP.

Size 6 only
Next row (RS): K to m, SM, *k1, p1*, repeat *–* to 6 sts before end, k1, p3, sl1 wyif, k1.
Next row (WS): Sl1 wyif, k4, p1, *k1, p1*, repeat *–* to m, SM, p to end.
Repeat last two rows 3 more times.
Work rows 23–44, then rows 1–44 of RFP.

Size 7 only
Work rows 11–44, then rows 1–44 of RFP.

Size 8 only
Work rows 9–44, then rows 1–44 of RFP.

All sizes
Right front measures approx. 7 (7.25, 8, 9, 9.5) (9.75, 10.5, 10.75)" / 17 (18, 20, 22.5, 23.5) (24.5, 26, 27) cm, measured at the arm opening (not at the collar edge). Break yarn and place right front sts on a holder or waste yarn.

LEFT FRONT

Using US 6 / 4 mm circular needles, cast on 56 (61, 67, 72, 79) (84, 89, 94) sts using the Long-Tail Cast-On Method or method of choice.

Sizes 1, 4, 6 and 8 only
Row 1 (WS): P1, p2tog, p to 16 (–, –, 18, –) (20, –, 20) sts before end, PM, p1, *k1, p1*, repeat *–* a total of 5 (–, –, 6, –) (7, –, 7) times, k4, sl1 wyif. You should have 55 (–, –, 71, –) (83, –, 93) sts: 16 (–, –, 18, –) (20, -, 20) sts for collar, 39 (–, –, 53, –) (63, –, 73) sts for left front.

Sizes 2, 3, 5 and 7 only
Row 1 (WS): P to – (16, 16, –, 18) (–, 20, –) sts before end, PM, p1, *k1, p1*, repeat *–* a total of – (5, 5, –, 6) (–, 7, –) times, k4, sl1 wyif. You should have – (61, 67, –, 79) (–, 89, –) sts in total: – (16, 16, –, 18) (–, 20, –) sts for collar and – (45, 51, –, 61) (–, 69, –) sts for left front.

All sizes
Next, you will shape the shoulder slopes using German Short Rows.
Short row 1 (RS): K1, sl1 wyif, p3, k1, *p1, k1*, repeat *–* to m, SM, k1, turn.
Short row 2 (WS): MDS, SM, *p1, k1*, repeat *–* to 6 sts before end, p1, k4, sl1 wyif.
Short row 3 (RS): K1, sl1 wyif, p3, k1, *p1, k1*, repeat *–* to m, SM, knit Double Stitch (kDS), k4 (4, 4, 5, 5) (6, 6, 7), turn.
Short row 4 (WS): MDS, p to m, SM, *p1, k1*, repeat *–* to 6 sts before end, p1, k4, sl1 wyif.
Short row 5 (RS): K1, sl1 wyif, p3, k1, *p1, k1*, repeat *–* to m, SM, k to DS, kDS, k4 (4, 4, 5, 5) (6, 6, 7), turn.

Short row 6 (WS): MDS, p to m, SM, *p1, k1*, repeat *–* to 6 sts before end, p1, k4, sl1 wyif.

Repeat short rows 5 and 6, 7 (8, 8, 8, 8) (8, 8, 8) more times.

Next row (RS): K1, sl1 wyif, p3, k1, *p1, k1*, repeat *–* to m, SM, k to DS, kDS, k to end.
Next row (WS): P to m, SM, *p1, k1*, repeat *–* to 6 sts before m, p1, k4, sl1 wyif.

Sizes 5 and 6 only
Next row (RS): K1, sl1 wyif, p3, k1, *p1, k1*, repeat *–* to m, SM, k to end.
Next row (WS): P to m, SM, *p1, k1*, repeat *–* to 6 sts before m, p1, k4, sl1 wyif.
Repeat last two rows – (–, –, –, 1) (3, –, –) more time(s).

All sizes
START LEFT FRONT PATTERN (LFP)

Size 1 only
Work rows 39–44, then rows 1–44 of LFP.

Size 2 only
Work rows 37–44, then rows 1–44 of LFP.

Size 3 only
Work rows 31–44, then rows 1–44 of LFP.

Size 4 only
Work rows 23–44, then rows 1–40 of LFP.

Sizes 5 and 6 only
Work rows 23-44, then rows 1–44 of LFP.

Size 7 only
Work rows 11–44, then rows 1–44 of LFP.

Size 8 only
Work rows 9–44, then rows 1–44 of LFP.

All sizes
Place left front sts on a holder or waste yarn. Do not break yarn.

BACK

Note! Back sts are picked up from both front cast-on edges.

With a new ball of yarn and US 6 / 4 mm circular needles, starting at the arm opening edge of the left front (RS facing), pick up and k 56 (61, 67, 72, 79) (84, 89, 94) sts from cast-on, with RS of right front facing, continue to pick up sts, starting at the collar edge of the right front, pick up and k 1 st, PM, pick up and k 55 (60, 66, 71, 78) (83, 88, 93) sts from cast-on. You should have 112 (122, 134, 144, 158) (168, 178, 188) sts.

Set-up row (WS): P to m, RM, p2tog, p to end. You should have 111 (121, 133, 143, 157) (167, 177, 187) sts.

Next row (RS): K to end.
Next row (WS): P to end.

Sizes 5 and 6 only
Repeat last 2 rows – (–, –, –, 2) (4, –, –) more time(s).

All sizes
START BACK PATTERN (BP)

Size 1 only
Work rows 39–44, then rows 1–44 of BP.

Size 2 only
Work rows 37–44, then rows 1–44 of BP.

Size 3 only
Work rows 31–44, then rows 1–44 of BP.

Size 4 only
Work rows 23–44, then rows 1–40 of BP.

Sizes 5 and 6 only
Work rows 23–44, then rows 1–44 of BP.

Size 7 only
Work rows 11–44, then rows 1–44 of BP.

Size 8 only
Work rows 9–44, then rows 1–44 of BP.

All sizes
Break yarn. Turn work so that the WS is facing, lay the piece on the table and fold front pieces down at the shoulders (RS facing out). Place left front sts onto one end of your needle, the right front sts onto the other end of your needle. Be careful not to twist work. With the yarn still attached at the left front, ready to start working a RS row.

JOIN FRONTS AND BACK

Sizes 1, 2, 3, 5, 6, 7 and 8 only
Next row (RS): K1, sl1 wyif, p3, k1, *p1, k1*, repeat *–* to m, SM, k to 4 sts before end of left front, PM, k4, slide the back sts to needle tip of left-hand needle, k4, PM, k to 4 sts before end of back, PM, k4, slide right front sts to needle tip of left-hand needle, k4, PM, k to m, SM, *k1, p1*, repeat *–* to 6 sts before end, k1, p3, sl1 wyif, k1. You should have 221 (243, 267, –, 315) (333, 355, 373) sts: 51 (57, 63, –, 75) (79, 85, 89) sts for each front, 8 sts for each underarm and 103 (113, 125, –, 149) (159, 169, 179) sts for back.

Next row (WS) (dec row): Sl1 wyif, k4, p1, *k1, p1*, repeat *–* to m, SM, k to m, SM, p2tog, p to 2 sts before m, ssp, SM, k to m, SM, p2tog, p to 2 sts before m, ssp, SM, k to m, SM, *p1, k1*, repeat *–* to 6 sts before end, p1, k4, sl1 wyif. You should have 217 (239, 263, –, 311) (329, 351, 369) sts: 51 (57, 63, –, 75) (79, 85, 89) sts for each front, 6 sts for each underarm, 103 (113, 125, –, 149) (159, 169, 179) sts for back.

Next row (RS) (dec row): K1, sl1 wyif, p3, k1, *p1, k1*, repeat *–* to m, SM, k to m, SM, ssk, k2, k2tog, SM, k to m, SM, ssk, k2, k2tog, SM, k to m, SM, *k1, p1*, repeat *–* to 6 sts before end, k1, p3, sl1 wyif, k1. You should have 213 (235, 259, –, 307) (325, 347, 365) sts: 51 (57, 63, –, 75) (79, 85, 89) sts for each front, 4 sts for each underarm, 103 (113, 125, –, 149) (159, 169, 179) sts for back.

Next row (WS) (dec row): Sl1 wyif, k4, p1, *k1, p1*, repeat *–* to m, SM, p to m, SM, p2tog, ssp, SM, p to m, SM, p2tog, ssp, SM, p to m, SM, *p1, k1*, repeat *–* to 6 sts before end, p1, k4, sl1 wyif.
You should have 209 (231, 255, –, 303) (321, 343, 361) sts: 51 (57, 63, –, 75) (79, 85, 89) sts for each front, 2 sts for each underarm, 103 (113, 125, –, 149) (159, 169, 179) sts for back.

Next row (RS) (dec row): K1, sl1 wyif, p3, k1, *p1, k1*, repeat *–* to m, SM, k to m, RM, k2tog, RM, k to m, RM, k2tog, RM, k to m, SM, *k1, p1*, repeat *–* to 6 sts before end, k1, p3, sl1 wyif, k1. You should have 207 (229, 253, –, 301) (319, 341, 359) sts.

Size 4 only
Next row (RS) (dec row): K1, sl1 wyif, p3, k1, *p1, k1*, repeat *–* to m, SM, k to 4 sts before end of left front, PM, k4, slide the back sts to needle tip of left-hand needle, k4, PM, k to 4 sts before end of back, PM, k4, slide right front sts to needle tip of left-hand needle, k4, PM, k to m, SM, *k1, p1*, repeat *–* to 6 sts before end, k1, p3, sl1 wyif, k1. You should have 285 sts: 67 sts for each front, 8 sts for each underarm and 135 sts for back.

Next row (WS) (dec row): Sl1 wyif, k4, p1, *k1, p1*, repeat *–* to m, SM, p to m, SM, p2tog, p to 2 sts before m, ssp, SM, p to m, SM, p2tog, p to 2 sts before m, ssp, SM, p to m, SM, *p1, k1*, repeat *–* to 6 sts before end, p1, k4, sl1 wyif. You should have 281 sts: 67 sts for each front, 6 sts for each underarm and 135 sts for back.

Next row (RS) (dec row): K1, sl1 wyif, p3, k1, *p1, k1*, repeat *–* to m, SM, k to m, SM, ssk, k2, k2tog, SM, k to m, SM, ssk, k2, k2tog, SM, k to m, SM, *k1, p1*, repeat *–* to 6 sts before end, k1, p3, sl1 wyif, k1. You should have 277 sts: 67 sts for each front, 4 sts for each underarm and 135 sts for back.

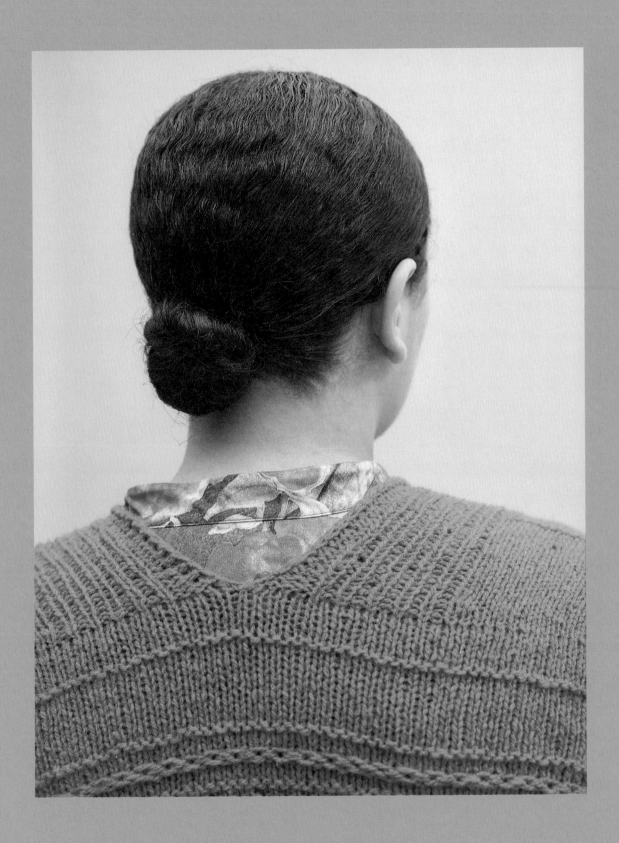

Next row (WS) (dec row): Sl1 wyif, k4, p1, *k1, p1*, repeat *–* to m, SM, p to m, SM, p2tog, ssp, SM, p to m, SM, p2tog, ssp, SM, p to m, SM, *p1, k1*, repeat *–* to 6 sts before end, p1, k4, sl1 wyif.
You should have 273 sts: 67 sts for each front, 2 sts for each underarm and 135 sts for back.

Next row (RS) (dec row): K1, sl1 wyif, p3, k1, *p1, k1*, repeat *–* to m, SM, k to m, RM, k2tog, RM, k to m, RM, k2tog, RM, k to m, SM, *k1, p1*, repeat *–* to 6 sts before end, k1, p3, sl1 wyif, k1.
You should have 271 sts.

Work rows 2–5 of body pattern.

BODY

All sizes
Work rows 6–44 of body pattern, then repeat rows 1–44 of body pattern until body measures approx. 12.75 (12.75, 12.75, 12.25, 11.75) (11.5, 11.5, 11.25)" / 32.5 (32.5, 32.5, 31, 30) (29, 29, 28.5) cm or 2" / 5 cm less than desired length, from underarm. End after a WS row.

Next row (RS): K1, sl1 wyif, p3, k1, *p1, k1*, repeat *–* to m, SM, k to m, SM, *k1, p1*, repeat *–* to 6 sts before end, k1, p3, sl1 wyif, k1.

Ribbing
Change to US 5 / 3.75 mm needles.
Set-up row (WS): Sl1 wyif, k4, p1, *k1, p1*, rep *–* to m, RM, k1, *p1, k1*, repeat *–* to m, RM, *p1, k1*, repeat *–* to 6 sts before end, p1, k4, sl1 wyif.

Row 1 (RS): K1, sl wyif, p3, *k1, p1*, repeat *–* to 6 sts before end, k1, p3, sl1 wyif, k1.
Row 2 (WS): Sl1 wyif, k4, *p1, k1*, repeat *–* to 6 sts before end, p1, k4, sl1 wyif.
Repeat rows 1–2 until ribbing measures approx. 2" / 5 cm. Bind off all sts in pattern with preferred bind-off method.

SLEEVES

With US 6 / 4 mm DPNs or circular needles (if using the Magic Loop Method), starting at the underarm, pick up and knit 72 (76, 82, 88, 98) (104, 110, 112) sts around arm opening at a ratio of approx. 2 sts per 3 rows (this means you will pick up *1 st from 1 row, the next st from the next row, skip the third row*, repeat *–*). Place m for the beginning of the rnd (BOR).

Rnd 1: K to end.
Rnd 2 (dec rnd): K1, k2tog, k to 3 sts before end, ssk, k1. You should have 70 (74, 80, 86, 96) (102, 108, 110) sts.
Repeat rnds 1 and 2, 2 (2, 2, 3, 4) (4, 5, 5) more times. You should have 66 (70, 76, 80, 88) (94, 98, 100) sts.

Continue working in Stockinette Stitch (k all sts), repeating rnd 2 every 14 (11, 8, 7, 5) (4, 4, 3) rnds [this means you will work 13 (10, 7, 6, 4) (3, 3, 2) rnds in Stockinette Stitch, then work rnd 2], 5 (7, 9, 8, 14) (17, 10, 20) times. You should have 56 (56, 58, 64, 60) (60, 78, 60) sts.
Sizes 4 and 7 only
Repeat rnd 2 every – (–, –, 6, –) (–, 3, –) rnds – (–, –, 3, –) (–, 9, –) more times. You should have – (–, –, 58, –) (–, 60, –) sts.

All sizes
Continue in Stockinette Stitch (k all sts) until sleeve measures approx. 14.75 (14.75, 14.75, 13.5, 13.25) (13, 13, 12.25)" / 37.5 (37.5, 37.5, 34.5, 33.5) (33, 33, 31) cm or 2" / 5 cm less than desired length from underarm.

Ribbing
Change to US 5 / 3.75 mm needles.
Next rnd: *K1, p1*, repeat *–* to end.
Continue to work in established 1 x 1 Ribbing until ribbing measures approx. 2" / 5 cm. Bind off all sts in pattern with your preferred bind-off method.

Repeat instructions for the second sleeve.

FINISHING

Weave in ends. Wet block to measurements.

Category Index

P.S. As knitting patterns are made by humans and not machines, errors can sometimes occur. On our website (*lainepublishing.com/pages/errata*) you will find an Errata list, in which we gather possible mistakes and their corrections.

This edition published in 2023 by Hardie Grant Books, an imprint of Hardie Grant Publishing
First published in 2022 by Laine Publishing Oy
Published in agreement with Ferly Agency

Hardie Grant Books (Melbourne)
Wurundjeri Country
Building 1, 658 Church Street
Richmond, Victoria 3121

Hardie Grant Books (London)
5th & 6th Floors
52–54 Southwark Street
London SE1 1UN

hardiegrant.com/books

 A catalogue record for this book is available from the National Library of Australia

52 Weeks of Easy Knits
ISBN 978 1 74379 970 3

10 9 8 7 6 5 4 3 2 1

Concept: Jonna Hietala & Sini Kramer
Photography: Riikka Kantinkoski & Sini Kramer
Graphic design: Tiina Vaarakallio
Editors: Maija Kangasluoma, Sini Kramer, Pauliina Kuunsola, Tiia Pyykkö
Translation: Sini Kramer, Pauliina Kuunsola
Stylist: Anna Komonen (except pp. 18, 62, 65, 78, 117, 119, 193, 195)
Hair & makeup: Miika Kemppainen
Models: Salomé & Yousra / As You Are Agency
Clothing: Beamhill, COS, Reserved, Rains, R/H Studio, Stockmann, Unisa, Vamsko, Vimma

Colour reproduction by Splitting Image Colour Studio
Printed in China by Leo Paper Products LTD.